W9-DGR-665

The DEER HUNTERS

THE TACTICS, LORE, LEGACY AND ALLURE OF AMERICAN DEER HUNTING

EDITED BY

PATRICK DURKIN

Book design by Allen West, Krause Publications.

Cover Photo Credits:
Front Cover: *Ian McMurchy*
Back Cover: *Brad Herndon (left), Greg Miller (top), Patrick Durkin (right)*

Published by

**krause
publications**

700 E. State St. • Iola, WI 54990-0001

Please call or write for our free catalog of publications. Our toll-free
number to place an order or to obtain a free catalog is (800) 258-0929.
Please use our regular business telephone (715) 445-2214 for editorial
comment and further information.
Library of Congress Catalog Number: 97-73778
ISBN: 0-87341-537-X
Printed in the United States of America

DEDICATION

Penny, you're the best. Now, let's talk about those hunting trips.
Please remember one thing when I'm continually gone from your
side: It was on a solitary bow-hunt in Virginia's Blue Ridge
Mountains in November 1979 that I knew I couldn't go through
life without you.
That's when I proposed marriage.
You just weren't there to hear it.

CONTENTS

FOREWORD

Honesty compels me to admit I don't remember the first time I met Pat Durkin. He said it was at a public hearing in Wausau, Wis., in March 1985, at which anti-hunters were trying to convince legislators to outlaw bear hunting.

I'll take his word for it. Sometimes he has a good memory.

I do, however, recall meeting him a couple of years later at yet another meeting, this one closer to our homes in east-central Wisconsin. By that time Pat was the outdoors editor for a nearby newspaper, and we were both at a public meeting relating to another fish or wildlife issue. Pat was there to report on it for the newspaper and I, being involved in the biopolitics of fish and wildlife management, was listening and presenting my views on the issues.

> FROM ITS INCEPTION IN 1977, *Deer & Deer Hunting* ALWAYS ATTEMPTED TO PROVIDE DEER HUNTERS WITH A DIVERSE BLEND OF ARTICLES ABOUT WHITE-TAILED DEER AND THE HUNTING OF THEM. *The Deer Hunters* CAPTURES THE ESSENCE OF *Deer & Deer Hunting* MAGAZINE.

After the meeting, Pat introduced himself and the talk quickly shifted to deer hunting. Pat recognized me as the editor of *Deer & Deer Hunting* magazine, and said he tried to buy and read every issue. He also offered some kind words about its content, appearance and overall approach. We became good friends in the intervening years, but that night neither of us realized that about five years later, Pat would join the magazine's staff, and then become its editor in 1992 shortly before the magazine was acquired by Krause Publications.

Early in this book's planning process, Pat contacted me and asked for some advice about making the compilation of this book flow smoothly. He thought my experience in editing a similar book, *Deer & Deer Hunting: A Hunter's Guide to Deer Behavior and Hunting Techniques* (1993), would prove helpful.

Pat probably received less helpful advice than he had hoped. We talked at length about many of the mundane aspects of book publishing and, perhaps, I provided a useful tip or two about how to avoid some of the potential stumbling blocks. When I told Pat the most difficult part of compiling an anthology of material published during the first 15 years of *Deer & Deer Hunting* magazine was selecting the articles and photos to include in the book, it was something he already knew. The only difference was that Pat had to select about 30 articles published in a span of not 15, but 20 years. That's one of those rare jobs that only gets more difficult with experience.

Do not misunderstand. The problem Pat faced was the same one I faced: the number of articles worthy of inclusion far exceeded the book's space limitations. As you read *The Deer Hunters: The Tactics, Lore, Legacy and Allure of American Deer Hunting*, I believe you'll agree Pat succeeded admirably when he made his final selection of articles and photographs.

Pat captures the essence of the magazine in this book. From its inception in 1977, *Deer & Deer Hunting* magazine always attempted to provide deer hunters with a diverse blend of articles about white-tailed deer and the hunting of them. Like the magazine, this book is much more than a how-to-hunt manual, even though articles on hunting methodology form an important part of it. But equally important are the chapters that cover an array of topics relating to deer biology, behavior and management; the deer hunting experience; the multiple satisfactions derived from pursuing whitetails; and the relationship between hunters and the whitetail. I believe this diversity of subjects contributed significantly to the success and popularity of *Deer & Deer Hunting* magazine. And for the same reason, this book should be well-received.

In the section titled "The Deer Hunter's Ethic," the authors explore many of the prickly, philosophical and thought-provoking issues deer hunters confront.

These chapters might not enable hunters to become more skillful or proficient during their days in the deer woods, but they provide insight into some of the issues facing deer hunters who desire to pursue this pastime in a responsible and ethical manner.

In "The Deer Hunter's Tactics," readers benefit from the combined knowledge and experience of many accomplished deer hunters from throughout the country. They share the fine points of time-honored hunting techniques, such as stand-hunting and still-hunting. Additionally, readers will learn about relatively modern tactics that can be added to their repertoire. If you agree that experience is the best teacher, you cannot help but learn much from the centuries of combined deer hunting experience of the authors in this section.

Today, human hunters are the most significant predator of deer in all but the most remote parts of the whitetail's range, but we are certainly not the only threat to individual members of a herd. "The Other Deer Hunters" examines many of the threats posed by other species, including other deer sharing the same range, and the environment itself in which deer live. As most hunters learn early in their hunting lives, the natural world can be competitive and often downright brutal.

In this book's final section, "The Deer Hunter's Bonds," the authors become more reflective, somewhat philosophical and even whimsical at times. Most of us who take our deer hunting seriously know there is much more to the total deer hunting experience than simply filling a deer tag. The authors included in this section would certainly agree. They show how

seemingly insignificant events can often make a deer hunt memorable. And they also reveal what motivates the deer hunter, and why so many of us return to the deer woods each autumn regardless of our successes or lack thereof.

Pat has assembled this anthology in a way that, I believe, makes it a first-rate volume that should be included in every deer hunter's library. *The Deer Hunters: The Tactics, Lore, Legacy and Allure of American Deer Hunting* can be read for pure enjoyment, to make you a more educated hunter, to increase and improve your hunting skills, and to make you more appreciative of the white-tailed deer and the opportunity to hunt them.

And because of the way the book is structured, it does not have to be read in order, from beginning to end. If the deer have you baffled during your next hunt, you might find the assistance you need in the hunting tactics section. Or if, at the end of your day's hunt, you're in the mood to sit in your favorite recliner in front of the fireplace with a good book, you'll find plenty in this one to keep you stimulated.

— Al Hofacker
Athelstane, Wis.
June 7, 1997

INTRODUCTION

I still remember the first time I read about the Stump Sitters study group and *Deer & Deer Hunting* magazine. I was reading one of the "Big Three" outdoor magazines in the late 1970s while overseas in the Navy. I took notice because the Stump Sitters were based in my home state, Wisconsin. The brief article noted the ground-breaking insights this group was providing into white-tailed deer. I remember a sense of respect being shown its two leaders.

Just a couple of years later, I got my first look at the magazine while visiting a cousin. Her husband pointed to the latest copy of *Deer & Deer Hunting* on the table and said: "That's my bible. I read every issue cover to cover."

The next time I saw *Deer & Deer Hunting* at a nearby gas station, I bought it. After that, I seldom missed an issue each time a new one appeared on the rack. I should have just subscribed, as had thousands of other North American deer hunters who consider themselves Stump Sitters. It would have been cheaper in the long run.

Therefore, I was a bit overwhelmed when returning from a deer hunt in November 1990. My wife met me at the door and said a guy named Jack Brauer had called, and that he wanted to hire me as an associate editor. Just like that. I was happy in my work as a newspaper outdoor writer and editor, but pursued the job with all my heart, hoping to work beside its editor, Al Hofacker. I reread old issues and reviewed Rob Wegner's *Deer & Deer Hunting* books. It paid off. I showed up for work on Jan. 2, 1991, and never looked back.

This award-winning magazine is now 20 years old, and I've been in its employ the past 6½ years. Even with that many years and 53 issues of the magazine now under my editorial belt, I still feel honored to be editing the work of people whose articles and photographs appear in *Deer & Deer Hunting* magazine, and now, in this book, *The Deer Hunters*. At times, when working long-distance and unending hours with people like Charlie Alsheimer, Larry Weishuhn, John Ozoga, Jay McAninch and Greg Miller, I remind myself that I'm working my dream. They're all certified deer nuts, each in their own way, and none apologizes for it.

In preparing for *The Deer Hunters*, which honors the magazine's 20th anniversary, I first talked with Hofacker and then reviewed again his 1993 compilation, *Deer & Deer Hunting: A Hunter's Guide to Deer Behavior and Hunting Techniques*. Soon after, I was tempted to call him back and say, "You muskrat, you took all the good stuff."

Two minutes later, however, as my mind churned, I recalled some long-lost favorites from the 1980s by people like Lee Nisbet, Dick Thomas, Professor Valerius Geist, and Hofacker himself. Within a few hours I realized Al's book had only flicked away a sliver of the magazine's history. I also realized a lot of quality material had appeared since he was in this chair, so the challenge wasn't finding good stuff. It was finding the right combination of good stuff. Like Al before me, I soon had a long list of potential articles, and dreaded winnowing them down.

The task was made a bit easier when I decided on the book's theme: the deer hunters themselves and why they hunt, be they two-legged or four-legged predators. From there, I decided the book would look at four areas that we've examined in-depth in *Deer & Deer Hunting*:

✓ "The Deer Hunter's Ethic"
✓ "The Deer Hunter's Tactics"
✓ "The Other Deer Hunters"
✓ "The Deer Hunter's Bonds"

The Deer Hunters began to take shape in my mind. I then looked for articles that would best complement and enliven each section. I know I'll second-guess every article and photo that didn't make the final cut. But more importantly, I hope you'll enjoy the ones that made it.

One thing you've probably already noticed about this book: It's not short on photos of hunters with deer they've killed, be they human hunters who used bullets or arrows; or wolves, bobcats, bears or coyotes that used tooth and claw. There's two reasons for that: One, life in the wilds isn't all ferns and trilliums. Life's cycle is built upon death, and we should appreciate nature's brutal harmony. And two, hunters should not feel shame in a kill, as long as it's done ethically and humanely, and they honor the animal by consuming its venison.

Further, I've been disturbed in recent years that books and magazines often act as if deer don't die in the woods. Some outdoor publications even ban photos of deer killed by hunters. An editor of one told me, "No deer is pretty after it's dead." I don't know. It works for me, as long as the animal is displayed with respect and the hunters are humble in their accomplishment. I think most deer hunters, for whom this book is intended, feel the same.

OK. The sermon is over. Thanks for indulging me. I hope you'll enjoy *The Deer Hunters* for years to come.

— *Patrick Durkin*
Waupaca, Wis.

ACKNOWLEDGMENTS

I realize it's obligatory to open an acknowledgment with a sincere apology to all those influential people I will forget to mention in the paragraphs to follow. Believe me, I love you and deeply value the insights, praise, criticisms and suggestions you've offered over the years. Whether you're a writer, editor, friend, teacher, professor, family member, hunting buddy or co-worker, or a former co-worker, shipmate or school chum, you can rightfully share the credit — and blame — for the book that follows. All of us are shaped by those around us, even though we too often forget positive influences and dwell on irritants.

With that said, allow me to point out the obvious: This book wouldn't be possible without *Deer & Deer Hunting* magazine, and the people, places, philosophies, mystique, gut feelings, and reader involvement that have shaped its existence since its birth in 1977. I've always said the magazine is bigger than any person — past, present or future — who works on it, and I'm confident it will outlive all of us.

I'm also indebted to Al Hofacker, Debbie Knauer, Jack Brauer and Rob Wegner for making me a part of *Deer & Deer Hunting* in January 1991. Any one of them could have nixed my job application, but each seemed sure I would mesh with the magazine. I like to think I've proven worthy of their trust. And, of course, I offer a heartfelt thanks to Krause Publications, which took that foursome's word that I was worth keeping when *Deer & Deer Hunting* changed owners in April 1992.

I also deeply appreciate the field editors and contributing editors — past and present — whose work has appeared regularly in *Deer & Deer Hunting*. Each has provided regional and national insights that give the magazine its depth and breadth. I salute New York's Charlie Alsheimer, New Jersey's Leonard Lee Rue III, Alabama's Kent Horner, Minnesota's Jay McAninch, Texas' Larry Weishuhn, Michigan's John Ozoga and Richard P. Smith, and Tennessee's Bill Bynum. These creative individuals have shouldered much of the magazine's writing load, and provided the perspectives that separate *Deer & Deer Hunting* from the rest of the magazine pack on the rack. Even though some of those folks' names won't appear again in this book, know their imprints are throughout.

I'm especially appreciative of Alsheimer, Knauer and the magazine's readers, who continually provide the reminders and insights I need to keep *Deer & Deer Hunting* true to its roots. Alsheimer and Knauer have been on watch almost from the magazine's start, and they've endured nerve-racking changes in editors, publishers and owners since signing on in 1979 and 1981, respectively.

It's impossible to list all the talented free-lance writers and photographers who also vividly shape *Deer & Deer Hunting*. One of the greatest pleasures of editing this book was rereading many of the nearly 1,000 articles the magazine has featured over the past 20 years. It's truly a remarkable collection of deer hunting research and literature. Reading all those articles from the past made me again value the free-lancer who never asks: "What kind of material is *Deer & Deer Hunting* looking for?" or "How can I get more articles into *Deer & Deer Hunting*?" Those whose work is regularly published already know the answers because they're regular readers of *Deer & Deer Hunting*. Chances are, those who don't read the magazine for its pleasure and insights won't be able to write the insightful articles or photograph the awesome scenes that give the magazine its distinctive personality. Anyway, it's a thought.

No doubt, though, one of the most gut-wrenching, time-consuming but richly rewarding aspects of *Deer & Deer Hunting* magazine is developing ideas and relationships with North America's gifted free-lance outdoor writers and photographers. I've never met most of you, and know you only by your creations and, occasionally, your telephone voice. I thank you for your patience, perseverance and persistence, and wish we had 500-page magazines to publish all of your amazing work. Hey, we can dream, can't we? Seriously, we're nowhere without you.

It's also crucial that I thank the associate editors, editorial interns, artists and proofreaders who have made me, the magazine and this book look so good. To Dan Schmidt, Gregg Gutschow, Al West, Chris Mork, Sandy Sparks, Jeanette Sawall, Dave Beauchaine, Kathy Dugan, Seiche Sanders, Jodi Wolfe and Amber Paluch, I can tell you now in confidence: You are/were the best in your field. Just don't tell the others. Let it be our little secret.

And finally, I dig deeply to offer heartfelt thanks to Penny, Leah, Elle, Karsyn, my parents, grandparents, brothers, sisters, lifelong friends and teachers who fanned the small spark. Again, thanks for your prodding, love and support. And yes, that includes you, Uncle Terry, Mary Bergin, Kathy Hoveland, Peggy Davidson, Scott Peterson, Shirley Rogers and Mary Martin. Each of you helped make possible my sincere appreciation of everyone above.

THE DEER HUNTER'S ETHIC

*I*n naming this first section and selecting its collection of articles, I tried not to sound like a nag or scold. That would belittle the work of the people whose articles appear in these first 10 chapters.

  The deer hunter's ethic is more than choosing between right and wrong, even though that is part of it. To borrow and paraphrase from Aldo Leopold, the deer hunter's ethic is a cooperative process that is always evolving to guide us in our thoughts and actions. While the deer hunter's ethic involves the way we cooperate with other hunters, it also has much to do with the way we hunt deer, and how we view them and the land they inhabit.

  One of the challenges in editing this book was deciding which articles best belonged in Part 1, "The Deer Hunter's Ethic," and Part 4, "The Deer Hunter's Bonds." Both ideas guide and borrow from the other. Nowhere was that decision more difficult than deciding where to place Greg Miller's two-piece tribute to one buck, "Until Next Year," and "Next Year." I had a similar problem with Val Geist's "Three Threats to Wildlife Conservation." No doubt these articles deal with the hunter's bonds to the deer, the land and how deer should be valued and hunted. But they also deal with the ethical decisions hunters make in how they administer death to a respected quarry, and how easily and unintentionally we can sunder the fabric upon which modern wildlife management is based.

  But, just to warn you, along the way and in between, some of us do some scolding, too. Then again, maybe we'll learn and evolve from it. Read on.

  ■ *PATRICK DURKIN*

ALL WHO HUNT WITH JOE LEE THE FIRST TIME GET HIS LECTURE ABOUT SHOOTING LEGAL DEER. AND HIS NEPHEW GOT THE LECTURE THE MORNING BEFORE THE HUNT. IT DIDN'T TAKE.

HOW MUCH IS A DOE WORTH?

I hope one day the penance for that wasted doe will be paid, because I don't like hunting alone anymore.

■ BY CHARLIE SMITH

At first glance, Thomas and Joe Lee are your typical Southern white-tailed deer hunters. They work hard, take care of their families and go to church. But after midsummer each year their lives are dominated by bows, guns, scouting, shooting and, most of all, counting down the days until the Oct. 1 opener.

But Thomas and Joe Lee don't stop there. Some say ethics are what you do when folks are watching, but character is what you do when no one else will ever know. Call it what you want, Thomas and Joe Lee have it in spades.

It might come from their Christian upbringing, or maybe from something deep in their genes that no one understands. Thomas and Joe Lee just don't break game laws, period.

In fact, this is one of the reasons I hunt with them. There are no surprises. I have accepted many invitations to hunt deer, only to find that "ground-checking" and "camp-meat does" are acceptable behavior. Because I can't handle folks who shoot a deer without first identifying its sex, or sneaking an illegally killed doe back to camp, I was usually the odd man out.

Eventually, I came to accept hunting alone. That is

Tom Tietz

until I met Thomas, Joe Lee, and a third friend, Wayne. Ten years ago around a campfire, we learned we all shared a desire to do it right. It seemed we all understood the future of hunting was in our hands, and would somehow be determined by how well we followed the rules.

Since then, there have been no surprises. We have tracked each other's deer late into the night. Wayne, especially, has rolled out of bed more than once to pull my old truck out of a mud hole.

But two years ago I learned just how deeply ingrained this thing called character can be.

A New Acquaintance

While scouting different areas, Wayne and I teamed up while Thomas and Joe Lee hunted another farm. At the last minute, Joe Lee's 20-year-old nephew asked to be included in the hunt.

All who hunt with Joe Lee the first time get his lecture about shooting legal deer. And his nephew, Chad, got the lecture the morning before the hunt. It didn't take.

About 8 a.m., four does fed underneath Joe Lee's stand and angled off toward the ladder stand where he had left

As I write this article, it's the evening after a deer season opener. It has been two years, and neither Thomas nor Joe Lee has hunted since that day.

didn't know what else to do."

In a subdued voice, Thomas explained what happened, and then got into the truck and drove away. "Charlie, if it had been Thomas or Joe Lee who made an honest mistake, I'd have given them that dang doe tag. But that boy shot it on purpose, and he ain't even sorry."

A Heavy Weight

On stand that afternoon, I wondered if they had tried to retrieve the illegal doe. Wasting game was a serious sin in our camp. But I knew if they got caught, they could lose the truck, their guns, pay a fine, and destroy a reputation that had been years in the building.

I came down from my tree earlier than usual and drove to Thomas' house. Wayne was already there. He again said he was sorry for not giving up his doe permit, and Thomas again apologized for asking. It seemed there were no hard feelings.

The doe had been left in the woods, and it was weighing heavily on Thomas. A stop by Joe Lee's house found him equally depressed. Because it was the first day of the season, I was surprised to find him storing away his gear.

"I just don't feel like hunting anymore right now," Joe Lee said. "Maybe later."

As I write this, it's the evening after a deer season opener. It has been two years, and neither Thomas nor Joe Lee has hunted since that day. Last season, Wayne and I stopped by their homes nearly every day. They agreed with all of our reasons to put the incident behind them. In fact, Thomas still shoots his recurve bow every afternoon. But they just don't hunt.

Begging Off

Our families all remained close friends. We watched deer hunting videos together, and we planned hunts, just like the old days. But when the time came to hunt, Thomas and Joe Lee always begged off.

Last spring, Wayne's job transferred him out of state. I hope one day the penance for that wasted doe will be paid, because I don't like hunting alone any more.

"How Much is a Doe Worth?" was originally published in the November 1994 issue of Deer & Deer Hunting *magazine.*

Chad before daylight. About five minutes later, Chad's .30-30 cracked. Fearing what had happened, Joe Lee hurried down the ridge and found Chad standing over a yearling doe.

The first I knew anything was wrong was when I came out of the woods to find Chad and Joe Lee sitting in the truck, and Thomas holding a quiet conversation with Wayne. Wayne was the only one who had drawn a doe permit that season. As I walked up, I heard Wayne say: "Thomas, I'm sorry. It just wouldn't be right." Thomas replied, "Wayne, it wasn't even right to ask, but I just

THE TERM "PRIVATIZATION OF WILDLIFE" SOUNDS INNOCENT ENOUGH, BUT IT IS SO DEADLY THAT DEER AND DEER HUNTING AS WE KNOW IT WILL BE HISTORY IF WE FAIL TO TAKE COUNTERMANDING MEASURES NOW.

CHAPTER 2

THREE THREATS TO WILDLIFE CONSERVATION

North America's success in conservation is based on three mighty pillars which support the laws, regulations, beliefs and attitudes that benefit wildlife. Will these pillars soon collapse?

■ BY VALERIUS GEIST

On the face of it, wildlife conservation is a healthy, thriving enterprise. The success of North American wildlife conservation is staggering. The success of North Americans in conserving wildlife, though known elsewhere and imitated abroad, remains a well-kept secret in America.

We take wildlife management so much for granted that we long ago forgot why we follow certain strategies, why we are successful, and how we differ in our approach from other systems of wildlife management.

We might pay dearly for our ignorance! A deadly cancer is growing in wildlife conservation, and we must not wait before performing surgery. Like many illnesses that creep into a healthy body, this cancer has deep roots and has had time to get established. It can be labeled "privatization of wildlife." That sounds innocent enough, but it is so deadly that deer and deer hunting as we know it will be history if we fail to take countermanding measures now.

To understand the nature of the illness, we must review the forgotten principles of our system for

THE THREE PILLARS

North America's success in wildlife conservation is based on three policies and beliefs:

1) No legal market for the meat, parts and products of vulnerable species of wildlife (and plants).

2) The material benefits of wildlife are allocated by law, not by the marketplace, birthright, land ownership or social position. The state is the owner, guardian and manager of wildlife resources.

3) Wildlife is a food resource to be cropped annually for subsistence, making wildlife management a form of food production.

conserving and managing wildlife, the principles we fail to ingrain into our wildlife managers and the public alike. If I had my druthers, every school child would learn them as a part of North America's history, a work of which to be proud.

The Three Pillars

North America's success in wildlife conservation is based on three primary policies, three mighty pillars that support the superstructure of laws, regulations, beliefs and attitudes. These are:

1) There is no legal market for the meat, parts and products of vulnerable species of wildlife (and plants). This is the largest and most important pillar, a policy established about 70 years ago after grim, bloody battles on behalf of wildlife.

2) The material benefits of wildlife are allocated by law, not by the marketplace, birthright, land ownership or social position. Ours is a complementary policy arising from the first, which automatically places wildlife into the public domain, making the state the owner, guardian and manager of wildlife resources. This policy ensures broad interest at the local level in wildlife and its conservation, and generates political clout on behalf of wildlife.

3) We hold the belief (not a policy, alas!) that wildlife is a food resource to be cropped annually for subsistence, making wildlife management a form of food production. That idea generates broad public consensus, by hunters and non-hunters alike, for the management and harvest of wildlife.

Today, those three pillars supporting wildlife conservation are deeply eroded, so much so that collapse within a

> BY INSISTING THAT HUNTING IS A NOBLE FORM OF RECREATION, A SPORT, THE OLD AMERICAN IDEA THAT HUNTING IS FOOD HARVESTING IS LOSING GROUND.

generation is highly probable. The first policy is being eroded by short-sighted efforts to "game ranch" wildlife so venison can be sold to the public, while velvet antlers, sex organs, glands and sundry other parts can be sold in a lucrative Oriental market for folk medicine. The second policy is eroded by hunting leases, private trophy fees, trespass fees and "Texas-style" game management. The third policy is eroded by the notion that hunting is killing for "sport" or "fun," and, therefore, is frivolous blood-sport; and that wildlife is primarily a "recreational," not a food resource.

These subjects are complex, full of potential for confusion, and require a cool, level head to be dealt with properly.

Game ranching is often advertised as a superior way to raise exceptional meat, provided predators can be curtailed or eliminated, and the public alienated from large tracts of land. That claim is supported by scientific research. To allow game ranching and venison marketeering, New Zealand expropriated deer from the public in favor of private users, and prohibited public access on large tracts of public land. Moreover, New Zealand has no deer predators! How all this happened is recorded by Graeme Caughley, a premier wildlife biologist, in his book *The Deer Wars* (1983). Because game ranching is more productive than cattle ranching, it's logical to think it will displace cattle ranching — and the public — on ranchlands, private or public.

Most insidious is the need by game ranchers for a market in venison and in parts of wildlife. When the meat of a wildlife species is marketed and various parts of deer fetch high prices, it attracts poachers. This has happened historically in many countries, and protecting wildlife against illegal killing and marketing requires draconian policing efforts.

Policing Wildlife

Few Americans remember that during the heydays of market hunting, when wildlife was rapidly decimated everywhere, the United States cavalry protected Yellowstone and other national parks. We owe the United States Army a continent-wide vote of gratitude for their efforts on behalf of wildlife, having guarded Yellowstone's wildlife from 1886 to 1918. The soldiers left only after venison markets were outlawed. It's all explained in Professor Duane Hampton's book, *How the U.S. Cavalry Saved Our National Parks* (1971).

The Germans are even more draconic. They make every lessee or owner with hunting land a deputized policeman with a right, in law, to shoot to kill in cases of justifiable doubt. In 1985, Germany had 65,000 armed wildlife protectors for 85,000 square miles of land, which is divided into 40,000 hunting territories. Moreover, any of Germany's remaining 190,000 tested, registered hunters can be deputized by any of the 65,000 primary deputies. Germany also has about 1,000 full-time professional hunters employed to manage and protect the hunting leases of wealthy lessees. On state land, foresters are charged with protecting wildlife. Together with strict food-protection laws, an army of food inspectors with policing powers controls the flow of wildlife to the retail market. In these ways, and with strict gun-control laws, Germany maintains a venison market while minimizing poaching.

How many game wardens protect wildlife in your state or province? In most of North America, each warden patrols literally tens of thousands of square miles.

New Zealand did not even wait for poaching to begin. Together with the 1977 Wild Animal Control Act, New Zealand's lawmakers passed legislation giving state foresters powers exceeding those of its regular police forces. Those powers and stiff penalties for violators were designed to deter citizens from hunting on public land, where deer were reserved for venison marketeers.

A Distant Threat?

If a venison market becomes established in North America, the lives of our deer are not worth a plug nickel. Stocks of public and private wildlife can coexist with a lucrative market in venison only with severe policing powers and gun control. If Americans don't swallow those bitter pills, a venison market will destroy North America's wildlife. That would be the penalty for ignoring history, our very own history at that!

If you think a market in wildlife venison is a distant threat, you err. Game-ranching interests work relentlessly on uninformed, well-meaning, civil servants and politicians.

Some of the most determined support for game ranching comes from unexpected quarters: from wildlife biologists and professional wildlife managers. I know. I was one of them! I fell for game-ranching lock, stock and barrel, and it took me eight years to realize how damaging are its consequences. I held, with Dr. F. Walther (then of Texas A&M University), a conference in 1971 that dealt in significant part with game ranching. The conference attracted

Patrick Durkin

DENY THE HARVEST AND THE HUNTER/CONSERVATIONIST TURNS INTO THE CONSERVATION ROMANTIC, AND WILDLIFE BECOMES THE LOSER. NO MATTER HOW MUCH HE DENIES IT, THE CONSERVATION ROMANTIC STANDS, ULTIMATELY, FOR BRUTALIZED LANDSCAPES AND DEPLETED WILDLIFE POPULATIONS SQUEEZED INTO TINY, PROTECTED ENCLAVES OVERRUN BY PEOPLE — OUR NATIONAL PARKS.

more than 250 big-game biologists, including game ranchers from South Africa and Rhodesia. Even then it took a year or two for me to realize how unacceptable are the consequences of game ranching. My only regrets are that I failed to speak against it then, before matters reached the stage they have.

We need, continent-wide, a reaffirmation that there shall be no markets in venison and wildlife parts. It will not be easy because creeping marketeering has infiltrated many states and Canadian provinces and territories.

Further, illegal markets in urban centers educate the public that wildlife is available, without the effort of hunting it. Professional poachers already are evident in de-antlered Yellowstone Park elk and in bears killed for paws, claws and gall bladders. Pressures are increasing to legalize the sale of bear parts and deer antlers. It's time to awaken our sleeping publics!

The Consequences

Nearly as vicious as the consequences of venison markets are the long-term repercussions of lease hunting and paid hunting to our system of wildlife conservation. This is what history teaches us about lease hunting:

Very slowly, paid hunting concentrates access to wildlife in favor of a smaller segment of an increasingly affluent, politically powerful people. They use wildlife as a badge or symbol of their social status. This excludes an ever-larger segment of the public from benefiting from wildlife. In rural areas it mainly creates resentment and envy against the privileged landowners. In urban areas it creates a sentiment against hunting fueled by the questionable "sporting" activities of the privileged few, and it redirects attitudes regarding wildlife conservation into the hands of the "romantics" or Greenpeace-style wildlife "protectors." In the long run, it slowly but surely alienates the public from wildlife altogether, because wildlife becomes a symbol of detested privilege and power. This has, historically, had severe consequences.

First, significant segments of the public are not happy to see their hunting curtailed, and illegally take the path of wildlife acquisition. They poach, less for gain than for defying the privileged, not to mention the thrills involved. Poaching in that case, however, would have public support! Now poachers become local folk heroes, not unlike Robin Hood! Landowners, jealous of their valuable wildlife, respond, usually in draconic fashion! They protect their land and wildlife with arms. Inevitably, that leads to bloodshed. In the long run, an alienated public, unpracticed in regarding wildlife as theirs to cherish, use and protect, exterminates wildlife the moment the powers of land and wildlife owners slacken. Unless strenuous efforts somehow restore effective wildlife protection, the country remains depopulated of wildlife, with citizens killing wildlife

> MANY PEOPLE TODAY HAVE NOT EXPERIENCED THE PROCESS OF FOOD PRODUCTION THAT FEEDS THEM, AND HAVE SUCCESSFULLY SUPPRESSED IN THEIR MINDS THE REALIZATION THAT HUMANS, IN ORDER TO LIVE, MUST KILL.

competitively, void of conservation considerations.

History Repeats

The above scenario is recorded repeatedly in history. It has happened so often that one can declare it a law of restricting access to wildlife to a privileged few. It has happened in Europe and Asia, it happened in the distant past and in modern history, and it is happening today in parts of the United States. The ruthlessness and brutality with which the rich have protected their privileged access to wildlife is, historically, startling!

American sportsmen and conservationists face a grim battle in which they have everything to lose. When they threaten the privileges of the mighty few, hunters will first be inundated with disinformation. This will also trigger political skulduggery of gargantuan proportions. Returning control of wildlife to the public will be a task not for the faint of heart. Already, the remorseless grinding of events has made wildlife in vast stretches of North America the defacto property of a few, of the powerful. Not only wildlife conservation stands to lose from the current drift of events, but so do the many industries that support hunting.

How to Define Hunting

The third threat to wildlife conservation arises from the notion of "sport" hunting. That one is painful, and must be faced calmly. The notion that hunting is "sport" is a medieval European idea, although similar notions existed in all civilizations where hunting rights were restricted to the ruling minority. Originally, it had none of the connotations of honorable conduct associated with it today. Medieval nobility were not "sportsmen" in our sense, certainly not in their attitude toward wildlife they so brutally pursued and slaughtered for pleasure. They practiced little sportsman-like restraint. Unfortunately, the notion of hunting as sport spread because lower classes notoriously imitate upper classes! They imitate the rich and powerful no matter how unworthy the values. The idea of honorable conduct toward wildlife, the idea of noble, self-imposed restraint, the very idea of sportsmanship itself is of fairly recent vintage, but also of upper-class origin.

To the public, however, sport-hunting means killing for

the pleasure of killing, not hunting in order to feed a family. The public accepts subsistence hunting, much as it also accepts agriculture's arguments that it fulfills the noble role of food production. Meanwhile, the public excuses the ecological havoc raised by modern agriculture. By insisting that hunting is a noble form of recreation, a sport, the old American idea that hunting is food harvesting is losing ground. As little as a few decades ago, access to private land to harvest wildlife was commonplace, but access for sporting enjoyment is today increasingly restricted.

Two reasons explain this. First, some landowners perceive sport-hunting to be a frivolous killing of wildlife, which is dear to their hearts. Second, some find it easy to charge a fee to strangers who want to use their land, a fee they would never charge a neighbor who wants to kill a deer for food. Hunting for "fun" offends the work ethic. Killing a deer for the family table does not.

However, sport hunting does worse things than create a lease hunting market and trespass fees, with all their sordid consequences. It alienates broad segments of an urban, wildlife-loving public from good wildlife management and conservation. Killing creatures just for "fun" and flouting trophies as some sort of a sporting achievement generates revulsion. It creates the passionate "antis" and, worse, it creates the conservation romantics who see no place for wildlife on the dinner table. These people have not experienced the process of food production that feeds them, and have suppressed in their minds the realization that humans, in order to live, must kill. They have suppressed the recognition that every potato chip they munch is a dead slice of a once-living organism, that granola bars are dead children of plants, that raw cabbage is a living, breathing organism.

The Hunter/Gardener

When I note in discussions that I no more hunt to kill deer than I garden to kill cabbages, I get strange looks. But usually the coin drops when I add that my wife loves to garden for sport: She grows flowers! The conservation romantic, who would rather eat beef or who has turned vegetarian, in reality denies deer — and all things wild and beautiful that go with deer — a place to live. There is no vacuum on land! Unless there is local political support for deer and deer habitat, forestry, agriculture, mining, transportation and urban sprawl take over and destroy deer habitat. When cattle replace deer, the coyote and black bear that

> WHEN I NOTE IN DISCUSSIONS THAT I NO MORE HUNT TO KILL DEER THAN I GARDEN TO KILL CABBAGES, I GET STRANGE LOOKS FROM THOSE LISTENING.

preyed on deer fawns start attracting unwanted attention when they start killing calves. The conservation romantic is happy deer are alive and well if some survive in a national park; a hunter/conservationist is livid if he does not have deer nearby, and lots of them. The strength of America's system of wildlife conservation, that the conservation romantic so thoroughly enjoys, was built and is still maintained by the efforts, sweat and blood of local hunter/conservationists with a real, very personal stake in wildlife, namely a part of the wildlife harvest.

Deny the harvest and the hunter/conservationist turns into the conservation romantic, and wildlife becomes the loser. No matter how much he denies it, the conservation romantic stands, ultimately, for brutalized landscapes and depleted wildlife populations squeezed into tiny, protected enclaves overrun by people — our national parks.

That's the long-term cost of making a "sport" of hunting and of restricting public access to the harvest of wildlife. The Germans have long, deep hunting traditions. Do they hunt for sport? You would offend a German hunter to suggest such a disgrace! No, he does not hunt for sport. He does not regard pheasants as sporting targets. He regards hunting as a necessary harvest of the land, as his chance to commune with nature and be part of it.

Return to Our Roots

We must get back to wildlife as food and wildlife management as food production for the benefit of all, and forget the statistics of "recreation days" and other data that detract from wildlife's worth.

Markets in venison and wildlife parts, lease hunting and trespass fees, and hunting for "fun" represent three grim horsemen of destruction riding down on the best system of wildlife conservation the world has seen.

We had better take up arms and meet them. Helpless we are not!

"Three Threats to Wildlife Conservation" was originally published in the January 1987 issue of Deer & Deer Hunting *magazine.*

CHAPTER 3

Where Silence Once Rang

When the ravens were quiet all I could hear was the odd ringing in my ears that can only be known in places far removed from roads, radios, voices and TVs.

■ BY PATRICK DURKIN

IF YOU THINK ABOUT THE RINGING SILENCE TOO MUCH, YOU WONDER IF IT'S A PHENOMENON OF MODERN-DAY HUMANS WHO ARE ALWAYS BOMBARDED WITH NOISE, OR IF FOREST DWELLERS EONS AGO KNEW THE SAME SOUND.

A n hour had passed since shooting light had spread through the dark cedar bottoms. The only sound in this small portion of a vast forest in Michigan's Upper Peninsula was oddball calls from passing ravens.

My hunting partner and I always joke that if we can't identify the origin of a call, croak or chirp, blame it on ravens. We're seldom wrong.

When the ravens were quiet, though, all I could hear was the strange ringing in my ears that can only be known in places far removed from roads, radios, voices and TVs. If you think about the ringing too much, you wonder if it's a phenomenon of modern-day humans who are always bombarded with noise, or if forest dwellers eons ago knew the same sound.

When you're hunting deer in the balsam and cedar forests of the North Woods, you tend to have ample time for pondering. That's because you typically don't see many deer. I've always said three deer sightings in a full day of hunting such country qualifies as a good day. But one sighting is just as common, and, therefore, zero doesn't surprise me.

Richard P. Smith

IN THE NEXT INSTANT, THE DOE LEAPED AND DARTED ABOUT 30 YARDS, AND THEN ABRUPTLY STOPPED TO LOOK AT ME, STILL NOT SURE WHAT I WAS. HER CHEST NOW EXPOSED, I TOUCHED THE TRIGGER WITHOUT GUILT.

A Busy Morning

Not this day, though. About 7:30 a.m., I saw movement 40 yards in front of my ground blind. An adult deer stepped from behind a fallen cedar and looked away. I quickly shouldered my .35 Whelen and looked through its low-power riflescope.

I had a bonus tag for antlerless deer, so I scanned the deer's head to make sure it didn't carry antlers. Before pushing in the safety, I glanced again at the deer's head. A sliver of an antler was tucked against its left ear.

"A sub-legal spike," I thought, as the yearling turned to look at me. I could have used my bonus tag on him, but I wanted a mature doe. Shooting a malnourished adolescent buck would do little to stop the herd's growth and ease the forest's burden. He soon walked out of sight.

Thirty minutes later, I had another spike in the cross-hairs, one that qualified for the buck tag. I passed on him, too. I wanted to shoot a mature buck or doe, or go home empty-handed.

Another hour had passed when I heard hoofs breaking shell ice. Puddles in the forest behind me had frozen, and the ice now telegraphed the deer's approach. When a doe and her two fawns pranced into view, I was waiting, my rifle shouldered.

The doe got within 30 yards before spotting me. The cross-hairs jumped between her extended neck and the back of her rib cage. A cedar blocked her chest. My heart racing, I hesitated as she dropped her head and jerked it up, trying to make me move.

In the next instant, she leaped and darted about 30 yards, and then abruptly stopped to look at me, still not sure what I was. Her chest now exposed, I touched the trigger without guilt. Her fawns had been weaned two months ago, and could take care of themselves, despite what Disney's disciples believe.

The Revelation

After tagging and field dressing the doe, I pulled her viscera to the side and exposed the rumen, one of her four stomach compartments. It's there that deer pack in their food and store it until they have time to regurgitate it, chew their cud, and reswallow it for digestion.

I slit the rumen and examined its contents to see what the doe had been eating. With forest deer, it's usually woody browse, leaves and acorns. I found such matter in the doe's rumen. But along with it, I also found a heavy mixture of shell corn.

"Baiters," I said aloud, half-amused. There probably wasn't a cornfield within 30 miles of me. Obviously, someone in the area was baiting deer.

That's perfectly legal, of course.

Still, I no longer noticed the ringing of solitude in my ears.

"Where Silence Once Rang" was originally published in several Wisconsin newspapers in December 1995.

Len Rue Jr.

WHEN DEALING WITH TWICE-SHOT DEER, MANY BELIEVE THE HUNTER WHO DRAWS FIRST BLOOD IS ENTITLED TO THE ANIMAL. OTHERS ARGUE THE DEER SHOULD GO TO THE HUNTER WHO MADE THE KILLING SHOT. WHILE SOME HUNTERS CAN CALMLY AND DIPLOMATICALLY RESOLVE THESE CONFLICTS, CONSERVATION WARDENS ARE SOMETIMES ASKED TO SETTLE DISPUTES.

CHAPTER 4

THE TWICE-SHOT DEER: WHO KEEPS IT?

"The surrender of a previously hit deer to the first shooter is in direct proportion to the size of the deer. The larger the antlers, the less the chance of that deer being surrendered."
— *South Dakota warden*

■ BY BRYCE M. TOWSLEY

Dick Spooner faced demons most of us won't meet in our worst nightmares. From the Viet Cong bullet that put him into a wheelchair to a devastating disease that sucked out his life one piece at a time, his journey through life has not been easy.

Last summer, shortly before Lou Gehrig's disease ended his 48 years of turmoil, Spooner sent me a copy of his autobiography. Like its author, the book is rustic and unpolished. But also like him, if you dig deeper you'll find an underlying story of strength and perseverance.

Spooner never gave in to despair. Instead, there was always a thread of optimism that tomorrow would be better, that hope might bring him through. He used his love of deer hunting to form hope's foundation. But as I read his book, I was shocked to learn even that let him down.

Spooner had a 4-wheel-drive truck with hand

WHOSE DEER WAS IT?

A volley of shots broke the midmorning silence and drew my attention to a grass field.

There he was, charging straight at me: the huge buck that was responsible for all the area's remarkable rubs, including one on a telephone pole.

I couldn't help but be struck by the massive size of his body, and his gray coat. But his antlers were simply incredible. He bulled across the field like an NFL fullback, somehow avoiding what I assumed were my brother's shotgun slugs.

I was on stand near a beaver dam, a popular deer crossing on a steeply banked stream. I hadn't seen a deer in the past day-and-a-half of hunting. The jolt I felt as adrenaline rushed through me can't be described.

The buck jumped a barbwire fence as if it weren't there. He angled upstream, apparently heading for another crossing. I prepared to sprint up the opposite side of the wooded stream in a long-shot effort to head him off. Just then he turned toward me and, in seconds, was gingerly crossing the beaver dam.

I let him get well onto the dam and then shot. He didn't flinch. I shot again. He continued to methodically cross the dam, seemingly fearful of taking a wrong step.

I couldn't believe I had missed, but surmised buck fever was causing my problems. I took a deep breath, knowing this would be my last shot at him while he was slowed by the dam. I squeezed the trigger this time, and he went down hard.

I watched to make sure he stayed down, and then yelled up the ridge to my buddy, who was nearby. He called back that he was on his way.

I then saw my brother sprinting across the field from where the buck had come. Just as I was about to yell, I noticed it wasn't my brother.

The unidentified hunter continued to sprint for the dam. I ran to beat him to my deer, which was on its back, not quite dead. With each huge breath he drew, the buck's body expanded to even greater proportions. He dwarfed a 180-pound buck I had helped a friend drag out only a few weeks earlier. This animal was massive.

Suddenly, from across the creek, the other hunter pulled out his knife, presumably, to slit the buck's throat. I told him to put his knife away, because this buck's head was going on my wall. He didn't say a word, and was soon joined by a second hunter. I asked them to step to the side so I could dispatch the buck.

Soon, my friend was at my side, and the other two hunt-

WALT LARSEN POSED FOR THIS PHOTO BEFORE RELINQUISHING THE BUCK TO A GROUP OF HUNTERS WHO CLAIMED TO HAVE SHOT IT FIRST.

ers were joined by five more. My brother was a ridge over, curious as to what was happening, but he continued with his still-hunting.

The other hunters claimed to have already shot the big buck, having driven it over a few ridges and flung a lot of lead at him. A closer look revealed three holes: one in the right side of his neck, my shot; one in the left antler, one of their shots; and one behind the left front shoulder, their shot.

I asked my friend to give his opinion. He said they had made a lethal shot on the buck. I replied that the deer hadn't seemed seriously hurt, and that he had to have traveled at least several hundred yards with that hole. None of their hunters in the field had been shooting at the deer's left side. Probably so, he said, but he had seen the buck limping at times as it crossed the field, and it was a lethal shot, nonetheless.

I considered the politics: We were outsiders, albeit landowners, and they were locals. Considering this, along with my friend's assessment of the wounds, I relinquished the deer.

Fortunately, although in shock, I had enough sense to demand a photo of this amazing deer. My friend retrieved my camera from my daypack and snapped a few shots. He remarked later that he had never before witnessed such a Mona Lisa smile on a deer hunter. Except for the memory and the roller coaster of emotions I felt that morning, the photo is all I have to show for the experience.

Several nights later, I awoke in a cold sweat, believing my finishing-off shot hadn't been accounted for when my friend examined the buck. I thought the left-side "lethal shot" that cost me the deer could well have been my slug's exit hole.

I was sick. I called my friend, but he assured me he had checked the hole carefully. It wasn't an exit hole, he said. It bore the characteristic pucker of an entry wound.

In the weeks after the episode, the story was told and retold. Many hunters said I did the right thing. Nearly as many insisted it was my deer because I had reduced it to possession. Nobody lacked an opinion.

If nothing else, it inspired me to write this article. And so now, I ask you: Whose deer was it?

I still can't decide with certainty, even though more than a year has passed.

— *Walt Larsen*

controls. He and his father had driven deep into the mountains of Chittenden, Vt., one day late in the 1981 deer season. They sat together watching a logging road, neither really expecting to see a buck, but content they were deer hunting as best they could.

Suddenly, a buck was standing in the snowy road. Spooner fired his shotgun as the buck started to run. When it came out from behind a small rise, Spooner's father hit it through the heart with his .33 Winchester. The buck made it over a sharp ridge, and started tumbling down the steep hill. They heard another shot, and saw a hunter running along the bottom of the hill.

With Spooner paralyzed from the waist down and his father crippled by the infirmities of age, they couldn't make it through the snow and rough terrain to the deer. By the time they drove around the hill and made their way to the deer, the other hunter already had the buck field dressed and was dragging it out. Even though it was obvious the big Winchester had made a killing shot, the hunter refused to give them the buck.

An old man and a paralyzed war veteran were hardly a match for the strapping young hunter, so the Spooners left without a fight.

An Enduring Debate

Questions surrounding twice-shot deer are often debated when deer hunters meet. Rules and traditions vary by region, and even by camp. Some say the hunter who draws first blood owns the deer, regardless of the wound's location. Others claim the hunter firing the first obviously lethal shot gets the deer. Others argue the hunter who administers the final shot claims it. Still others insist that whoever first tags it or cuts its throat is the rightful owner.

It seems, too, that such "rules" are often subject to interpretation, which will vary depending on the sex and size of the deer.

I was hunting a few years ago in New Brunswick when a man from our camp wounded a buck late in the day. This quiet man never asked for assistance, but his friend jumped in and helped track the deer until dark.

That night we discussed the situation over dinner. Within that group, we agreed that because the man had drawn first blood, and the wound would likely lead to a dead buck, the deer was his, regardless of how the track unfolded the next day. The next morning, however, the taciturn fellow deferred to his friend, who was refusing all offers of help. They returned to the track at daylight.

A few hours later, they heard a horn blowing. The buck had stumbled onto a logging road and collapsed

WHAT OUTFITTERS SAY

What follows are some comments on twice-shot deer that we solicited from a sample of outfitters who regularly guide deer hunters:

"It was always an unwritten law that whoever draws first blood and seriously wounds the deer gets it. But then we found out that this is breaking the law. Instead, it is whoever actually kills the deer. If that deer has even 1 ounce of breath left when you shoot it, you have killed it and the law says you must tag the deer."
— *Carman Kelly, Kelly's Sporting Lodge, Fredericton, New Brunswick*

"We have always considered the hunter who makes the first lethal hit owns the deer. For years it was the unwritten law that applied, but today in much of Pennsylvania, it has become so cut-throat during our gun season that it's usually the first one to the deer. That is one of the primary reasons we concentrate on archery hunting. There are a lot fewer hunters in the woods then."
— *Brian Post, Full Fan Lodge, Montrose, Pa.*

"It has always been the first one that hits the deer well and has an expectation of collecting it. Common sense applies. A superficial hit is different than a solid hit. With the latter, it is usually obvious who owns the deer.

"Sadly, though, this is changing. We are seeing a different kind of hunter in the woods today. The ethics and morals are not in the forefront as they were only a few years ago. Some hunters will stoop pretty low to tag a buck. I think this is a reflection of changes in our society. When I started hunting almost 50 years ago, everybody hunted, and it was considered an honorable thing to be doing.

"The ethics that rule in the woods and apply to situations such as a twice-shot deer should be taught early but, sadly, they are often ignored in today's changing society."
— *Bob Beaupre, Vermont Sportsman Lodge, Morgan, Vt.*

"We have never encountered it here with our customers, but it occurs in the area now and again. The rules of fair play say the first hunter to hit the deer well owns it, but in the disputes that we know of, usually one party gives up and walks away. So, it seems the one inclined to argue the longest and loudest often gets the deer."
— *Roy & Cynthia Petrowicz, Lamplighter Lodge, Sturgis, Saskatchewan*

near death in front of the outfitter's truck. The "friend" was younger and faster than the quiet man. He sprinted over and put a killing shot into the downed buck, which was truly a huge animal. In fact, the buck would later score almost 180 points gross Boone and Crockett. Friendship and ethics took a back seat as he tried to claim the buck. The outfitter would have no part of such foolishness, and instructed the first hunter to tag the buck.

Still, the deer now seemed tainted, the victory hollow. It was perhaps the largest buck the man would ever see, let alone shoot, but there was no celebration in his heart that night. He was too much a gentleman to complain publicly, yet when I asked him about it privately, he said he wished things had turned out differently.

Too often in today's woods, such incidents ruin what should be a great day. Worse, there seems to be no universal way to solve these problems. Further, with the deer woods becoming more congested with hunters, such problems seem certain to escalate.

> THE BIG DEER NOW SEEMED TAINTED, THE VICTORY HOLLOW. IT WAS PERHAPS THE LARGEST BUCK THE MAN WOULD EVER SEE, LET ALONE SHOOT, BUT THERE WAS NO CELEBRATION IN HIS HEART THAT NIGHT.

Opposite Example

In an opposite example, my cousins Stephen and Philip Baker heard a shot early in the morning on the last day of Vermont's 1992 black-powder season. They went in that direction to see if the hunter needed help dragging the deer. In the fresh snow they found footprints trailing a bleeding deer. My cousins followed, but soon they saw where the tracker had broken from the deer's trail and headed toward the road.

My cousins followed the deer all day, covering several miles without any sign of the first hunter. Finally, just before dark, Philip spotted the deer and ended the chase with a well-placed shot.

Later that night, he received a phone call from a man who heard they had "found" his deer. He wanted to claim it, even though he admitted he had abandoned the trail and realized they had worked hours to recover the deer. I doubt anybody would say the first hunter had a legitimate claim, but my cousins gave the deer to him.

Some years ago, I noticed that some hunters I met from Pennsylvania often used rifles most hunters consider too big for whitetails. They told me that because of intense competition in the hunter-infested Pennsylvania woods, they try to "wreck" a deer to drop it in its tracks. I can't view a big-bore rifle as a real solution.

Who Has the Solution?

Instead, the remedy would seem to be hunter education and better ethics. Or perhaps the answer can be found in a state's rules and regulations.

To see how the problem is addressed in North America, *Deer & Deer Hunting* magazine sent a survey to each state and Canadian province to see if conservation wardens had an established policy, or if they knew of local customs that usually applied. We also asked how the two, if different, were used to settle disputes.

The survey questions follow:

1: Does your state or province have any laws or administrative rules that specify who is legally entitled to a deer that has been shot by two different individuals or parties?

2: Are there local customs or "unwritten laws" that help determine who is entitled to a twice-shot deer? If yes, please elaborate.

3: When conservation wardens are asked to intervene in disputes over twice-shot deer, do they follow a standard procedure in determining who claims the deer? If yes, please elaborate.

4: What factors help a warden decide who should claim a twice-shot deer? (Examples: Location of wounds, time/distance between shots, type of weapon, adherence to trespass laws, etc.)

5: We often hear three opposing justifications for claiming a twice-shot deer. Which of the following beliefs best describes how you would settle disputes over twice-shot deer:

A: First Blood — Whoever inflicts the first wound claims the deer, regardless of the circumstances that follow.

B: First Lethal Hit — Whoever puts the first shot though a vital organ or artery claims the deer.

C: Final Shot — Whoever fires the killing shot claims the deer, regardless of previously inflicted wounds.

Wardens Respond

Several officers wrote that if the dispute could not be settled to mutual agreement, then the law enforcement officer would take the deer.

Many other officers said this was not an area that often required their intervention and, further, many of them liked it that way. Kentucky's respondent simply

WILL COOL HEADS PREVAIL WHEN ARGUING OVER A TWICE-SHOT DEER? EMOTIONS SOMETIMES TAKE CONTROL. "SOME HUNTERS WILL STOOP PRETTY LOW TO TAG A BUCK," SAID ONE OUTFITTER. "I THINK THIS IS A REFLECTION OF CHANGES IN OUR SOCIETY."

Bryce Towsley

WHAT THE WARDENS SAY

What follows are select comments from conservation wardens who answered our survey about twice-shot deer:

"Possession claims favor the person who actually puts the deer down. However, the more ethical gentleman would offer the deer to the person in immediate pursuit of the injured animal.

"Unfortunately, the surrender of previously hit deer to the first shooter is in direct proportion to the size of the deer. The larger the antlers, the less the chance of that deer being surrendered.

"As you might expect, relinquishing a deer to the person initially hitting it is much greater between parties of the same hunting party than between competing parties. Ethical standards are much more easily compromised for a stranger than for a person whom you know and expect to encounter with some regularity."
— *Ron Catlin, Enforcement Specialist, South Dakota Division of Wildlife*

"If the first hunter hits a vital organ, but the deer runs another half-mile and was dropped by a second hunter, it would be my opinion that the second hunter would tag the deer. There will always be situations with twice-shot deer, however. Most are settled between sportsmen in a very sportsman-like manner. Those few situations that lead to problems usually involve at least one game hog.

"Basically, it is the hunter who makes the fatal shot, unless the deer was lying down and the hunter walked over and put a round through its neck."
— *Col. Wayne Brewer, New York Division of Law Enforcement*

"Game has no ownership until legally reduced to possession. Possession can't occur until the game is dead."
— *Larry Bell, Chief of Law Enforcement, New Mexico DNR*

"What makes life interesting is not the first shot, first lethal hit, or final shot.

"All of the above are extremely inconclusive. ... You raise a more important subject about life. That is, things are rarely black or white, just shades of gray."
— *Major Ronald P. Alie, chief of law enforcement. New Hampshire Fish & Game Department*

"The 'reasonable expectation of following through to the kill' would be the deciding factor. The 'first blood' might eventually be lethal, the 'lethal shot' might be abandoned, the 'final shot' disturbs me: If someone runs up and shoots my downed — but not yet dead — deer in the head, he should claim it? I think not."
— *Lt. Don Starbard, Alaska Fish & Wildlife*

"I am not aware of a problem with twice-shot deer in Alberta. It might have happened, but common sense should dictate the outcome."
— *Officer Neil Maki, Alberta Energy & Natural Resources*

"Generally, the person who puts the animal down to stay gets it. However, English Common Law puts ownership of fallen game into the hands of the landowner and would prevail if no permission to use the land was granted."
— *Guy Winterton, Manager, Compliance Operations, Ontario, Canada*

"Legally, the person who administers the fatal shot is entitled to the deer."
— *Lt. Robert J. Rooks, Vermont F&W Department*

"The older, more experienced wardens stay completely out of such incidents where the warden's and only the warden's opinion is used to make such controversial decisions.

"But fallacies exist because of the many variables associated with (deer hunting) scenarios. I saw a man shoot a nice buck (one shot) with a .30-06. The deer did not fall, but ran close to a man who shot at it with double-ought buckshot. The deer fell dead instantly, but upon gutting and skinning the deer, it was shown the only shot to hit the deer was the .30-06.

"The most nightmarish scenario would be two hunters, unacquainted, using 150-grain Winchester Silver Tips in .30-06, simultaneously shooting and killing a Boone and Crockett trophy buck having massive, symmetrical antlers with 16 points and a 29-inch inside spread. As none of the above-mentioned beliefs would be applicable, would they simply flip a coin? I think not.

"However, at no time should a game warden be expected to make a determination of lawful or proper ownership under any circumstances."
— *Harold Oates, assistant commander, Texas Parks & Wildlife Department*

"Washington Fish and Wildlife officers have no legal authority to declare an animal belongs to either hunter. We enter the dispute as a mediator and attempt through actual evidence and reason to resolve the conflict."
— *Investigator Ron Peregrin, Washington Department of Wildlife*

"First lethal hit, if verifiable, would be my judgment because a lethally shot deer might run 100 yards or more before falling. However, a killing shot is hard to argue with because we cannot, without extensive professional necropsy, determine whether a previous shot would have been lethal."
— *Capt. Keith LaCaze, Louisiana Department of Wildlife & Fisheries*

"The shot that felled the animal is the one that counts. We encourage both hunters to be ethical in this process by making a decision that they can live with."
— *Major Mike Howard, Maryland Forest, Park & Wildlife Service*

wrote, "Don't get involved" as his complete response. Most wardens, however, suggested that hunters should be able to work it out among themselves if they applied common sense. Several wardens believe they're seldom called into such disputes because hunters usually do work things out themselves. Only Maine's respondent said the state's wardens often receive calls to mediate such matters.

Several wardens pointed out that no laws in their state or province specifically address the problem, and they could only act as mediators without enforcement powers. Further, because such disputes could escalate into civil court or formal complaints, wardens are often wary of getting involved. Texas's respondent said that because of such concerns, "The older, more experienced wardens stay completely out of such incidents."

In reviewing the responses, it seems that only Quebec has dealt with this issue in court. The court found in 1960 and in 1977 that the hunter who first inflicts a serious wound to the animal "in such a manner that he can anticipate imminent capture, regardless of the circumstances that follow," is entitled to the animal.

Of the 59 responses we received, 42 wardens provided a definitive answer about how they would determine who's entitled to a twice-shot deer. By far, they said the hunter who administers the final shot gets the deer, with 27 listing this as the option they would choose. Many explained that the law states the hunter who "kills" the animal or "reduces it to possession" is required to tag it. Therefore, they must choose that option or risk being in violation. The next most common response — 10 votes — was to favor the hunter who administered the first lethal hit. The "first blood" option drew only three votes, and two respondents said the "first to tag" the deer owned it.

For the record, the National Bowhunter Education Foundation, recommends the "first lethal hit" option. This seems in keeping with the tendency among bow-hunters to wait 30 minutes or more before trailing a deer they've shot. Also, bow-hunters tend to enjoy less crowded and less competitive hunting conditions than firearms hunters. It's our guess that this option is more likely to grow in popularity with hunters and wardens than the other two, especially if it becomes a concept taught in hunter education classes.

> THE NATIONAL BOWHUNTER EDUCATION FOUNDATION RECOMMENDS THE "FIRST LETHAL HIT" OPTION BE USED TO DECIDE DISPUTES. THIS SEEMS IN KEEPING WITH A TENDENCY AMONG ARCHERS TO WAIT 30 MINUTES OR MORE BEFORE TRAILING A DEER THEY'VE SHOT.

How Far to Push?

While it wasn't recommended by any of the wardens, one solution is often suggested by hunters. How many would actually carry it out, however, is debatable. In a 1970 *Sports Afield* article on Larry Benoit, this legendary deer hunter described an incident in which he applied the concept.

"I shot this deer, wounding it and was trailing him. Killed him from a cliff, and two hunters came up and were going to dress him out.

"I hollered to leave him alone, that I'd be down to take care of him, thanks anyway. They yelled up that the law of the woods says that a man sticks him first and it's his deer and I said you go right ahead and stick him and I'll blow the stock off your rifle.

"He started to stick him and I blew the stock off his rifle. I said, 'Now get!' and they got. I had no trouble, But I stayed there till dark to make sure."

The article continued, "Larry keeps his word."

Still, this isn't an option we recommend. No deer is worth risking property damage or personal injury.

"The Twice-Shot Deer: Who Keeps It?" was originally published in the March 1996 issue of Deer & Deer Hunting *magazine.*

Bill Marchel

CHAPTER 5

WHO WOULD KNOW?

Hindsight would clear up any lingering ethical questions. Or would it? What good is hindsight to ethics? It is ethics, after all, that guide us through temptations of the moment.

■ BY LAURIE LEE DOVEY

When the 180- to 190-class Boone and Crockett whitetail stepped into sight 80 yards away, I instinctively placed my scope's cross-hairs on his vitals. The buck's antlers spread far beyond his ears. The bases of his main beams were easily half again as big around as my wrists. The ivory-tipped tines of his symmetrical 14-point rack glowed in the burnt-orange evening sun.

My record-book buck of a lifetime stood before me. My .270's safety was off, and I knew my aim was true. The deer was mine, all right.

But I couldn't shoot.

Thirty minutes before rattling in this huge-racked king, I had shot at a smaller 10-point buck. I saw the 10-pointer bow up under the impact of my shot, yet, out of reflex, it jumped a barbwire fence. The deer ran only 30 yards before it dropped out of sight. I believed I had hit the deer, but I couldn't hop the fence to look for its blood trail.

When the owners of the ranch where I was hunting

MY RECORD-BOOK BUCK OF A LIFETIME STOOD BEFORE ME. MY .270'S SAFETY WAS OFF, AND I KNEW MY AIM WAS TRUE. THE DEER WAS MINE, ALL RIGHT. BUT I COULDN'T SHOOT.

dropped me off, they had told me not to cross that fence no matter what happened. If I crossed, I would have to walk across a county road that bordered another rancher's land. If law enforcement officials spotted me, big trouble was certain.

So Close, So Far

I desperately wanted to see that 10-pointer lying in the brush just over the knoll on the other side of the road. But the rise blocked my view. Although the buck was certainly just a few yards, it might as well have been a continent between us. This was the final hour of a five-day hunt and 12-day road trip. I had been hunting hard and was now exhausted. I had passed up numerous big deer, mainly heavy-racked 8-pointers, waiting for a super deer. I wanted desperately to return home successful. After shooting at the 10-pointer, I left my setup position and walked along the fence to where the deer had stood when I shot. I didn't find blood.

Immediately, I began doubting everything I had seen. Because the deer was moving toward the fence when I fired, I thought I might have misjudged either my timing or shot placement. After reassessing everything, I decided my chances of a hit were 50-50.

But two events continued to nag me. I clearly saw the deer bow up immediately after the shot, and I saw it disappear 30 yards away as if it had fallen. The buck could be lying just a short distance from where I now stood.

But I had no way to tell. There were no trees to climb for a better view over the knoll in front of me. Frustrated, I retreated to my stand site and waited for my companions to pick me up. I knew we could then search for the buck because they had permission to go onto the other land.

While I waited, I decided to try a new rattling box I had picked up six days earlier. I had nothing else to do but wait, and only 30 minutes of daylight remained. I also knew I had nothing to lose by trying a new product.

Rattling In a Dream

So I rattled the box. Unfortunately, it worked like a dream. A magnificent whitetail raged out of the brush along a drainage 100 yards upwind of me. The huge buck was stomping, grunting and snorting, looking for his inferiors. I gasped at the sight. Never before had I seen an animal equal to this buck. Not even the mounted head on the ranch-house wall that measured 26-plus inches across

THERE WASN'T ANY BLOOD. SURELY I MISSED THE FIRST DEER. I CAN SQUEEZE ON THIS OTHER BUCK AND TAKE HIM WITH NO PROBLEM.

the main beams could compare. The buck created such excitement and intensity that I felt entranced. He was mine! I began to squeeze the rifle's trigger when reality gripped me firmly.

"You can't shoot," I whispered to myself. "You might have hit the 10-pointer. It might be lying 30 yards past the fence. The law says one deer per hunter. If you kill this buck, you're breaking the law. But look at him! You'll never get this chance again!"

Instantly, the corners of my mind engaged in an ethical battle I'll never forget. In retrospect, some of my thoughts not only embarrass me, they shame me. Here's a synopsis of the struggle between my ethics and desires:

I missed that 10-pointer. He jumped the fence. No deer hit by a .270 bullet would or could jump a fence. But wait! Remember the conversation last night with Judd Cooney? He said a wounded deer can, out of reflex, jump a fence. He knows what he's talking about. He's been hunting forever. He's right.

But there isn't any blood. I missed. I can squeeze on this deer and take him without a problem. He's still standing there. He's calmed down. Heck, he's starting to feed along the fence line. This is the surest shot I've ever had on a whitetail!

I start to squeeze. I back off again.

No! I won't be able to live with myself if I illegally kill two deer.

But I can easily lie about what happened. This is *the* deer I've always dreamed of. When they come to get me, if anyone heard two shots, I can say the buck was the first shot, and a coyote I missed was the second shot. That's believable. I simply won't mention the other deer. Who would know the truth? No one.

Am I crazy? Now I'm thinking about lying to myself and to friends. Maybe I don't have to lie. With a buck like this, everyone would understand why I shot. Heck, any other hunter would shoot, right?

A Virtue Tested

I was possessed. I considered every side of the situation as my mental skirmish continued for nearly 15 minutes. All the while, the record-book deer sauntered closer while my cross-hairs followed. With the buck at 65 yards, I could wait no longer. The sun was on the horizon and darkness was moments away. I had to decide now! My hands shook. I was sweating and breathing heavily.

I knew I couldn't live with a lie. I knew I'd never be able to look at the beautifully mounted deer hanging on my wall without remembering the circumstances of its death. I sighed as I dropped the butt of my rifle to my knee. I was disappointed, distraught and highly emotional. The buck hadn't moved. Still, it taunted me.

I begged: "Lord, if I'm the person who's supposed to take this deer, have it stand there a few more minutes. If I'm not the hunter who's to take him, please make something happen."

Instantly, the buck took three steps, just enough to move behind thick brush and out of sight.

He was gone.

Still, my disappointment deepened, even though I knew I had done right.

After dark, five of us searched for the 10-pointer without luck. We searched again the next morning. We found tracks down a deep drainage, but no blood trail.

Hindsight's Clarity

Reality sliced my heart. I had cleanly missed the 10-pointer. I could have shot the 14-pointer without breaking any man-made laws. And the clarity of hindsight would have even cleared up any lingering ethical questions.

Lance Krueger

UNFORTUNATELY FOR ME, THE RATTLING BOX WORKED LIKE A DREAM. A MAGNIFICENT WHITETAIL RAGED OUT OF THE BRUSH ALONG A DRAINAGE 100 YARDS UPWIND OF ME. THE HUGE BUCK WAS STOMPING, GRUNTING AND SNORTING, LOOKING FOR HIS INFERIORS. I GASPED AT THE SIGHT. NEVER BEFORE HAD I SEEN AN ANIMAL EQUAL TO THIS BUCK.

Or would it? What good is hindsight to ethics? It is ethics, after all, that guide us through pressures of the moment, and tell us to shoot or flip the safety back on.

Yes, I came close to killing that buck. And I've had dozens of hunters more experienced than I am say they would have had no internal debates. They say with conviction that they would have killed that buck. But they're making their judgments in retrospect, knowing the first deer wasn't down. I listen to them, but say you can't know how you'll react until you're living the situation, weighing uncertainties, both legal and ethical.

Several years later, that Mexican buck still haunts me continuously. I close my eyes and see him in vivid detail. I wish he were a trophy hanging in my office over the computer as I record this story.

Yes, I wish my name were in the record books. But if I had taken the shot, and I had never told another soul the

whole story, I would have been stuck with a lie I could never reveal. And every time I looked at the majesty of that incredible buck, I would be living a lie.

I would know the truth. The record-book entry would mock me.

And I could never escape my own stare.

Editor's Note: Shortly after writing this article, Laurie Lee Dovey received word from her hosts that a buck they believe to be the same 14-pointer was shot the year after her hunt. The buck scored 186.

"Who Would Know?" was originally published in the November 1994 issue of Deer & Deer Hunting *magazine.*

Patrick Durkin

WE REVEAL OUR NATURES IN THE CHOICES OF THE SPECIES WE HUNT, THE MANNER IN WHICH WE HUNT THEM, AND ESPECIALLY IN THE SPORTING STANDARDS WE IMPOSE ON OURSELVES AND THE DEGREE TO WHICH OUR HUNTING MEETS THESE STANDARDS.

THE ETHICS OF PURSUIT

Pursuit must always take precedence over killing, or we destroy the important meanings and values essential to the activity.

■ BY LEE NISBET

To know a man is to know what activities he chooses to pursue and the manner in which he pursues them. It is through activities that our character is formed, deformed and reformed. In reflecting on our activities, we recognize who we are and what kind of person we're becoming. Such reflection represents the essence of moral or ethical thinking.

The activity of hunting, the pursuit of other species with the intention of killing them, provides a compelling opportunity for moral insight. To know what attracts a man to hunting, and especially how he carries on his hunting, is to know much about his character.

We who choose to hunt, and who make it a preferred activity and a living piece of who we are, have a revealing means of self-assessment in this activity. We reveal our natures in the choices of the species we hunt, the manner in which we hunt them, and especially in the sporting standards we impose on ourselves and the degree to which our hunting meets these standards.

These choices also reveal the strengths and weaknesses of our character. Never have I been so tested as a man as in my hunting.

The Significant Choice

I am concerned here with a specific kind of hunter, a man who finds the qualities of the hunt so immediately attractive, so compatible with who he is that his hunting becomes a focal point in his life. Such a man could not imagine a life without hunting. The mere thought of such a life would depress him.

I choose this kind of hunter for several reasons. Ethically, as Aristotle noted, for a choice to be significant it must be an expression of one's character. Activities and choices that are merely sporadic or forced count for nothing. Further, to have ethical importance, a man's choices must be made freely and knowledgeably.

With these criteria in mind, it's obvious that ethical significance attaches only to activities of the natural hunter, one for whom a predatory relationship is scintillating; one who thrills to pursuit and killing within pursuit; one who dreams, recollects and delights in recounting the adventure of the chase; one who studies and knows the habits and habitat of his prey. Such a man is the hunter and all others are pretenders. We can numerically count these others, but the moral significance of their hunting does not count.

What are the qualities of hunting that compel such attention in the kind of hunter I am talking about? Hunting and the predatory relationship is obviously rooted in a man's nature. There is, however, no instinct for hunting, for not all men are moved to hunt. But in human nature there is one salient trait that all men share: the need for drama. As John Dewey, the philosopher, observed, it is historically

I DID NOT FIRE. I LACKED THE SKILL TO PULL OFF THAT PISTOL SHOT WITH CERTAINTY, AND I KNEW IT. I FELT BAD THAT HE HAD SLIPPED BY ME, BUT I ALSO FELT STRONG. I KNEW THAT ON THIS OCCASION I WON AN IMPORTANT VICTORY.

Bill Marchel

common that temples were built before people were fed and clothed, that any occasion served as an excuse for a celebration, and that men hunted while women and other "inferiors" were confined to practical endeavors. Whenever men have had the opportunity, they seized and still seize the opportunity for dramatic experience.

Sport Hunting

Dewey noted further that animals have always captured man's imagination. They fed and clothed ancient man, they were adept at avoiding capture, but not perfectly adept. They, therefore, were and are material for the drama called sport hunting. Through varying kinds and degrees of restrictions upon our tactics and weapons, we can vary the degree of diffi-

culty in pursuing and killing the animal. Degrees of difficulty can also be varied by the kind of animal hunted and the terrain where we choose to hunt. Different species attract attention because of some special characteristics they possess: size, grace, wariness, massiveness of antler, ferocity, succulence of flesh, and so on. The hunted species, for the serious hunter, are objects of aesthetic appreciation, objects with qualities of form, temperament, habit and habitat that make them beautiful, desired.

But there is something else, and here we come to the essential feature hidden to all but the true hunter that makes hunting so compelling. When a predatory man is attracted to a species, what attracts him most are its qualities that emerge when it's pursued. We understand now why a man can find an animal beautiful and want to kill it, for it is the very wanting to kill it in a difficult chase in the animal's habitat that makes the animal attractive. A superbly racked but penned whitetail is ultimately of no more interest to a deer hunter than a bovine confined to a pasture. The deer is attractive to the hunter insofar as he can imagine the great buck in the woods walking past his stand. That image makes the deer hunter's eyes widen and his hands tighten around his imaginary weapon. The hunting urge is so strong that he can hardly resist adopting his shooting posture toward the imagined animal. The animal becomes beautiful, attractive, compelling — that is, dramatic — when we imagine hunting it. That is why we are predatory men.

> ETHICALLY, AS ARISTOTLE NOTED, FOR A CHOICE TO BE SIGNIFICANT IT MUST BE AN EXPRESSION OF ONE'S CHARACTER. ACTIVITIES AND CHOICES THAT ARE MERELY SPORADIC OR FORCED COUNT FOR NOTHING.

We predatory men, those of us who find compelling drama in the hunt, share characteristics with men of other natures. No matter what the formed activity, if it aims to achieve an end, there exists dramatic tension between the successful achievement of the desired end and the process of achieving that end. The hunt becomes truly revealing of who we are because we will have the opportunity to decide whether we are more interested in killing the animal or more interested in hunting it well. Allow me to explain.

Predatory Relationships

The predatory relationship is an aggressive relationship toward the animal. Every predatory man, every true hunter, delights in a certain kind of killing. When we seek to pierce a deer with an arrow, slug or bullet, we do not want to hurt the animal. We want to kill it. So we can say every true hunter delights in killing quickly and cleanly within the context of the hunt. This sort of killing is what we are talking about when we acknowledge our aggressive relationship toward the animal. Without the hunting, the killing would have no drama, no special meaning or value. Without the hunting, the killing would merely be the extinction of an animal, which would hold no special interest or appeal. The hunting, then, does not justify the killing. Rather, it gives the killing its meaning and value.

Therefore, the question often raised by those hostile to hunting, "How can you justify killing an animal for sport?" is meaningless. We don't justify it. We do it. Whether we experience the killing as good or not depends on how effectively or ineffectively we kill, and how well we hunt the animal. One cannot deny that we hunters are willing to sacrifice something valuable and important: the life of an animal we admire. Again, however, the conflict between killing and admiration is resolved by the fact that our admiration grows out of what the animal gives us in the process of hunting it.

The relationship of pursuing to killing determines an important ethical standard intrinsic to sport hunting. If we kill the animal sloppily, or worse yet, wound it and fail to retrieve it, or take shots that are beyond our skill level, then we violate the essence of sport hunting, the relation of pursuing to kill that makes the killing good and the pursuit exciting.

We ruin the act and drama of hunting when we value the killing of the animal more than its pursuit. In sum, pursuit must always take precedence over killing or we simply destroy the important meanings and values essential to the activity.

Shots Not Taken

How do I know this about hunting? My hunting, especially my deer hunting, taught me these lessons. I have hunted and killed many deer, but not all my hunts have been equally good. My best hunts were those in which I deliberately exercised judgment that resulted in a clean kill or no shot at all.

Two of my most memorable deer hunting moments involved deliberately not shooting at two white-tailed bucks that I wanted to kill.

In the first instance, a series of novel running tactics designed to confuse the deer, combined with still-hunting and use of a noisy creek, allowed me to stalk within 20 yards of a superb buck that first spotted me at about 200 yards. When he exploded from his hiding place, I was on him quickly with my 12-gauge, which was equipped with a red-dot optical sight. This combination had allowed me to cleanly kill running deer before. On this hunt, though, I didn't complete the trigger squeeze. It just struck me there was too much brush for a sure, killing shot. Immediately after, I felt wonderful. The stalk itself made my day. In fact, that stalk made my deer season. That stalk was simply the best hunting I had ever done.

I felt excited about my hunting and absolutely proud that I chose not to shoot. I had chosen, in this instance, the greater of two goods. Had I shot and killed the buck, I would have known that the killing was more luck than skill. Conversely, wounding an animal of that size and savvy would have been sickening. I had chosen well and I knew it.

A few years later, however, within a stone's throw of the earlier hunt, I had a different experience. I killed a doe by permit earlier in the season, but I was having no success getting a buck, especially a particular buck I wanted. Preseason scouting allowed me to jump him on opening day, but he ran out of sight too quickly for a shot. As the season progressed, I studied the problem, thought about it night after night, and finally developed a plan. I knew where he bedded and where he likely spent most of his time, especially as the season progressed. I began to think that if I killed him in a predetermined manner, this would prove I was as excellent a buck hunter as I conceived myself to be. It was the last Saturday of the deer season, about 4:15 p.m., with daylight fading fast.

With my back against a tree, the wind at an angle in my face gave me two directions the buck could travel on his run without detecting me. A movement to my right snapped me to attention. There he came, grazing and walking slowly on a course that would take him in front of me. I decided not to make a move until he came from behind a huge oak 30 yards away. I watched as he slowly grazed his way toward the oak. He took forever! My heart pounded. I started a breathing exercise to relieve the tension. At last his head went behind the massive trunk. I raised my scope-sighted shotgun. His head, then his neck, appeared. The cross-hairs centered on his neck and I squeezed the trigger. Unbelievably, I missed!

The buck bolted down the trail and the scope's

> I HAD PULLED THE TRIGGER IN AN IMPULSIVE, DESPERATE ATTEMPT TO MAKE UP FOR MY FIRST MISS. I LURCHED, CONSEQUENTLY, FROM A FAILURE IN SHOOTING TO A FAILURE IN CHARACTER.

black cross-hairs got lost in his dark coat in the failing light. In desperation, I fired anyway. He hunched at the shot, then disappeared. I found hair but that was all I ever did find. That was the last cheap shot I ever took at a deer. Walking back to camp in the blackness of the woods, I felt as I never want to feel again. What a failure of ethical judgment! I had so valued success, so needed to prove my skills, that I had pulled the trigger in an impulsive, desperate attempt to make up for my first miss. I lurched, consequently, from a failure in shooting to a failure in character. I wounded and lost a magnificent animal and, thereby, ruined my deer hunting for that season.

Conclusion

I have, however, used that failure and others to good advantage. I remember them, go over them and acknowledge my mistakes in attitude and judgment. My reflections served me well this past season. A massively built, well-racked buck got by me on a trail I discovered while grouse hunting. I was hunting with my scope-sighted .44 Magnum revolver. Just as he came over a ridge to my right I glanced to my left. When I turned and spotted him he was moving quickly through thick woods about 65 yards away. I pulled back the hammer on my single-action. At the click he stopped and looked through a small hole in the brush. The cross-hairs of my scope settled on the patch of white throat hair, the only target that presented itself as he looked at me.

I did not fire. I lacked the skill to pull off that pistol shot with certainty, and I knew it. I felt bad that he had slipped by me, but I also felt strong. I knew that on this occasion I won an important victory.

In this instance, I was a hunter.

And a better man for it!

"The Ethics of Pursuit" was originally published in the October 1987 issue of Deer & Deer Hunting *magazine.*

CHAPTER 7

A CHEAP RESOURCE?

Where do we draw the line between the importance of having numerous opportunities to shoot a deer, and the quality of the deer herd, its habitat and our deer hunting experiences?

■ BY DICK THOMAS

The value of a wildlife resource, such as the white-tailed deer, cannot be judged solely on its renewability. The enjoyment and quality experience one derives from the use of that resource — whether as a hunter, a photographer or casual observer — must be deemed equally as important as a wildlife agency's annual harvest figures concerning that resource.

Yet each year wildlife managers in most states face the question, "Do we want to manage for as many deer as biological and social factors allow?" The usual answer from the deer hunting public is, of course, a resounding yes, and fish and wildlife agencies usually respond by doing just that.

Too Many Deer?

But, herein lies another question: "Are we cheapening the resource and our deer hunting experiences by allowing for too many deer on the landscape?"

Most of today's deer management systems call for the controlled harvest of a certain percentage of the herd's females. This, in turn, provides the tool for

WHAT DEGREE OF SATISFACTION CAN HUNTERS DERIVE IN SITUATIONS WHERE IT'S POSSIBLE — EVEN OBLIGATORY — TO HARVEST SEVERAL DEER?

Bill Marchel

raising, lowering or maintaining the herd's population. By maintaining deer numbers at or just below the range's carrying capacity, biologists can manage for a healthy herd and, consequently, increase reproduction rates. The result is more deer available each year for hunters to harvest.

Because the ultimate responsibility is not to exceed the range's carrying capacity, biologists must rely on hunters to harvest the required number of female deer each year. To do that, states use various methods based on hunter success rates, the number of licensed hunters, the herd's size and density, and social acceptance of the herd's size. These methods include doe-only days, separate antlerless deer seasons, liberal seasonal or daily bag limits, and special deer-management permits that allow a certain percentage of hunters to shoot additional deer.

Consequently, a gleeful deer hunting public often applauds these measures for an obvious reason. The more deer there are available, the better one's chances of harvesting a deer or, better, several deer.

Drawing the Line

Many hunters, however, remain ignorant of biological facts and oppose the deer manager's system, believing a doe harvest causes population declines, meaning less reproduction and, ultimately, fewer deer to hunt.

In essence, almost everybody wants the most deer possible. But where do we draw the line between the importance of having numerous opportunities to shoot a deer, and the quality of the herd, its habitat and the deer hunting experience? Several states allow hunters to harvest one deer or more per day throughout a liberal season. Even if a state allows one hunter to harvest only two or three deer the entire season, is that two or three too many? Or is it two to three deer too few?

Some states boast a success rate of more than one deer per licensed hunter per year. I can't help but think back to a time when only one out of every 10 hunters killed a deer each year in my state.

When I was the one, by skill or luck, I was proud. My whole season, my whole year, in fact, centered on that one brief moment where patience, knowledge and practice paid off. I can look up at a set of antlers on my wall and remember all of the details of that hunt. My memories remain sharp when it's a single affair. Few

> ARE WE CHEAPENING THE RESOURCE AND OUR DEER HUNTING EXPERIENCES BY ALLOWING FOR TOO MANY DEER ON THE LANDSCAPE?

details are lost: the weather, the initial sighting of the deer, my racing pulse, the joy (and sorrow) of killing the animal, and the personal satisfaction of internal instincts fulfilled.

Most importantly, however, are the strong feelings I retain in support of the justification for my actions. The serious deer hunter's personal code of ethics is magnified each time he harvests a deer that required significant time and effort.

Nowadays, I wonder what degree of satisfaction a hunter derives in situations where it's possible — even obligatory — to harvest several deer. In addition, a hunter and his family can only store and consume so much venison each year without losing their high regard for the luxury of deer meat. And isn't that one of our primary reasons for harvesting deer: to enjoy them as a renewable resource in the form of table fare?

And where do we balance such concerns with the almost moral duty hunters often feel to remove as many deer as necessary to keep the herd in tune with its range? These are the questions we will increasingly encounter in the years ahead.

Conclusion

I urge those interested merely in having increasingly more deer available to shoot to evaluate what you receive, or want to receive, from your deer hunting experiences. Contemplate the possibility that there can be too many deer. And consider how you, as a person and as an appreciative admirer of the outdoors, are affected by the quality of a day or season afield in pursuit of deer.

We should be more concerned with that aspect of our hunting heritage, not with how many animals we can each shoot. Let's not cheapen our sport by forcing it to remain a numbers game.

"A Cheap Resource?" was originally published in the March 1989 issue of Deer & Deer Hunting *magazine.*

CHAPTER 8

DR. JEKYLL & MR. DEER HUNTER

Because of irresponsible behavior by some licensed sportsmen, our deer hunting privileges face greater opposition every year. It's the hunter inside each of us that will ultimately decide deer hunting's future.

■ BY DICK THOMAS

D eer poachers are found everywhere you find the whitetail. With little or no respect for the magnificent animal they pursue, the sporting arms they use, and the art of hunting itself, these people kill deer year-round with total disregard for laws.

Sportsmen frown on these criminals and cheer when a poacher is arrested and prosecuted. Some of these same sportsmen then go afield during deer season and break every game law and rule of ethical deer hunting.

I call this the "Dr. Jekyll and Mr. Deer Hunter Disorder," and for years I've sought to unravel the mysteries of this annual syndrome, which afflicts thousands of otherwise responsible people.

Analyzing the Disorder

Most of the data I've collected on this disorder has come through detailed field observations. By stepping

FRIENDS, NEIGHBORS, RELATIVES, LAWYERS, EXECUTIVES, FARMERS AND EVEN POLICE OFFICERS HAVE BEEN BESET WITH THE DR. JEKYLL AND MR. DEER HUNTER SYNDROME. FOLKS WHO ARE OTHERWISE RATIONAL, ETHICAL, HARD-WORKING PEOPLE SUDDENLY TRANSFORM INTO SLY, SNEAKY BRUSH-BUSTERS OVERFLOWING WITH IRRATIONAL THOUGHTS AND ACTIONS.

back and taking a broader look at my years of notes, I came up with these generalizations:

1) The disorder appears to coincide with the white-tailed deer's annual rutting period. It begins shortly before deer season and abruptly ends the evening of the last day.

2) Contributing factors affecting the severity of a hunter's disorder include sightings of polished antlers, buck rubs and scrapes, fall foliage, temperature changes, the urge to test a firearm's abilities, visions of tenderloins in a frying pan, and, perhaps most importantly, peer pressure to be successful.

3) The disorder can plague anyone in the deer hunting community. Friends, neighbors, relatives, lawyers, executives, farmers and even police officers have been beset with the Dr. Jekyll and Mr. Deer Hunter syndrome. Folks who are otherwise rational, ethical, hard-working people suddenly transform into sly, sneaky brush-busters overflowing with irrational thoughts and actions. I've witnessed victims of the disorder suffer incredible mood swings, harshness toward others, and an inability to tell the truth.

Let Me Tell You ...

My field notes concerning the disorder go back several years. By sharing some of my experiences, I hope to also convince you to share my concern over the disorder and the future of deer hunting.

Several years ago, while jogging on a country road during bow season, I was enjoying the autumn air and fall colors. Suddenly, I heard a car crest the hill behind me. It soon slowed and pulled alongside me.

Its driver was a man I knew from town. He was a respected small-business owner. He was also a deer hunter. He was wearing a sport jacket and tie, with dress slacks and shoes. He looked as though he had been to church. At about the same time he was saying hello, two does bolted out of the brush, ran across the road, and stood broadside to us 50 yards out in a hayfield. The well-respected businessman leaped from the car and grabbed his compound bow.

Leaving the vehicle in the center of the road just over a blind hill, he ran toward the deer, nocking an arrow as

> One gentleman flipped his Jeep while paying more attention to deer in the hayfield than the road. Amazingly, he had an arrow already out of the quiver and nocked when he and his broadhead took flight inside the Jeep's cab.

he went. The deer, of course, bounded away and offered him a splendid 75-yard shot at a dead run. He missed, the deer disappeared, and I continued jogging at a much faster rate.

Hard to believe? I thought so too.

That same year, at the same spot, another gentleman flipped his Jeep while paying more attention to deer in the hayfield than the road. Amazingly, he had an arrow already out of the quiver and nocked when he and his broadhead took flight inside the Jeep's cab. A trip to the hospital was inevitable.

Gun Tales

That year's firearms season was loaded with Dr. Jekyll disorders. A neighbor and I spent several hours one day pursuing one buck. My neighbor, an older man who hadn't shot a deer in several years, finally was positioned so that when I walked through a little swale the buck ran past him. He shot it, he gutted it, we dragged it, and that night someone stole it. Right out of his barn. Deer hunting will never be the same for my neighbor.

I can recall another infamous season that seemed like the year of the road warrior. One day, my father and I noticed several does running toward us. In the distance we heard a noise similar to that made at a drag race. Before long a pickup truck, whose driver had seen the deer, careened off the road and across the field toward the brush, the deer and us. Finally, he saw us and turned back, oblivious to the posted sign he ran over on the way in. A few days later, two truckloads of men in orange stopped on our road long enough to shoot 23 times at a big buck I had watched for three years. They hit him, but all they found were pieces of the 14-point rack they shattered.

A favorite tree stand of mine is at the intersection of several hedgerows, and it looks out over a few hundred acres of open field. I've killed two deer from this stand. From its upper branches I've also seen all sorts of hunters take shots at running deer at distances I estimated to be 200 yards or more.

From that same tree, I once spoke to an elderly man walking under me. In the pre-dawn light I said, "Sir, you're on private property." His reaction was to bring the gun barrel up in an alarming fashion and wave it at me while looking wildly about for the voice from the dark. Talk about irrational! I'll never do that again!

But one year in particular was the best for observing the Dr. Jekyll disorder. While tracking a buck I had wounded, six other hunters shot at the deer 18 times. Not one shot hit it. I finally killed that deer and, as I sat next to it wondering how I had survived the slug-fest, I heard a shot nearby. A hunter, excited about seeing me bag the buck, had climbed out of his tree stand without first unloading his gun. The slug entered his pants above the knee and exited just above his boot sole-without touching him. I never realized you could get all the color to leave your face as that guy did.

Through these and many similar experiences, I believe the Dr. Jekyll disorder is the single most damaging mark against deer hunting. It is the root of most problems that deer hunting faces. Because of irresponsible behavior by some licensed sportsmen, our deer hunting privileges face greater opposition every year. Hunter education programs, hunter safety courses, organized sportsmen's groups, and law enforcement officers have taken their toll on other harmful factors, which include poaching, hunting fatalities, and limited access to private lands.

Conclusion

But the fact remains, it's the hunter inside of each of us that will ultimately decide deer hunting's future. It is each hunter's sense of ethics and responsibility that make

DR. JEKYLL DISORDER

1) The disorder appears to coincide with the whitetail's rutting period. It begins shortly before deer season and abruptly ends the evening of the last day.

2) Factors affecting the severity of the disorder include sightings of polished antlers, buck sign, autumn weather, and, perhaps most importantly, peer pressure.

3) The disorder can plague anyone in the deer hunting community. Friends, neighbors, relatives, lawyers, executives, farmers and even police officers have been beset by it.

us remember last deer season as "the year I matched wits with that deer" and not "the year I filled my tag and those belonging to three others."

This next fall, if you suddenly feel the urge to trespass, take a ridiculously long shot, or shoot 30 minutes before legal shooting time, sit down on the nearest stump, breathe deeply and talk yourself out of it.

And when you're done talking to yourself, decide then and there how much you truly love deer hunting. The depth of that love will determine deer hunting's future.

"Dr. Jekyll & Mr. Deer Hunter" was originally published in the March 1988 issue of Deer & Deer Hunting *magazine.*

IF YOU SUDDENLY FEEL THE URGE TO TRESPASS, TAKE A RIDICULOUSLY LONG SHOT, OR SHOOT 30 MINUTES BEFORE LEGAL SHOOTING TIME, SIT DOWN ON THE NEAREST STUMP, BREATHE DEEPLY AND TALK YOURSELF OUT OF IT.

Lance Krueger

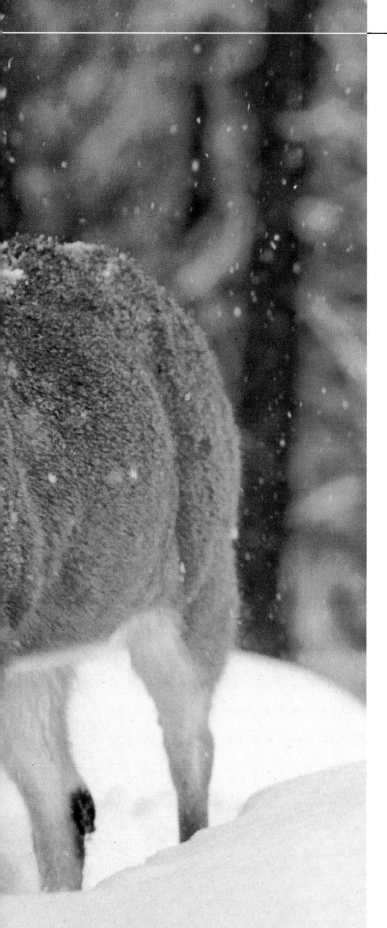

CHAPTER 9

Until Next Year, *Part 1*

Is any sight quite as grand as a monstrous white-tailed buck, completely unaware of your presence, simply being himself?

■ BY GREG MILLER

The inside of my hunting cabin is silent, save for the hissing of logs in the fireplace. I stand and stare at the burning embers a few seconds. It's been a long season. Three months ago I began pursuing the monster buck I will hunt this evening.

We've come to know each other well, this big buck and I. His ability to stay one step ahead of me has, so far, kept the score in his favor. But the game is quickly ending. This is the final day of archery deer season.

The warm, pleasant days of September and October are forgotten, replaced by the harsh early-winter cold of December. It was 15 degrees below zero yesterday evening when I went to the stand, and 10 below the evening before. I check the thermometer outside the cabin. The mercury sits dead center on 12 below. That's OK. I'm getting accustomed to the cold. Or maybe it's more a case of knowing how to deal with it.

Frigid Ritual

Slowly, I start the ritual of layering my clothing. I know I'll have at least a two-hour wait on my stand before the buck shows. My apparel must be warm but not restrictive. Experience from many seasons of hunting in frigid conditions serve me well. Long underwear first, then a layer of thermals. Wool atop that. I pull on a pair of light cotton socks. Two more pairs of wool socks cover these. Heavy Canadian pac-type boots, specially designed for extreme cold, engulf my sock-encased feet. I then pull on a pair of down-filled mittens, which I can remove quickly and quietly at crucial moments. I'll carry a set of insulated coveralls in my backpack. They'll be put on just before I climb into my stand.

After getting dressed, I hesitate. My mind drifts back to a cool, frosty October morning. I was in a stand not far from the one I'll occupy tonight. He walked through that morning, but out of range. I was reduced to being a mere spectator instead of a participant in nature's game. Still, is there any sight so grand as a huge white-tailed buck, unaware of a human's presence, simply being himself?

His body size was massive. He had not yet lost any weight from pursuing does. The rut was still a couple of weeks away. And what antlers! Ten long, evenly matched points and main beams as fat as my wrist! That buck was a grand representative of the whitetail.

As quickly as he appeared, he just as suddenly vanished, swallowed up by brush around my stand. It made no difference. I had seen enough to be hooked. I paid that area a lot of attention the next few weeks. Once the big fella started rubbing and scraping, I had gotten a much better feel for his movements.

Back to the Present

I'm brought back to reality by the pop of dry oak in the fireplace. It's time to head out to my stand. My nostrils just about freeze shut as I step from the cabin and into the subzero cold. I wonder how much someone would have to pay me to do this if a big whitetail weren't involved.

The drive to my hunting area is less than one mile. I park my truck, grab my gear and start my walk. It's about a quarter-mile to my stand. Plodding along, I notice the cold makes the snow squeak underfoot.

Arriving at my tree, I see several fresh deer tracks nearby. There's no mistaking one set of tracks. The wide, splayed print belongs to my buck. So, he passed through here after I left last night. I'm optimistic he will

> AS QUICKLY AS HE APPEARED, HE JUST AS SUDDENLY VANISHED, SWALLOWED UP BY BRUSH AROUND MY STAND. IT MADE NO DIFFERENCE. I HAD SEEN ENOUGH TO BE HOOKED.

show up earlier tonight. My stand is near a prime feeding area. The cold surely will prompt him to hurriedly try to restore his depleted fat reserves.

I pull the insulated coveralls out of my backpack and put them on. My gloveless hands tingle from the cold during the short time it takes to climb into my stand. After pulling my bow up with the tow rope, I nock an arrow and take a couple of practice draws. The bulk caused by my cold-weather clothing doesn't interfere with my shooting style. I check to ensure everything is OK on my bow, and then hang it on a dead stub of a limb.

Settling onto my stand's seat, I prepare for my motionless vigil. Yesterday, I had found the antler of a small buck on a nearby runway. Last evening, the little deer, with frozen blood hanging from his right pedicel, walked under me. With no desire to shoot him, I watched as he browsed within bow range for almost 30 minutes. That helped the time go by! Will he return to entertain me tonight?

Recalling November

A half-hour after settling in, my thoughts again return to the big buck. I think of an early November morning when he nearly made a fatal mistake. A doe had run into view, and I knew a buck was following. With her mouth hanging open and tail tucked tightly, the doe left no doubt she was in heat. I soon heard him coming. He was busting brush and emitting deep-pitched grunts.

The doe looked back toward the buck and trotted toward me, passing less than 10 yards away. "This is it," I thought. "He's going to follow right in her tracks and give me a shot." It seemed a bit too easy.

Everything was going fine. My dream buck was walking along, head down, following the doe's trail. If he took just a few more steps I would get my shot.

Suddenly, he stopped, snapped his head up, and looked in my direction. I dared not breathe. I soon realized he wasn't looking directly at me. Still, he knew something was amiss.

How do they know?

Instead of continuing his route, the buck turned and quickly took about five quick steps to his right. He got behind a blowdown and stopped 25 yards away, but all I could see was his huge rack and a single eye peering

Len Rue Jr.

through dead branches. A shot was out of the question.

Five minutes dragged by, then 10. All the while, the buck moved nothing except his head. He was trying to pinpoint the danger. I waited. If he came out either side of the blowdown, I would get a clear shot. If he turned and went straight away, keeping the blowdown between us, he was safe.

That's what he did.

The big monarch didn't panic or act nervous. He simply turned and walked straight away. When he had walked perhaps 30 yards, he stopped and looked back. What a sight! His neck swollen to an absurd size and antlers polished a mahogany brown color, he was the epitome of a rutting buck. He stood 15 seconds and then turned and trotted off, tail held high. He had won the round.

I collapsed onto my stand's seat. The nerve-racking ordeal had exhausted me. Even though I had been there only an hour, I got down and left. I knew it would be impossible to hunt effectively any longer that morning.

Time Flies

My mind returned to real time. Glancing at my watch, I was surprised to see more than an hour had passed. So far, the cold hadn't bothered me, other than creating a nasal drip that wouldn't quit.

It was about this time yesterday when the little buck showed up. Not today, though. I wonder if I spooked him by crawling down from my stand last night when he was so near. If so, did I tip off the big buck to my presence?

He had dropped out of sight one other time, during our nine-day firearms season. Fearful he might have been shot by another hunter, I had spent days searching for his sign after gun season. Finally, a week ago, I found something better than sign. I saw him with my own eyes. In fact, he was right here, at the food source my stand overlooked.

It was Christmas Eve day when I walked up on that 10-pointer. The wind was blowing hard from him to me. He had his head stuck in the brush, browsing. Never have I been so close to a mature buck who was so completely unaware of me. The range was 35 yards. I paced it off later. Of course, my bow was back at the truck. I had walked into the woods merely to check for his sign. It was midday and I didn't expect to walk up to him.

So, he was alive! All my fears of him dying during rifle season were erased. He looked at me one time, but I remained motionless. Convinced he had nothing to fear, the buck kept feeding. When his head went back into the brush, I turned and slowly walked away. When I was out of his sight, I quickened my pace. I returned to my truck, grabbed my bow, and headed back into the woods.

He was gone.

His home turf was a small corner of a huge chunk of land. Undoubtedly, gun-hunters had poked and prodded every square foot of his stomping grounds except this one 40-acre parcel. I didn't doubt he had spent the entire gun season here. Now I had found him.

Finding him and killing him, however, were two different things. After seeing him Christmas Eve, I spent many hours on my stand without another sighting. Still, his huge, fresh tracks continued to appear around my stand. It was just a matter of time before he walked by during shooting hours. I just hoped it happened before the season ended.

> MY BOW HAND GOES FROM FEELING NUMB TO FEELING NOTHING. I PERSIST. IF HE TURNS HIS HEAD TO LOOK IN ANOTHER DIRECTION, I MIGHT BE ABLE TO DRAW AND SHOOT. IT'S BEEN TOO LONG OF A SEASON TO GIVE UP NOW!

Reappearing Act

So, here it is: The last day of the season and, so far, after nearly two hours of watching, I've seen nothing of the 10-pointer.

Wait! He's here! A few seconds earlier, there was nothing. But mysteriously, he has appeared. He's slowly turning his head, surveying the surroundings. There's no doubt it's him. His tremendous body looks black against the snow. Even at 75 yards, I can easily see his heavy, long-tined rack. Shucking the heavy mittens, I grab my bow and get positioned for a shot. He starts walking toward me.

At 40 yards, he stops and looks around. He sticks his nose straight into the air and sucks in the air currents. Satisfied all is well, he drops his head and continues toward me. My heart hammers, making it seem someone is beating a bass drum inside my ears.

After closing the distance to 20 yards, he stops once more. This time, he appears to be staring up at me. I shut my eyes to avert his stare and to thwart his sixth sense.

It works! Once more he drops his head and walks closer. A hundred thoughts rush and tumble through my head. How big are his antlers? No doubt they'll make Pope and Young easily. Boy, his mounted head will look great on my wall! I wonder if someone is around to help

track and drag him out. Should I draw now?

He suddenly stops at 15 yards and snaps his head up. He looks into my eyes. This isn't the plan! The gloveless hand holding my bow begins to go numb from the cold. I think about trying to draw while he's looking at me. Forget it!

More time passes. My bow hand goes from feeling numb to feeling nothing. I persist. If he turns his head to look in another direction, I might be able to draw and shoot. It's been too long of a season to give up now!

Three or four more minutes pass. I'm in trouble. No longer worried about drawing my bow, my biggest concern is whether I'll be able to descend safely from my stand. Both hands seem detached from my arms. Yet I can't bring myself to move or do anything that would scare the deer. It just goes against everything I've learned to intentionally spook a big buck away from my stand.

No Choices Remain

Finally, I realize I have no choice. Looking the buck in the eyes, I speak: "You win this time." Instantly, he wheels and bounds away. Feeling dejected, I sit down and try to warm my hands. The process is slow and painful. Eventually, enough feeling and mobility return to allow me to climb down. Once on the ground, I gather my gear and start to walk out. Something compels me to turn and look back.

There he is, 60 yards away, watching. In the fading daylight we have another brief stare-down. Then he turns and walks off. I watch until he disappears from sight, feeling that awesome hollowness of being so close but coming up empty.

For some reason, still unknown to me, I holler after him: "You're the winner!

"Until next year!"

"Until Next Year" was originally published in the March 1990 issue of Deer & Deer Hunting *magazine.*

MY EYE WANDERED BRIEFLY FROM THE KILL ZONE TO THE ANTLERS. THE GLANCE CONFIRMED MY SUSPICION. IT WAS HIM! I COULDN'T MISTAKE THOSE ANTLERS. I HAD SEEN THEM MANY TIMES. LONG BEAMS, FAIRLY WIDE, WITH MORE THAN EIGHT POINTS.

Bill Kinney

CHAPTER 10

NEXT YEAR, *Part 2*

Next year is here. Would the big 10-pointer I had been chasing two years make a fatal mistake? Apparently so. The red evidence in the snow looked promising. Still, I couldn't risk everything by being impatient now.

■ BY GREG MILLER

I don't know what made me turn and look over my left shoulder. Perhaps it was some sixth sense, honed by countless hours spent pursuing whitetails. Or maybe it was just that I know better than to concentrate in one direction. Deer always seem to appear exactly where "they ain't supposed to."

The buck had already walked by and was quartering away when I saw him. Three inches of fresh snow allowed the big deer to pass silently behind within 20 yards of my tree stand. I was lucky to have glanced that way. The buck was unlucky in that if he had been moving faster, he would have been safely into thick cover before I turned.

The early morning's heavy clouds were rapidly dissipating, giving way to a clear sky. Soft midmorning sunlight filtered through the trees, illuminating small patches of the woodlot. Just as I shouldered my .270, the buck stepped into a patch of sunlight. His rack, which at first had looked dull and dark against the snow, now seemed to glisten.

The Confirmation

He suddenly stopped, head erect, looking and listening for anything that might be a threat. Peering intently through the scope, I was ready. But my eye wandered briefly from the kill zone to the antlers. That glance confirmed my suspicion.

It was him!

I couldn't mistake those antlers. I had seen them often in the two years I had pursued this buck. Long beams, fairly wide, with at least 10 points. Then there was the deer itself. He was big-bodied and heavy through the chest and neck. And rather than the slate-gray color of most North Woods bucks, he had a rusty hue.

My mind returned to my goal. The buck was walking again, heading toward a small opening. I moved the rifle slightly, aligning the scope's cross-hairs in the middle of the opening. The buck's rack loomed into view, then his neck and finally his chest. After one more step I saw a shoulder. I centered the cross-hairs and squeezed the trigger. The recoil knocked my vision off line a second, but when I recovered, the buck was on the ground. As I bolted in another round, he suddenly got his legs under him and was gone. I waited, rifle at the ready, hoping to catch him moving through some small opening in the underbrush. Nothing. No sound, no movement, no buck.

After five minutes, I climbed down and slowly walked to where the buck had fallen. Blood and hair littered the snow. Staggering, running tracks led away into the thick cover. Even without snow, it would have been easy to see that the deer was well hit. I felt no need to push things. He wasn't going far. Breathing a sigh of relief, I leaned against a giant poplar tree and recalled what had transpired the past two seasons.

The First Sighting

My mind raced back to that cool October morning when he first showed himself. He was out of bow range and obviously wasn't coming closer. All I could do was watch, but that was enough. I guessed he was close to 250 pounds on the hoof, and his antlers did justice to

his gigantic body. Ten evenly matched points adorned a dark, long-beamed rack. He grazed around me nearly five minutes, but suddenly disappeared as quickly as he had appeared.

Almost three weeks passed before I saw him again. His love for the ladies nearly killed him that November morning. A doe had run into sight, "hot" and fleeing earnest advances. Soon after, I heard him coming. He was busting brush and breaking branches, making no attempt to conceal his approach. He grunted deeply with each step.

> I HAD RECENTLY DISCOVERED THE BUCK'S WHEREABOUTS. HE WAS LIVING IN A SMALL CORNER OF A LARGE TRACT OF LAND. THE CORNER WAS ATTRACTING ONLY LIGHT HUNTING PRESSURE.

The doe looked once in the buck's direction and trotted toward me, passing within 10 yards. My heart jumped into my throat. I quickly scanned my equipment, got into a comfortable shooting position, and waited.

The buck kept coming, but then he suddenly stopped, raised his head and looked in my direction. I didn't twitch, but he knew something was wrong. He quickly moved behind a large blowdown and stood behind it about 10 minutes, moving nothing except his head. If he came out either side, I would have had a shot.

After a prolonged wait, he turned and slowly walked away, keeping the blowdown between us. At 30 yards, he stopped and looked back, making me wish I were carrying a camera instead of my bow. His huge, swollen neck accented his dark rack, giving the exact picture of what a rutting white-tailed buck should look like. He posed for perhaps 15 seconds, turned and trotted out of sight.

The Wait

My mind is jogged back to the present by the sound of someone walking through the brush. The orange-clad figure is my longtime hunting companion, Dan Dyson. Quietly, he asks what I shot. Even before I speak, I think he knows the answer. He's well aware of my pursuit of this buck.

"It was him, Dan," I said. "He almost got away again. I turned my head just in time to see him sneaking toward this thick brush behind me."

Dan glanced at the blood and hair. "From the looks of this, I'd say the chase might finally be over."

Larry Holjencin

I nod my head, adding, "I think we should wait a while before taking up the track, though."

Dan agrees and we speak no more. We stand in silence. I'm sure my partner knows what's going through my mind.

Nearly a year earlier, the buck came close to making a fatal mistake during our third encounter. It was the last week of December's archery season. The temperature had stayed below zero for several days. Although the cold made hunting a bit tough, deer were moving during the day, browsing to bolster their winter fat.

The 10-pointer had remained hidden throughout the firearms season, but he had suddenly shown up again in December. I was doing some late-season scouting on Christmas Eve when I walked up on the big fellow, but I wasn't carrying my bow. The next morning, I sneaked back in and put up my stand.

Six afternoons of below-zero temperatures passed before I saw him again during the bow season's final minutes. When he approached within 20 yards, he stopped. Soon after, he dropped his head and walked closer.

Just as he began to turn broadside, he stopped again. This time, he looked right at me. We exchanged stares until my body was numbed with cold, forcing me to move.

I told him aloud that he had won, and he ran off the way he had come. Once on the ground, I saw him watching from a distance. Before leaving I even yelled something about coming back for him next year.

Next Year Arrives

Now, next year is here. Would the buck make a fatal mistake? Apparently so. The red evidence in the snow looks promising. Dan sees me looking at the blood. "Think we should go after him now?" he asks. Without raising my head I reply, "Let's give him a few more minutes."

Just a month before I had been all-fired confident the buck was mine. The rut was just getting under way, so I had carried my rattling antlers to my bow stand one morning. About 30 minutes after getting settled, I performed a 45-second sequence of smashing and grinding the antlers. Before I had time to hang them up,

I heard a deer approaching.

As soon as he came into view, I decided not to shoot. He was a small 8-pointer. The little buck stayed nearby nearly five minutes, looking for the antagonists he had heard. Before leaving, he walked to the edge of a grassy swamp. He stopped and looked across the swamp toward a small spruce stand 50 yards away. I followed his line of sight, and nearly lost my breath. Standing knee deep in the frost-covered grass, was the buck.

I thought he would walk right to me. After all, he had obviously come to the rattling and could see a buck under my stand. Surely he would walk over to see if this buck had been fighting over a sweet-smelling doe.

I stared at the big buck. Twin columns of steam billowed from his nostrils in the frosty air. He glared at the 8-pointer. The small buck, intimidated, turned and

skulked away. As the little guy retreated, he walked under my stand. I remember thinking: "This is great! That big guy is going to come over here and run off this small buck." Not so. The monster buck watched only long enough to see the subordinate leave. Then he turned and melted into the spruce. My light rattling and grunting couldn't coax him back out.

I never saw him again during bow season. Still, huge rubs continued appearing almost daily, persuading me to hunt the area during gun season.

Also, I had discovered the buck's favorite haunts. Best of all, his favorite pocket of cover attracted only light hunting pressure.

I hunted him off and on during the gun season's first four days, but only when conditions were perfect. It was 9:30 a.m. on the fifth day when he finally walked by. If not for that casual glance over my shoulder, my hunt for this deer likely would have stretched into a third year.

Time to End It

I break the silence: "We've given him enough time, Dan. Why don't you circle around the patch of brush he ran into, just in case he isn't hit as hard as we think. I'll give you a few minutes to find a place to set up."

Dan merely nods his head and walks off. The tremendous amount of time we've spent together in the woods often creates unspoken understandings of each other's moves. I wait 10 minutes for him to get into position, and then ease ahead on the buck's trail.

At first the wounded deer made fairly big bounds, but within 50 yards, he had slowed to a walk. About 25 yards farther, I walk up on him.

He's in the middle of a tiny clearing, lying under the low-hanging branches of a small white oak. Amazingly, his head is up, but he doesn't look at me as I approach. Death is near. Quickly, the .270 comes to my shoulder and I put a finishing bullet into his neck.

Walking up to the deer, I feel greatly accomplished. I've waited two years for this moment. Kneeling down, I grab an antler and slowly lift his head from the snow. It appears age has caused his rack to stub out a bit. Also, he has grown an extra tine on the right side, which now makes him an 11-pointer. I admire him a few moments and then lay his head back into the snow.

Conclusion

After a bit, I hear a soft, low whistle. Dan wants to know what's going on. I don't answer right away. I need to be alone a few more minutes with the buck. Taking my gloves off, I run my hands over that beautiful rust-brown coat, smoothing the hair where it was ruffled by the brush.

The elation I first felt is replaced by a sadness. But there is something else, too. If there is such a thing as respect in death, that must be the emotion I'm feeling.

I silently straighten up, still looking at the buck. For some reason, my mind returns to that subzero

Greg Miller

GREG MILLER DISPLAYS THE **11**-POINT BUCK THAT FELL TO HIS **.270** AFTER TWO YEARS OF HUNTING WITH A BOW AND RIFLE. **I**F NOT FOR A CASUAL GLANCE OVER HIS SHOULDER, HIS HUNT FOR THIS DEER LIKELY WOULD HAVE STRETCHED INTO A THIRD YEAR.

December evening a year ago. I had hollered something about being the winner, until next year.

I now realize killing the buck didn't put the score in anyone's favor. Hunting isn't about winning or losing.

In my heart and soul, where the only true scores are kept, he'll always be the winner.

"Next Year" was originally published in a briefer format as "You'll Always Be the Winner" in the November 1992 issue of Deer & Deer Hunting *magazine.*

Patrick Durkin

THE DEER HUNTER'S TACTICS

*I*t was easy to picture Charlie Alsheimer's wry smile at the other end of the telephone line as he told me what I was already thinking: "Pat, there's only so many ways to hunt a deer. After that, it's just a new twist on an old idea."

He's right, of course, but it's always fun to hunt for those twists, and to uncover variety in routine occurrence. Those who succeed in such hunts will consistently bring home more deer than those who remain captive to habit. And don't let him fool you: Alsheimer knows that better than anyone.

Among my most difficult hunts each year is finding the unique "how-to" articles that are not only instructive and original, but fun to read. The master of such writing was Larry Koller, whose 1948 book, Shots at Whitetails, *is a deer hunting classic.*

It's safe to say most writers whose work appears in Part 2 of The Deer Hunters *are well-acquainted with Koller's book. Like Koller, they're serious deer hunters who forever seek an edge — however slight — that will put them in place for their next kill. Their searches will make them track down not only deer, but every new whiff of insight offered. Most of these hunts turn up only myth and corkscrewed assumption, but occasionally they'll return the wiser, even if they can't put their wisdom into words. Invariably, the next time they hunt they'll drag out a buck when they had no right being near a deer. They'll concede it to luck, and begin their next hunt grateful for another chance to learn.*

Me? I trust in persistence. It's hardly novel, but it's a trait that aids all tactics, proven and otherwise.

■ *PATRICK DURKIN*

PART 2
CHAPTER 1

WHY DO THEY CALL IT STILL-HUNTING?

" 'Still-hunting' is, as a term, slightly ambiguous. It is not to be confused with the common practice of sitting on a deer run all day — day after day — hoping a buck will come along, sooner or later."

— Lawrence R. Koller, Shots at Whitetails

■ BY CHARLES J. ALSHEIMER

People from other countries often view the American lifestyle as a bit odd. For one thing, unlike most of the world, we Americans live life at break-neck speed. Patience does not come naturally to us.

We also use confusing descriptive terms. For example, where else on earth do people drive on parkways, park on driveways, and live in mobile homes that are anything but?

Deer hunting is not immune from curious terminology. In fact, it has one of the most ambiguous terms any of us has ever heard. It's a term that raises questions almost every time it's used. In fact, many people each year seek an answer to this puzzle from *Deer & Deer Hunting*'s staff. Hence, this article.

This confusing term is "still-hunting." It's a clas-

"TO FIND A DEER ON FOOT YOU HAD BETTER BE IN THE WOODS ABOUT THE TIME THE MORNING STAR BEGINS TO FADE IN THE FIRST SMILE OF THE COMING DAY."

—T.S. VAN DYKE, *THE STILL-HUNTER*

THOUGHTS ON STILL-HUNTING

"I will say that, with whatever proficiency in still-hunting any mortal ever reaches, with all the advantages of snow, ground, wind, and sun in his favor, many a deer will, in the very climax of triumphant assurance, slip through his fingers like the thread of a beautiful dream."
— *T.S. Van Dyke, The Still-Hunter*

"The still-hunter works over the grounds with his eyes. He uses his legs only to carry him over the terrain he has carefully scrutinized. Each time he comes upon a change of grounds he must pause to scan the area about him."
— *George Mattis, Whitetail: Fundamentals and Fine Points for the Hunter*

"True still-hunting will ever be a solitary effort, one in which the successful hunter can take the greatest pride of accomplishment. He has outwitted our most cautious and instinctively clever species of wildlife at its own game. The satisfaction of taking a whitetail buck by still-hunting methods alone can never be approached by killing a buck that has been driven to the stander to be killed."
— *Lawrence R. Koller, Shots at Whitetails*

"Examine all the surroundings; see which is the best way to approach. But above all things, positively don't hurry, for in still-hunting Hurry is the parent of Flurry. There is no occasion for haste."
— *T.S. Van Dyke, The Still-Hunter*

"The strong factor favoring the man still-hunting in remote or neglected areas is that here he might hope to find his game relaxed to the point where daytime browsing is not unusual for the species."
— *George Mattis, Whitetail: Fundamentals and Fine Points for the Hunter*

"The true still-hunter ... does a great deal of watchful waiting as he moves over deer country. Looking, stopping, and watching with patience and care has many times filled a deer license, oftener indeed than has barging through deer country without regard or respect for a deer's keenness of vision, hearing and olfactory senses."
— *Lawrence R. Koller, Shots at Whitetails*

"Of the thousands who enjoy the still-hunt, the majority are backwoodsmen. One great reason is that the art is one requiring more proficiency for life in the forest than the average city man can spend there."
— *T.S. Van Dyke, The Still-Hunter*

"One of the best opportunities the still-hunter has for coming upon a walking or browsing deer is during a heavy mist or gently falling rain in the absence of any wind."
— *George Mattis, Whitetail: Fundamentals and Fine Points for the Hunter*

"Deer driving and club hunting, while highly productive, never reap the reward of glowing inner satisfaction gathered by still-hunting."
— *Lawrence R. Koller, Shots at Whitetails*

"It might be truthfully said that the inveterate still-hunter gets as much satisfaction from the hunt itself as he does from bagging his quarry. He is actually more than just a huntsman out to get his deer, and he is a man with more than ordinary love for the solitude of autumn woods. So content is he with his lot that he is unwilling to share it with others."
— *George Mattis, Whitetail: Fundamentals and Fine Points for the Hunter*

"Before one can expect any success in still-hunting, he must know something about the daily life and movements of the game."
— *T.S. Van Dyke, The Still-Hunter*

"The best snow conditions the still-hunter can hope for ... is a quiet falling snow with a thin white blanket already underfoot. This is it, and the man leaving the woods at this time simply admits his love for comfort is greater than his love for the hunt."
— *George Mattis, Whitetail: Fundamentals and Fine Points for the Hunter*

"Primarily, the still-hunter is most concerned with seeing or hearing his deer before the deer sees him. His every movement must be directed to this end."
— *Lawrence R. Koller, Shots at Whitetails*

"Heavy pine cover often shelters a pretty fair concentration of deer, and the still-hunter can well afford to be on his best mettle when he knows the animals are there. Walking over the lush bed of pine needles is most ideal for stalking your game."
— *George Mattis, Whitetail: Fundamentals and Fine Points for the Hunter*

"Relax not an atom of either vigilance or caution on account of advantages. Mark this well. In still-hunting you have never an advantage to spare. It will do you no harm to retain every one, and you may lose by throwing away a very slight one that you think quite needless."
— *T.S. Van Dyke, The Still-Hunter*

"Most hunters prefer to clear the woods during a rain, but the avid still-hunter properly attired for the occasion is willing to suffer some discomforts in return for the better odds of success."
— *George Mattis, Whitetail: Fundamentals and Fine Points for the Hunter*

sic example of words that can mislead. To American Indians, still-hunting in its truest sense meant waiting in silence to ambush prey. This is similar to the way we hunt from stands today. In some areas, many deer hunters retain that definition, even though "still-hunting" means nothing of the sort in most regions.

For modern deer hunters, the proper definition of still-hunting reads like this: "The hunting technique of slowly and silently slipping through the woods while looking for deer, with the intention of seeing the quarry before it sees the still-hunter. After spotting the animal, the hunter tries to 'stalk' within shooting distance."

Notice the distinction between "still-hunt" and "stalk." By today's definition, we still-hunt while still looking (no pun intended) for unseen deer. After still-hunters spot a deer, they either shoot or attempt to stalk within shooting range.

History of the Term

Since the late 1800s, several noted authors have written extensively about still-hunting. As a result, historians find it a bit confusing when trying to decipher the evolution of the term, "still-hunt." This confusion comes from the way American Indians, Europeans and modern Americans describe the term.

History has a way of being written and rewritten with the subject or event changing to suit the writer. It appears still-hunting is a term born in this manner. Before Europeans arrived in North America, the continent's Indian tribes had several refined ways of hunting. Done mostly by males, hunting was a difficult and time-consuming task because of the weapons used. Indians relied primarily on the bow and arrow. Before the bow and arrow, the weapons of choice were spears and clubs. Because of such short-range "tools," Indians relied heavily on communal hunting methods to meet the tribe's needs. Two popular methods were fire and water drives, where more than one deer could be killed at a time. The Indians used fire to drive the animals to a confined killing point. In the water method, they drove deer into or toward water, where they were more easily killed with clubs and other weapons.

The Indian Influence

However, the tribes used many other techniques to secure meat. From southern Canada to Florida, Indians were often said to have "stalked" their quarry. In many ways, this strategy was similar to

EXTRAORDINARY STILL-HUNTERS

Finding a person who excels at deer hunting is not always difficult. That is, unless you're looking for a deer hunter who excels at still-hunting. Three men who are at the head of today's class are Larry Benoit of Vermont, and Paul Daniels and Jim Massett of New York.

Benoit is almost already legendary, not only in the New England states, but across much of the whitetail's range. Since the early 1970s, deer hunters have been reading about the still-hunting experiences of Benoit and his sons as they still-hunt the big woods of Maine and northern Vermont. Benoit is an expert at tracking big white-tailed bucks in snow. His abilities are renowned, whether it's sizing up a buck's track, or knowing when to cover ground or prepare for the moment of truth.

Paul Daniels is not a household name to America's deer hunters. That's because he doesn't write, and he hunts without fanfare near his home in western New York. I've been fortunate to hunt with some of North America's best deer hunters, and Daniels would easily fit into that select group. But what sets him apart from all other hunters I've known is his still-hunting ability with a bow and arrow. Further, until recently, he always hunted with a recurve. Until he became a selective big-buck hunter a few years ago, he killed a white-tailed buck 17 years in a row with a recurve while still-hunting. I find that feat incredible.

As Daniels says, "My success is knowing where the deer will be, working the wind, and having the patience to move at a crawl when I know deer are close."

Daniels has brought down several big whitetails over the years, and he killed a 180-class 12-pointer when he was a teen-ager.

Massett is a New Yorker who is well known throughout the Northeast for his ability to still-hunt whitetails in New York's Adirondack Mountains wilderness. Because he's a long-distance runner, Massett stays in top shape. That allows him to hunt whitetails in the Adirondacks' most remote portions. When snow covers the ground, Massett tracks a buck until he catches up with it. In the process, he covers a tremendous amount of ground, and often must jog to keep up. Like Daniels and Benoit, Massett knows when he is close to a buck, and he slows his pace to get the shot.

Massett has killed several 140-class bucks with his time-proven stop-and-go still-hunting technique.
— *Charles J. Alsheimer*

what we now call still-hunting. Stalking, as done by the Indians, had many variations, just as still-hunting does today.

Virginia's Roanoke Indians used a "sneak" method of stalking. They moved slowly through the forest looking for bedded deer. The Chippewa Indians of the upper Midwest and Canada intentionally jumped whitetails. They followed a deer until it tired, and then moved in for the kill. Like the Roanokes, the Assiniboine Indians of the Dakotas slowly circled resting deer and killed them in or near their beds.

The Indian How Book by Arthur C. Parker is a fascinating work on the ways Indians lived. Parker also wrote a book called, *Parker on the Iroquois*. Both books were brought to my attention by Ted Keir, an outdoor writer from Athens, Pa. Keir has studied the ways of American Indians most of his life, and knows much about how they hunted. Keir believes today's modern deer hunter has nothing on yesterday's American Indians when it comes to hunting strategy. Nearly every technique we rave about today — whether it's lures, cover scents, deer calls or decoys — was perfected by Indians and incorporated into their hunts. And when it comes to stalking (what we call still-hunting) the Indians were masters of the craft.

> NOTICE THE DISTINCTION BETWEEN "STILL-HUNT" AND "STALK." BY TODAY'S DEFINITION, WE STILL-HUNT WHILE STILL LOOKING (NO PUN INTENDED) FOR UNSEEN DEER. AFTER STILL-HUNTERS SPOT A DEER, THEY EITHER SHOOT OR ATTEMPT TO STALK WITHIN SHOOTING RANGE.

Keir, drawing on his research and the work of Parker, said Indians could walk as silently as ghosts. "They knew how to feel the ground," as he puts it. He also said they knew the feeding, movement and bedding habits of whitetails, and successfully still-hunted them in all haunts. Keir believes the American Indian was as good a hunter as the world ever knew.

Still-Hunting and Decoys

I was particularly interested in how Indians used decoys to hunt. After reading several books on the Indians' methods, it became obvious they were masters at "deercoying," and took still-hunting to a higher level by the way they decoyed deer.

Unlike our current methods of deercoying where we set up the decoy and wait for a deer to approach, Indians slipped into the tanned hide of a whitetail — complete with a deer head — and stalked or still-hunted them with great success. This quote from Lowell K. Halls' book, *White-tailed Deer — Ecology and Management*, illustrates the Indians' decoying/still-hunting prowess:

"John Lawson (1967:29), who traveled extensively through the Carolinas in the first decade of the 1700s, witnessed the expertise with which Indians in disguise stalked whitetails, noting that the practice was not without peril: 'An Indian will go as near a deer as he pleases, the exact motions and behavior of a deer being so well counterfeited by 'em, that several times it hath been known for two hunters to come up with a stalking head together, and unknown to each other, so that they have kill'd an Indian instead of a deer.'"

Such skill today is almost unimaginable. Accounts like that exemplify the ultimate in still-hunting and deercoying.

The Indians' versions of still-hunting were not always done at a slow pace. Many Northern tribes, like the Winnebagos of the upper Midwest, hunted whitetails with the aid of snowshoes in winter. With deep snow covering the ground, they quietly slipped into yarding areas, and ran down and killed foundering deer with their tomahawks.

The Early Writers

When Europeans arrived in North America, they saw and chronicled the Indians' hunting methods. Many of these writers made references to "deer-stalking," a term preferred by the English.

In the early to mid-1800s, several American writers wrote about deer hunting. Henry William Herbert — known as Frank Forester — in his 1843 book, *The Deer Stalkers*, referred to many hunting strategies. Charles Dudley Warner was perhaps the first to use the term "still-hunting" in writing.

In 1885 he wrote the book, *A Hunting of the Deer and Other Essays*. Warner wrote: "(The) idea of still hunting is for one man to go alone into the forest, look about for a deer, put his wits fairly against the wits of the keen-scented animal, and kill his deer or get lost in the attempt. There seems to be a sort of fairness about this."

The Term is Born

But Theodore S. Van Dyke brought the term "still-hunt" to the fore when he wrote, *The Still-Hunter*, in 1882. Van Dyke elevated still-hunting to the level we

Patrick Durkin

know today with his book of still-hunting strategies. He didn't spend much space defining still-hunting. He basically said still-hunting was the American equivalent of what his "English cousins" called "deer-stalking," and didn't worry about splitting the hair any finer. No doubt it was Van Dyke's work that caused the term to stick and become popular with writers and hunters.

In *The Still-Hunter*, Van Dyke almost seems to peer into the soul of deer hunting by expounding at great length on the virtues of still-hunting. In his introduction, Van Dyke writes, "Not without hesitation have I undertaken to explore this 'dark continent' of the world of field sports." Still-hunting might have been a dark continent before *The Still-Hunter* was published, but it certainly wasn't after. The book became a classic, and is perhaps one of the best works ever produced on sport hunting.

The Term Reinforced

Those who grew up in the 1950s and '60s had Lawrence R. Koller to thank for their knowledge of deer hunting. Koller was a special writer who had a wonderful skill for using anecdotes to make his points. As with Van Dyke's *The Still-Hunter*, Koller's *Shots at Whitetails* became a classic. It's a book I refer to often, whether for pleasure or research. Though written 50 years ago, it remains a vast, relevant source of knowledge for modern deer hunters.

Of all the definitions I've heard for still-hunting, I like Koller's best: "The hunter who follows the still-hunting game alone adheres to a typical ritual. He works the lower feeding grounds during the early morning and late afternoon hours. When the sun climbs above the treetops he begins to look for bedded deer on ridgetops or along the edges of heavy swamp or thickets of evergreens. In any case, he covers ground slowly, traveling the route which will permit motion through the woods with a minimum of noise. Feet are placed carefully on moss or rock at every opportunity, keeping away from the noisy rustlings of dead leaves. He travels woods roads wherever possible to keep clothing from brushing noisily through the

small branches. On the credit side of the ledger, we can say that a smart still-hunter will often spot his deer before their alarm sends them crashing away."

Following closely behind Koller was legendary bow-hunter Fred Bear, who reinforced the modern distinction between still-hunting and stalking: Still-hunting, Bear said, was moving slowly through the woods, looking for deer. Stalking began after he located his quarry.

Bear provided the following definition in a 1968 interview with Curt Gowdy, which was recorded on an LP called, *Secrets of Hunting*: "The kind of hunting I like, and it is exciting, is still-hunting. You sneak around until you see an animal. ... You are invading the domain of the deer. This is his home. You're a stranger there, and it's very difficult."

By the time Wisconsin's famed deer hunter George Mattis wrote *Whitetail: Fundamentals and Fine Points for the Hunter* in 1969, defining the term in print almost seemed unnecessary. In fact, it was so common by Mattis' day that he didn't bother to define it the first few times he used the term in his 1969 book. But like Van Dyke, Mattis occasionally used the terms "stalker" and "still-hunter" interchangeably.

Still-hunting was so much a part of Mattis' life as a hunter that he opened his book with a 30-page chapter titled, "The Still-Hunter." His tribute to Van Dyke, perhaps? Mattis seemed more intrigued by defining the type of person who still-hunts than he was in defining how one should do it.

"It is (the) familiarity and love of the land which determines the still-hunter," he wrote when first using the term on Page 2 of his book. "Those relatively few men who take to the field alone today are the remnants of earlier days. They are usually old-timers whose sole pleasure comes from hunting rather than from any conviviality associated with the sport. ...

"The individual who goes it alone is unfettered by any time limits, appointments, or any of a dozen things that can come up when he is part of a group. Being strictly on his own, he is free to change his tactics or direction of travel to suit the occasion

> "THE STILL-HUNTER COVERS GROUND SLOWLY, TRAVELING THE ROUTE WHICH WILL PERMIT MOTION THROUGH THE WOODS WITH A MINIMUM OF NOISE. FEET ARE PLACED CAREFULLY ON MOSS OR ROCK AT EVERY OPPORTUNITY."
> — LARRY KOLLER, *Shots at Whitetails*

anytime he desires, and he suffers no loss of hunting time in making those changes. ...

"The still-hunter learns to become self-reliant, observing, and somewhat of a lay naturalist, and, as a consequence, he develops a keen appreciation for the outdoors."

Still, despite his emphasis on explaining the still-hunting personality, Mattis perhaps defines still-hunting most succinctly when he writes: "Regardless of their individual peculiarities, they all have one thing in common when they take to the field with their guns: They tax their eyes more than they do their legs."

> WORDS AND THEIR MEANINGS EVOLVE ON THEIR OWN. SELDOM CAN THEY BE REDEFINED OR REPLACED BY WHIM OR MANDATE. LIKE IT OR NOT, THE TERM "STILL-HUNT" IS HERE TO STAY.

The Variety Remains

As with yesterday's Winnebago tribe of Wisconsin, not all still-hunting today is the slow, almost lethargic movement Koller and Mattis describe. For many North American hunters, still-hunting tends to be fast-paced. When snows hit the Northern states, hunters take up the track of a white-tailed buck in hopes of putting venison on the table. In many cases, these hunters cover several miles in a day while trying to get a buck in their sights. This requires that they often move fast through the woods, and then slow to a snail's pace. Their pace depends on the terrain, and what the tracks tell them about the buck's movements. Perhaps some would call this technique "tracking," not still-hunting. In reality, this method is a modified form of still-hunting because it still involves moving silently through the woods, trying to spot the animal before it spots its pursuer.

After reading several books, pawing through many other volumes, and talking to numerous lovers of natural history, I've come to believe we use the term "still-hunting" because of the power of the pen. From Warner to Van Dyke to Koller to Mattis, notable writers have embraced the term and stuck with it.

Perhaps still-hunting could also be called "slip-hunting" or "sneak-hunting." Or maybe we could even revert to "stalking," as the Indians and English called it. In my opinion, any of those three terms would more accurately describe what we now call "still-hunting."

But the term has now been around long enough that most hunters of white-tailed deer understand its meaning. And I seriously doubt there would be much point in trying to agree on a more precise term and make it the standard. Words and their meanings evolve. Seldom can they be redefined or replaced by whim or mandate. Like it or not, the term "still-hunt" is here to stay.

Conclusion

Two things are certain about still-hunting. The technique has many variations but, more importantly, it's without a doubt the most challenging way to hunt whitetails, whether your favorite deer woods is in Maine, Alberta, Texas or Georgia. Simply put, pitting one's still-hunting ability against a whitetail's razor-sharp senses is deer hunting's ultimate experience.

SELECT REFERENCES

Benoit, Larry with Peter Miller 1975. *How to Bag the Biggest Buck of Your Life*, Duxbury, Vt.: The Whitetail Press.

Halls, Lowell K. (editor) 1984. *White-tailed Deer: Ecology and Management*, Harrisburg: Stackpole Books.

Herbert, Henry W. (Frank Forester) 1843. *The Deer Stalkers*, Philadelphia: T.B. Peterson & Brothers.

Koller, Lawrence R. 1948. *Shots at Whitetails*, New York: Alfred A. Knopf.

Kroeber, Theodora 1961. *Ishi*, Berkeley: University of California Press.

Mattis, George 1969. *Whitetail: Fundamentals and Fine Points for the Hunter*, New York and Cleveland: The World Publishing Co.

Parker, Arthur C. 1927. *The Indian How Book*. Dover Publishing.

Van Dyke, Theodore S. 1882. *The Still-Hunter*. New York: The Macmillan 10 Co.

Wegner, Robert 1992. *Wegner's Bibliography on Deer Hunting*, DeForest, Wis.: St. Hubertus Press.

"Why Do They Call it Still-Hunting?" was originally published in the September 1995 issue of Deer & Deer Hunting *magazine.*

BUCKS MIGHT DIFFER IN THEIR ABILITY TO DETECT ESTROUS DOES BASED ON THE CHEMICAL SIGNALS INVOLVED IN URINATION. ALTHOUGH MUCH OF WHAT BUCKS DO IS INSTINCTIVE, MANY ASPECTS OF THEIR BEHAVIOR CHANGE WITH EXPERIENCE, WHICH INVOLVES LEARNING.

SHOULD YOU DOCTOR SCRAPES?

Hunters must decide for themselves if doctoring a scrape with scents is worth it. The right urine lure might bring results. But it might be asking too much for one lure to consistently attract every rutting buck that passes.

■ BY JOHN J. OZOGA

Deer hunters today can choose from an amazing variety of paraphernalia that might help them bring down the big one. Estrous urines, often referred to as doe-in-heat lures or sex scents, are on my list of products that "sometimes will/sometimes won't" work.

Don't get me wrong. I'm not implying there aren't important biological messages in naturally deposited deer urine. There are, especially during the whitetail's breeding season.

I also know and respect the work of hunters, such as New York's Charlie Alsheimer, who spend much of the autumn experimenting with scents, doctoring scrapes and tending mock scrapes. The results Alsheimer and others achieve suggests something beyond mere coincidence.

Scents produced by the deer's various glands undoubtedly provide important communication. Further, there's good evidence deer communicate individual identity, dominance rank, physical condition, breeding status, and many other bits of information through urine deposits.

Deer of both sexes and all ages are attracted to scrapes, and males readily urinate in or near the pawed sites. Some speculate the estrous doe, especially, urinates at the scrape to advertise her ready-to-breed condition, but that theory is unproven. In fact, the exact messages exchanged via urine at the scrape have not been deciphered by scientists.

Bottling Lightning

Assuming important chemical signals are present in deer urine, the question becomes this: Can these critical messages be collected, preserved and locked up in a bottle with original and lasting "punch"? I ask this because pheromones produced by many species are known to be highly volatile and dissipate rapidly. You won't find scientific literature to be of much help in answering such questions.

Work being conducted by professors Karl Miller, Larry Marchinton and their students at the University of Georgia is an intriguing investigation into scent communication among whitetails. For example, these researchers have revealed the existence of three deer glands — the forehead, nasal and preputial — and one wonders what they'll discover next. But even they confess that scientists are a long way from truly understanding how and what deer communicate through scent.

"For us just to get a clue about what types of information deer get out of each whiff of air, we must spend months, or years, in the laboratory working with highly sophisticated analytical equipment," Miller said. "Even after we identify a number of suspected compounds, we still only have a guess as to what these compounds tell the deer, if anything."

In one experiment, which was part of Dan Forster's master's degree program, the Georgia researchers tested the attractiveness of bladder urine from bucks, does in heat, and does not in heat, as compared to a commercial doe-in-heat lure. In addition, they used saline solution as a control.

The researchers used automatic aerosol dispensers to release test materials about every 15 minutes into circular areas of lightly tilled soil. These sites measured about 3 feet in diameter, about the size of a dandy scrape. The researchers then tallied the number of deer tracks at each site after 24, 48 and 72 hours to see if deer were more readily attracted to any of the test solutions. The tests were repeated six times on two sites in Georgia and Florida.

The study revealed that deer visited about 25 percent of the test sites each day. However, the researchers could detect no great preference by deer for any of the solutions. Interestingly, however, buck urine scored highest in both study areas.

> THE ELABORATE COURTSHIP FINESSE DEMONSTRATED BY RUT-EXPERIENCED MATURE BUCKS DIFFERS GREATLY FROM THE "SEEK-AND-CHASE" COURTSHIP STYLE OF YEARLINGS.

But Why?

One could theorize that the commercial doe-in-heat urine used in the tests was of poor quality, or was maybe just a bad batch. But why shouldn't doe-in-heat urine drawn carefully from the doe's bladder bring bucks running?

The answer seems obvious. Even urine collected directly from the bladder of an estrous doe seems to lack the magical sex pheromones that attract bucks.

In another investigation, student Mark Whitney and the Georgia professors conducted a highly detailed series of trials with penned deer, wherein bucks were introduced to does artificially treated with water, estrous urine, non-estrous urine or estrous vaginal secretions. Although individual responses varied, bucks devoted significantly more attention to does treated with estrous vaginal secretions.

Therefore, these experiments provide evidence that the female reproductive tract and associated vaginal secretions during estrous, and not the excretory tract itself, are the primary sources of pheromones that serve as sexual attractants.

Follow-up studies by Brian Murphy, under the guidance of Miller and Marchinton, confirmed these findings. Using seven captive does and three adult bucks, they again anointed the does with test substances and monitored the bucks' behavior. In these investigations, however, they used naturally excreted urines, not bladder urine.

Once again, all three bucks devoted significantly more attention toward females treated with the estrous vaginal secretions, but didn't respond positively to does anointed with non-estrous urine.

Interestingly, one of the three bucks was more readily attracted than the other two bucks to does treated with estrous urine than he was to those treated with non-

Bill Lea

estrous urine or water. The investigators emphasize that this buck (2½ years old) had lived in association with does in a large outdoor enclosure. The other two bucks (2½ and 3½ years old) had been housed primarily in a barn. Consequently, experience and learning might have been involved in the one buck's ability to discriminate estrous and non-estrous urine.

On the other hand, one of the test bucks performed more courtship approaches on does treated with water than he did on those treated with non-estrous urine. This exemplifies the unpredictable nature of whitetails. It might also suggest deer show individual preferences and demonstrate mate selection.

Visual Cues

The Georgia researchers emphasize that deer urine used in commercial lures is collected after it's excreted naturally. Therefore, it likely contains other materials not found in unattractive bladder urine that was used in their studies. Whether those materials include pheromones presumably found in estrous vaginal secretions — and whether those pheromones get preserved in the bottle — remains unknown.

These and other studies make us realize that visual cues play an important role in deer scent communication. Using does to test the bucks' response to scents in the pen studies provided an initial strong visual attraction. Likewise, in Whitney's study, the bare soil apparently drew the deer's attention, with or without urine attractants. Wind direction and the deer's approach might also play a role.

The scrapes you commonly see during the whitetail's breeding season are highly complex signposts. The average scrape involves much more than urine and glandular secretions, which emit complex olfactory signals. The typical scrape also presents distinct visual cues that even humans can recognize.

We humans can't identify buck scrapes by smell at long distances, but experienced deer hunters can see one from a afar when they know what to look for. Even if you can't see pawed turf, the ever-present overhanging branch in the proper setting hints that a scrape is likely.

After studying hundreds, if not thousands, of natural

> DEER OF BOTH SEXES AND ALL AGES ARE ATTRACTED TO SCRAPES, AND BUCKS READILY URINATE IN OR NEAR PAWED SITES. SOME SPECULATE THE ESTROUS DOE URINATES AT THE SCRAPE TO ADVERTISE HER READY-TO-BREED CONDITION, BUT THAT THEORY IS UNPROVEN.

buck scrapes, I was convinced that bucks could seldom resist scent-marking a bowed limb that hung about head high over a frequently traveled deer trail. I suspected these limbs served as strong visual attractants, and that many such limbs scent-marked during the summer marked full-fledged scrapes during the rut.

Induced Scraping

In 1989, I published an article in The Journal of Wildlife Management which explained that mature bucks, under proper habitat conditions, could be induced to scrape at a site with reasonable regularity. All that was necessary was a properly positioned bowed overhead limb. In fact, 24 of 40 such sites I created in Upper Michigan's square-mile Cusino enclosure on Oct. 8, 1987, became full-fledged scrapes during a five-week period that followed.

Also, my observations suggested that preferred scrape sites had concentrated deer activity, open understory vegetation, relatively level ground, and moderately dry, easily exposed soil.

Many such places exist. The only missing ingredient is the right kind of overhead limb. I conducted a companion study that year to test whether adding a commercial doe-in-heat urine lure to artificially created scrapes increased their use by bucks.

Would lure-treated sites be scraped more frequently than untreated sites? Similar to my earlier tests, I selected 20 areas along deer trails that met my criteria for favored scrape sites. Then, at each site, I set up a pair of sugar maple limbs about 30 feet apart overhanging the same trail, and trimmed off the leaves and lateral branches. Each limb was 5 to 6 feet long, and bowed slightly downward when suspended horizontally. I positioned the small diameter terminal tips so they were centered about five feet above the ground. I then cleared the leaf litter beneath each limb to expose a circular area of soil about 12 inches in diameter.

Beginning Oct. 8, I applied a doe-in-heat lure beneath one randomly selected limb of each pair every Monday, Wednesday and Friday for three weeks. I compared weekly pawing rates beneath the treated and untreated limbs through Nov. 12, which covered the most active scraping period in northern Michigan.

During the test, bucks pawed 14 treated sites and 14 untreated sites. Six treated sites and seven untreated sites were repawed at least once. In other words, I couldn't prove treating scrapes made them more, or less, attractive.

Limb Attractants

In 1988 I conducted another study using 25 paired limb sites. This setup gave bucks the chance to paw a 20-by-30-inch oval of freshly exposed soil, which resembled an authentic large scrape, or to paw beneath a nearby limb in unexposed soil. I applied no urines or scents to any site.

Before the study, all 50 limbs were kept upright to prevent bucks from scent-marking them. On Oct. 8, I lowered the limbs, tilled the soil beneath one of each pair, and monitored scraping activity beneath each limb until Nov. 14. For whatever reason, deer pawing at the test sites was unusually high in 1988, possibly because most of the artificially established sites had been available, and many were pawed by bucks, in 1987. In 1988, 22 of 25 sites with a large area of exposed soil turned into real scrapes, but so did 23 of 25 sites without exposed soil. Further, many of the 50 sites — including 20 with only the limb and 16 with a limb and exposed soil — were repawed one or more times.

The results agreed with my earlier findings that suggested the overhead limb is more important than exposed soil in scrape site selection by bucks. Also, evidence suggests bucks are just as likely to develop their own scrapes than take over those made by other bucks.

These studies certainly don't represent the subject's last word. But they emphasize that scrapes involve some important visual attractions to deer, in addition to the strong olfactory stimuli that soon result at sites which are repeatedly reworked and rescented.

Learned Behaviors

Research into the whitetail's reproductive behavior has revealed considerable variation in rutting behavior among bucks, depending on their age and breeding experience. Although much of what bucks do is instinctive, many aspects of their behavior change with experience, which involves learning. The elaborate courtship finesse demonstrated by rut-experienced mature bucks, for example, differs greatly from the "seek-and-chase" courtship style

> HIGHLY ACTIVE SCRAPES, NO DOUBT, EMIT A GREAT DEAL OF AROMATIC ATTRACTIVENESS. BUT THE IDENTITIES OF THOSE POTENT OLFACTORY ELEMENTS — CALLED PHEROMONES — STILL ELUDE SCIENTISTS.

of yearlings.

Even among older rut-experienced bucks, however, there are considerable behavioral differences between individuals. The reasons for these differences aren't known. One buck might make many times more rubs or scrapes than the next. And now it appears bucks might even differ in their ability to detect estrous does based on the chemical signals involved in urination.

Highly active scrapes, no doubt, emit a great deal of aromatic attractiveness. But the identities of those potent olfactory elements — called pheromones — still elude scientists.

Logically, any deer urine should interest some deer sometimes, but so might Chanel No. 5. After all, deer tend to be curious. And if your lure somehow contains those elusive magical sex pheromones that researchers have yet to identify, it should do an even better job attracting the big one. But don't be surprised if your lure attracts one deer but repels the next.

Is doctoring the scrape with doe-in-heat lures worth it? I think it's iffy, but that's something each hunter must decide. The right urine lure — used in the right place at the right time for the right buck — might bring results. But I think it's asking a bit much for one lure to consistently attract every rutting buck in the region.

Conclusion

Maybe the neutral results I reported from my studies were caused by low-grade lures or the inevitable "bad batch." Maybe a different lure would have produced better results. I can't prove it either way.

But frankly, I see no substitute for developing a good understanding of deer biology and behavior, and then putting that knowledge to wise use. If you're looking for an easy way to success, I'm afraid your search won't end soon. I know mine won't.

"Should You Doctor Scrapes?" was originally published in the November 1994 issue of Deer & Deer Hunting *magazine.*

WHEN THE RED GODS CALL, THE DEER HUNTER MUST GO TO THE WOODS. SOMETIMES THE RED GODS SMILE ON THESE HUNTERS. AT OTHER TIMES THEY FROWN.

CHAPTER 3

WHEN THE RED GODS CALL:

THE ROLE OF LUCK IN DEER HUNTING

"Am I just hunting poorly this year? Is it all a matter of probabilities? Or has a deeper bond between the deer and me been severed?" — Richard Nelson, The Island Within

■ BY ROB WEGNER

When the Red Gods call hunters to the deer woods, some go to their cherished hunting lodges to smell wood smoke at twilight and to listen to birch logs burning.

Other hunters, however, go to the woods to bag a deer. All return "to the camp of proven desire and known delight," as Rudyard Kipling wrote in his verse, *The Feet of the Young Men* (1897). For when the Red Gods call, deer hunters must go to the woods.

Sometimes the Red Gods smile on these hunters. At other times they frown. Luck in deer hunting is as variable as the winds of the universe. Luck will be your steady companion some years. At other times, "it will

THE RED GODS CALL ...

This phrase, or some variation of it, recurs in literature on deer and deer hunting, but little is known about its derivation and original meaning.

I first encountered it in 1973 when I read Paul Errington's book, *The Red Gods Call*. In this book, this distinguished professor of wildlife ecology acknowledges, "I have heard the Red Gods all of my life." In the book's preface, Errington (1902-62) notes that as a youngster with restless feet he heard the Red Gods (presumably meaning the hunting gods of North American Indians) when he saw autumn colors, a canoe in choppy water, or the flag of the whitetail. The Red Gods called the young naturalist to go hunting, fishing, trapping, camping and prowling the back woods.

I encountered the phrase most recently as a chapter heading in James Kilgo's book, *Deep Enough for Ivory Bills* (1988). In this work of one man's spiritual reunion with the deer woods, Kilgo tells us the phrase comes from a poem by Rudyard Kipling (1865-1936), titled, "The Feet of the Young Men," dated 1897. In this poem, the Red Gods call the feet of young men to the Northland to hear the creak of snowshoes and birch logs burning, and to smell wood smoke at twilight. The Red Gods call deer hunters "to the camps of proved desire and known delight."

When the Red Gods call, deer hunters must go to the woods!

— *Rob Wegner*

pass you by, until you commence to feel as though you were haunted by malevolent spirits," as a deer hunter from the Adirondacks named Paulina Brandreth described it in her classic book, *Trails of Enchantment* (1930). When the Red Gods frown, Brandreth observed, "the less fortunate experiences will sometimes send you grousing homeward with the realization that you have been the unwilling victim of a mocking jinx of bad luck."

When that happens the deer hunter often asks the same questions that Richard Nelson, a cultural anthropologist/deer hunter, poses: "Am I just hunting poorly? Is it all a matter of chance?" But when Nelson asks whether a spiritual bond has been broken between the deer and the hunter, he asks a question that goes to the heart of the metaphysics of deer hunting.

State of Grace?

For the past 30 years, Nelson has studied hunters of the Northern Forest, the Eskimos of Alaska, and learned their hunting techniques through participation. In a paper titled, "Stalking the Sacred Game," Nelson places luck in the context of a spiritual bond between deer and hunter. Nelson's paper, delivered at the 1992 Governor's Symposium on North America's Hunting Heritage,

presents luck as it is followed in the American Indian tradition, and compares it to a state of grace with a devout, religious respect for the animal:

"For Koyukon hunters, one of the important rules is that you must never brag or say demeaning things about any creature. A man or woman who kills an animal should avoid taking credit or acting proud. Of course, they recognize the value of being skilled and having a good sense for the woods. But ultimately, hunting success comes from what Koyukon people call 'luck,' which means keeping yourself in a state of grace by showing respect toward every animal species. One expert Koyukon hunter said that after inadvertently mistreating a black bear's remains, he got no bears for more than 10 years; then his luck gradually returned. People will say of a successful hunter, 'Something took care of him.'"

In his book, *The Island Within* (1989), which won the 1991 John Burroughs Medal for outstanding natural history writing, Nelson insists our deer hunting behavior should follow a few simple principles: "Move slowly, stay quiet, watch carefully, be ever humble, show no hint of arrogance or disrespect.

"This is the source of success (or luck), for a hunter or a watcher; not skill, not cleverness, not guile. Something is only given in nature, never taken."

Luck is perhaps best perceived as a direct result of a bonding covenant between man, the hunter, and the animal being hunted, namely the deer. It's a spiritual covenant that entails a profound respect for the animal and its ways. To violate that respect brings misfortune and failure.

Joseph Campbell (1904-1987), one of America's most inspiring teachers, defines this covenant in his book, *The Power of Myth* (1988): "You see, the basic hunting myth is of a kind of covenant between the animal world and the human world. The animal gives its life willingly, with the understanding that its life transcends its physical entity and will be returned to the soil or to the mother through some ritual of restoration. And this ritual of restoration is associated with the main hunting animal."

In his detailed discussion of the great hunting mythologies of the world, *Primitive Mythology: The Masks of God* (1959), Professor Campbell tells the lesson to be learned:

"The lesson reads, by analogy: The sun is the hunter, the sun's ray is the arrow, the antelope (or deer) is one of the herd of the stars; ergo, as tomorrow night will see the stars return, so will tomorrow the antelope (or deer).

Nor has the hunter killed the beast as a personal, willful act, but according to the provisions of the Great Spirit. And in this way 'nothing is lost.'"

Timeless Tradition

Deer hunters have always discussed the element of luck and invoked the Great Spirit or Unseen Powers to aid their quest. The vagaries of the hunt, the uncontrollable elements that so frequently complicate it, sway the hunter's mind toward the Red Gods. That tradition is timeless, from the Cro-Magnon hunters of 25,000 years ago, communicating with their animal paintings in the caves at Lascaux; to deer hunters of today who seek luck through silent prayers to St. Hubert, patron saint of the hunt.

Early in the 20th century, William Monypeny Newsom (1887-1942), a Wall Street broker and a giant among deer hunters, observed that the deer hunter's list of equipment does not usually contain "luck" as a basic ingredient, but it should. Newsom wrote:

"We like to think we are so learned we don't believe in it. Nearly everyone I know says openly there is no such thing, and secretly nurses a huge respect for the left hind foot of a rabbit. Discuss the matter with them and they say everything is subject to the laws of mathematics.

"All of which I will admit, given the proper time element to complete the test. And lest someone bob up to spring Permutations and Combinations or Choice and Chance on us, let us state we agonized through those; and we still believe in luck!

"For this reason: I know that there are 52 cards in a deck; that if you stick to it long enough ... the rules of chance will even up the game and you will find an even distribution of

LUCK IS PERHAPS BEST PERCEIVED AS A DIRECT RESULT OF A BONDING COVENANT BETWEEN MAN, THE HUNTER, AND THE ANIMAL BEING HUNTED, NAMELY THE DEER. IT'S A SPIRITUAL COVENANT THAT ENTAILS A PROFOUND RESPECT FOR THE ANIMAL AND ITS WAYS. TO VIOLATE THAT RESPECT BRINGS MISFORTUNE AND FAILURE.

Patrick Durkin

cards in the end. But in a short period of time, before the mathematics really have a whirl at you, the cards run in streaks. So you may turn up four or five spades, one right after the other.

"If you stop there, you cannot figure on percentages at all. So it is in hunting. You do not have a chance to play out the game before the season closes — luck is either with you or against you.

"Consider the weather as part of it. Let those who disbelieve in luck hunt long enough, and they'll have to explain 'beginner's luck,' too. Then they'll sit up nights trying to show by logic what refuses to be governed by reason. In the meanwhile let us define luck as the Unknown Force that makes the biggest buck walk into the muzzle of the gun carried by the dullest man in camp. It's a comforting definition as it's so soothing to the rest of us."

> FATE, LUCK, CHANCE, THE SMILES OF THE RED GODS — CALL IT WHAT YOU WILL. YOU MIGHT BE THE BEST DEER HUNTER, BUT IF LUCK SHUNS YOU, AS IT FREQUENTLY WILL, YOU'RE CERTAIN TO FAIL WHERE LESS-EXPERIENCED HUNTERS SUCCEED.

Time and Chance

Shortly after Newsom wrote those words, Robert Vale, an experienced journalist who devoted most of his years to hunting and writing about the activity, acknowledged that chance plays a large part in deer hunting. As proof, he relays the story of his camp cook who "after washing the dishes and cleaning up camp ... walked up the side of the ridge several hundred yards and sat in the warm sun with his back against a stump. He lit his pipe and started to read a newspaper."

A buck soon appeared and the cook calmly shot it. When the unsuccessful hunters returned to camp later in the day his lofty comment was: "Deers like to associate with lit'rary folks; they abhors ignorance."

Yes, lucky breaks happen during the deer hunt, as George Mattis (1905-1982), author of *Whitetail* (1969), will tell you:

"One of the happy aspects of deer hunting is the indiscriminate manner in which Lady Luck metes out favors to the men in the field. All too often, the sallow-complexioned city cousin stumbles onto and bags a handsome buck his first time out, while his host, a veteran of the woods, is humbled with a blank season. This is often termed 'beginner's luck,' but if one thoroughly examines every situation in which a fluke kill was made, he might

discover the deer was caught off guard by something the hunter did, even though it was done inadvertently.

"These pleasant interludes brighten the prospects for every man in the woods, but somehow these lucky breaks seem more often to drop into the laps of novices.

"And it could be because the inexperienced hunter has not yet learned the accepted rules of hunting. The crafty buck might well cope with the standard strategy of the true-to-form hunter, but he often becomes confused and meets his doom at the hands of a blundering beginner. This element of luck seems far more prevalent in white-tailed deer hunting than in other outdoor pursuits."

Unseen Powers

The element of luck also plays a prominent role in securing trophy bucks. In collecting countless pictures and stories of various trophy whitetails killed in Texas, Robert Rogers reached two basic conclusions in his book, *Big Rack* (1980): Half of the successful hunters pursued a particular deer, and the other half killed their trophy purely by chance. Apparently, a little luck never hurt anyone.

The late Jack O'Connor, one of the nation's most distinguished shooting editors, also believed in chance and the unseen powers that control the fate of hunters:

"I constantly hear and read interesting sets of instructions on how to catch large trophy bucks with sensational antlers. I have shot some rather good bucks in my day, but for the most part I don't know exactly how I did it. If I had to give my best advice, I would say the smartest thing to do is to get lucky."

Fate, luck, chance, fortune, the smiles of the Red Gods, Lady Luck — call it what you will. But one thing remains certain. You might be the best deer hunter, knowledgeable on all aspects of deer behavior, an excellent shot, a practiced and careful hunter, but if luck shuns you completely, as it frequently does, you will certainly fail where other less-experienced hunters succeed. While luck means many things to different hunters, one of its best definitions lies in Brandreth's *Trails of Enchantment*:

"Luck may mean a number of things but primarily I should say it means a well-timed coordination of your own movements, and those of the animal you are hunting. If you are five minutes too early or five minutes too late at a given point, your deer will not be seen. If you experience a little good luck, you will be in the right place at the right time.

"You will catch a glimpse of him as he crosses that opening in the woods ahead, or observe him standing on the ridge to the left. But you either pass the spot before he gets there, or arrive shortly after he has left, although he may have been within a radius of 200 yards, unconcernedly feeding.

"You, of course, never knew it, and went on your way disappointed because you didn't run across a buck in such an excellent locality.

"Good luck is often of greater value in the pursuit of the whitetail, or any game animal, than a carefully planned campaign. The candid hunter when he looks back will own that, for the most part, the trophies he has worked hardest for are the ones he never got, and that more opportunities are grasped than made."

Staying Optimistic

Of all the deer hunters I have known or read about, no one more strongly believed in luck than Archibald Rutledge (1883-1973). Throughout his long deer hunting career, he remained an incurable optimist who always believed in the possibility of last chances. In his essay, "A Buck in the Rain," he wrote, "Men who know deer nature best know that the element of chance is perhaps about as great in the pursuit of this superb game animal as it is in the following of any other game in the world."

Rutledge steadfastly maintained that each deer hunt should make sporting history, not create mystery with hunters giving faulty, elaborate reasons why missing that buck seemed altogether reasonable. No, Rutledge didn't care much for refined dissertations on how the buck escaped into the eternal, inviolate sanctuary. Instead, he wanted to see the old boy fall to the forest floor with his last race run as if struck by lightning. Only then could the hunter get that special thrill of wrenching success from failure in the game's final minute. As a pragmatist, Rutledge wanted the buck on the meat pole, not a masterpiece in the way of the Great Excuse. In this regard, a primordial element of blood lust drove him until his dying day.

Rutledge stuck with the hunt until the dark sky set in on the season's last day. He believed many deer hunters go home too soon.

"So often has the very last chance afforded me the best luck that I have become almost superstitious about this business of last chances. ... Faith, superstition, persistence — call it what you will; but I know the luck of the last

chance has often taken the empty cup of bitterness and disappointment and brimmed it with the wine of achievement. I can recall killing no fewer than 16 bucks on last chances. ... The actual shooting of them is usually a thing of the moment; the only question is whether you have patience to wait for the moment.

"Often, the last moment is the moment."

Conclusion

Once you experience this victory in the last moments of deer season, it serves the rest of your life as a fine reminder of the possibilities of last chances, and the great rewards that come to the faithful.

Not only that, but it proves irrefutably that the buck hunter's insane faith reaps the medicine of success when the Red Gods smile.

REFERENCES

Brandreth, Pauline. *Trails of Enchantment*. New York: Watt, 1930.

Campbell, Joseph. *The Power of Myth*. New York: Doubleday, 1988.

_____. *Primitive Mythology: The Masks of God*. England: Penguin Books, 1959.

Kipling, Rudyard. "The Feet of Young Men." *In Complete Verse*. New York: Doubleday, 1939.

Mattis, George. *Whitetail: Fundamentals and Fine Points for the Hunter*. New York: Van Nostrand Reinhold Co., 1980.

Nelson, Richard. *The Island Within*. New York: Vantage Books, 1991.

_____. "Stalking the Sacred Game: Perspectives from Native American Hunting Traditions." In Governor's Symposium on North America's Hunting Heritage. pp. 22-32.

Newsom, William Monypeny. *White-tailed Deer*. New York: Scribners, 1926.

O'Connor, Jack. "Are Big Bucks Just Luck?" In *Hunting on Three Continents with Jack O'Connor*. California: Safari Press, 1987. pp. 291-296.

Rogers, Robert. *Big Rack*. Texas: Privately Printed, 1980.

Rutledge, Archibald. "A Buck in the Rain." In *An American Hunter*. New York: Frederick A. Stokes, 1937. pp. 10-20.

Vale, Robert B. *Wings, Fur and Shot*. New York: Stackpole Sons, 1936.

"When the Red Gods Call" was originally published in the September 1993 issue of Deer & Deer Hunting *magazine.*

RATTLING:

DO HUGE BUCKS FALL FOR IT?

Bucks are individuals and each responds differently to every situation. Therefore, no one can say it's impossible to rattle up a tremendous buck. Even if it rarely happens, it seldom hurts to try!

■ BY LARRY L. WEISHUHN

T he stage was set. I had spotted a large 10-point buck bedded under a juniper below the ridgeline. He was watching for movement in the valley. A slight breeze blew across his back. If danger approached from above, he would know it instantly and vanish. Ten yards to his right was a brushy draw that ran down from the ridgetop to dense brush in a creek bottom.

Farther down the ridge in another brushy draw I saw a second buck. Like the first, his neck was swollen and his hocks were darkly stained after several days of scraping and rutting activities. Scattered between those two large-racked bucks were four younger bucks, primarily 2- and 3-year-olds, judging by their body and antler characteristics. One was bedded, and the other three were rubbing their antlers in mock battles or working scrapes.

My position on the ridge's highest point gave me a grandstand view of our unfolding plan. By arrange-

DURING THE AUTHOR'S **40**-PLUS YEARS OF DEER HUNTING, HE HAS RATTLED UP A FAIR NUMBER OF BUCKS FROM CANADA AND INTO MEXICO. HE HAS SEEN MANY MORE RATTLED UP BY HUNTING PARTNERS. BUT OUT OF THE MORE THAN **1,500** BUCKS HE'S SEEN RATTLED UP, ONLY FOUR WERE MONSTER BUCKS.

Lance Krueger

MANY TOP HUNTERS BELIEVE MATURE BUCKS QUIT RESPONDING TO RATTLING IF TOO MUCH OF IT'S DONE IN A SMALL AREA. HOWEVER, THEY ARE LIKELY RESPONDING TO THE SOUNDS. UNFORTUNATELY, THEY'RE APPROACHING SLOWLY AND CAUTIOUSLY.

He cautiously walked to where he could scent-check the source of the sound. He seemed to figure out my hunting partner, even though Porter had used a natural juniper and buck scent. In fact, he had rubbed his clothes with the hocks of a freshly killed buck, and hung the tarsal gland on a nearby limb.

Even so, the buck never tried to move any closer to Porter's position. He simply stood statue-like, staring toward the mock fight for about 10 minutes. Eventually, he turned and walked back down the draw, disappearing into the creek bottom.

Porter, meanwhile, was playing with the younger bucks. When they started to leave, he grunted. They would immediately return, stare intently at the fully camouflaged hunter, and turn to walk away again. As this continued, I watched the other big buck. Up to this point he had never left his bed. Then I noticed a bigger-bodied buck, but with a mediocre 8-point rack, running nearby. He charged off the top of the ridge and ran down the draw close to where the big buck was bedded. When this buck was on the same level as the mock fight, he charged to where Porter was seated. Not once did the 8-pointer seem concerned about danger. The buck moved back and forth a few steps in front of Porter, and then charged at the younger bucks. When one of the 3-year-olds challenged him, a brief fight ensued.

At the same time I tried to watch the first buck's reactions. He simply stared toward the fight, but made no other effort.

Meanwhile, the mature 8-pointer started chasing the younger bucks, and they momentarily disappeared into the creek bottom.

Delayed Reaction

Twenty minutes later, Porter got up, walked to the creek bottom and headed back toward camp. No sooner had he left than the big buck stood up and stretched. Then, slowly and cautiously, the buck headed toward the spot where Porter had been rattling. I watched this buck, which carried a rack of record-book proportions, slowly and carefully circle the area. Not once would he

ment, my hunting partner, Ron Porter, was now entering the valley. I watched as he still-hunted, with the breeze in his face and sun at his back, to the edge of the brushy draw that held the second big buck. Once there, Porter selected a tree to sit beside. He could see a fair amount of country between him and the draw. After waiting a bit, he started rattling. Immediately, the four younger bucks responded, trotting toward the simulated fight and boldly entering the opening in front of Porter.

A Mature Response

While I found that amusing, I was more interested in how the mature bucks responded. Both stared intently toward the sounds of Porter's ruckus. Throughout the 15-minute rattling session, the big buck closest to Porter moved up the draw, yet never left dense cover.

have been in sight of Porter. At one point the buck stopped, smelled the ground, and momentarily followed Porter's departing scent trail. Satisfied, the buck circled the rattling site, then made his way through another brushy draw back up the ridge, stopping twice to freshen scrapes. He bedded again where he had several avenues of escape, should danger approach from any direction.

Both huge bucks I saw that morning carried incredible racks. I estimated each was at least 6 years old, and both had heard many actual fights and rattling sequences. The Texas ranch where they lived was one I managed several years. The overall deer population was fairly high, about one deer per five acres, with an excellent 1-to-1 adult buck-to-doe ratio. While I never shot a mature buck on the ranch, the site served as an ideal research area for me to study mature buck behavior. About 50 percent of the ranch's bucks were at least 4 years old. Some of the mature bucks produced extremely large antlers, and some simply turned out to be big 8-point bucks. None of the deer ever lacked good nutrition from the time they were conceived.

In many ways, the operation was Utopia for deer hunters. For that matter, it was Utopia for the whitetails. The interesting thing about being able to study mature deer was that it became clear they were all individuals, and reacted differently to each of the many situations they confronted.

Larry L. Weishuhn

CAROLYN WILLIAMS DISPLAYS THE HUGE TEXAS BUCK SHE SHOT AFTER IT RESPONDED TO LARRY WEISHUHN'S RATTLING SEQUENCE. THIS IS THE LARGEST BUCK WEISHUHN HAS EVER RATTLED UP. THE BUCK RESPONDED DURING THE PRE-RUT TO A COMBINATION OF BRUSH RUBBING AND LIGHT SPARRING SOUNDS.

What Responds?

During my 40-plus years of hunting white-tailed deer — 25 of which have been as a full-time wildlife biologist specializing in quality management — I have hunted and spent time in some of North America's best deer country. It has given me many opportunities to learn about mature bucks, and also how these large-antlered bucks react to different hunting situations, including rattling.

In recent years, it seems you can't be considered a true deer hunter unless you own a set of rattling "horns," even though we all know they're antlers! Over the years, I've rattled up a fair number of bucks from

Canada and into Mexico. I have seen many more rattled up by hunting partners. Out of the more than 1,500 bucks I've seen rattled up, only four were monster bucks. One of those bucks came in when I was rattling in Mexico. He responded slowly and came into view just as I was about to leave. Unfortunately, I was guiding that day, not hunting. The buck came in from upwind and my hunter was watching downwind, just as I had instructed. The buck walked up behind us, stared momentarily in our direction, and then simply disappeared into the thick brush. He was an extremely large nontypical. Whether he was record-book material I can't say for certain. However, he was large enough to fit into my book, with plenty of antlers to spare!

Two of the other huge bucks I rattled up were in

South Texas. The first was a long-tined typical 12, which looked as if he would certainly "gross book." He also showed up as we were about to leave. Sad to say, I got one shot at him and missed. I simply blew it. I was awestruck by his size and caught a bad case of buck fever.

The second South Texas buck was one we had hunted several years. I found his shed antlers on a couple of occasions, but could not find him during hunting season. I saw him only once in four years, and that was at night during a spotlight game survey! I later rubbed and passively rattled him up about two weeks before the start of the rut. He fell that day to the ranch owner's wife on the property I described at the beginning of this article. I was rubbing a tree with an antler, and then began timidly rattling the antlers to imitate an amiable sparring match. That's when he appeared, cautiously moving our way. The buck was at least 8 years old, and carried a basic 14-point rack with numerous nontypical points. In fact, he had 24 points that were just over 1 inch long. He barely missed the Boone and Crockett minimum.

The fourth huge buck I rattled up was in Saskatchewan. After a long walk into the provincial forest, I found a small open area. Around the perimeter were abundant rubs and two scrapes. I settled in for a while and watched. After about an hour I started working brush with my rattling antlers, and then gingerly put them together and started meshing the tines. Two yearling bucks immediately responded. When they lost interest, I again started rattling. I soon heard movement behind me in the dense conifers, and then could see the lower portion of a buck's legs. For someone accustomed to much smaller-bodied deer, those legs were so big they looked as if they belonged to a yearling steer. I could see most of his back legs from his tarsal glands on down. His back legs were stained almost a tarry black, indicative of a mature buck. For the next five or six minutes I tried to entice the buck to show me more of his body. I tried rattling, grunting and even snort-wheezing. Nothing worked. He was obviously content to stand and stare. I was certain it was a big, mature

buck, yet I could not see anything above his lower legs. After an eternity, he turned and started moving away. Cautiously, with rifle at ready, I raised up, just as he disappeared into the dense greenery. I got one glimpse of him, and he truly was big! By the time I recovered from the sight, he was gone.

Usual Happening?

I have often wondered if my experiences rattling huge bucks into range were typical. Over the years I have heard about hunters who consistently rattle up record-book and record-class whitetails. I've always been skeptical of such claims, but I still wanted to find out if hunters I respect have fared better than I have at rattling up huge bucks.

One of the first hunters I contacted was Al Brothers. Besides being an old friend, fellow biologist and white-tailed deer aficionado, Brothers is essentially one of the reasons for today's great interest in quality deer management and hunting. I asked Brothers, and the others who follow, if they believed a herd's largest bucks can be rattled up.

Brothers was quick to point out that in order to rattle up a huge buck, you must hunt where such bucks exist. Further, few such bucks exist even in the best places. In the research Brothers has done to locate hunters who rattled up and killed huge bucks, he found a few who have accomplished the feat twice, but none who had succeeded three times. His definition of such bucks is similar to mine: bucks whose antlers have a gross score higher than the record-book minimums. During all his years of hunting, Brothers believes he has rattled up one such buck, but he didn't get a shot at it. He believes few bucks of such proportions respond to rattling, and even fewer are shot.

What suggestions does he have for those who want to increase their chances of rattling up a monstrous buck? "Concentrate your efforts during the pre-rut, and I mean starting very early, before most people would think of being successful rattling or even trying. And stay in one place 30 minutes to one hour."

Brothers also mentioned another interesting possibility: Perhaps some of the biggest whitetails become non-

> I SOON HEARD MOVEMENT BEHIND ME IN THE DENSE CONIFERS, AND THEN COULD SEE THE LOWER PORTION OF A BUCK'S LEGS. FOR SOMEONE ACCUSTOMED TO MUCH SMALLER-BODIED DEER, THOSE LEGS WERE SO BIG THEY LOOKED AS IF THEY BELONGED TO A YEARLING STEER.

breeders, producing just enough testosterone to go through the antler cycle, but not enough to make them sexually active. That would explain why some huge bucks are seldom rattled up. They have no interest in fighting or breeding, so why would they want to respond to a simulated fight?

Another respected biologist offers a similar view. Valerius Geist, professor emeritus from the University of Calgary, believes some of the forest's most tremendous bucks are basically timid cowards. He has watched huge bucks walk to the edge of a clearing, see another deer already there, and then melt back into the woods, ensuring they don't draw the attention of any possible challengers.

Interference

Skipper Bettis manages the famed Sanctuary hunting lodge in northern Michigan, which is known for its huge white-tailed bucks. Throughout the autumn he rattles up many of them. Some bucks on the Sanctuary would certainly fit the category of "super bucks." I once visited with Bettis about the number of huge bucks he and his guides rattle up each year.

Bettis believes they rattle up one or two of the best bucks on their property each year, but these bucks are usually slow to respond. The biggest problem, Bettis believes, is that the area holds a great number of young bucks that respond. These bucks generally give the rattler away before the biggest bucks can respond.

"We have so many bucks that key in on the rattler's position that they screw up any chance of rattling up the biggest bucks," Bettis said. "It's extremely difficult to catch one of the huge bucks without a doe, if they indeed chase does. But that's what needs to happen before they respond."

I also contacted Richard P. Smith, former Midwest field editor of *Deer & Deer Hunting* magazine. Smith has hunted whitetails in all types of terrain across North America, and helps track down information about some of the biggest bucks killed in Michigan, his home state.

"I can recall at least two Booners that were taken with the help of rattling in Michigan, both by bow-hunters," Smith said. "One was a nontypical scoring

196-⅞. He was taken Nov. 8, 1993, by a bow-hunter on the ground.

The other buck netted just over 170, and was rattled in about the same time of year as the other one, but two or three years earlier.

> AFTER AN ETERNITY, HE TURNED AND STARTED MOVING AWAY. CAUTIOUSLY, WITH RIFLE AT READY, I RAISED UP, JUST AS HE DISAPPEARED. I GOT ONE GLIMPSE OF HIM, AND HE TRULY WAS BIG! BY THE TIME I RECOVERED FROM THE SIGHT, HE WAS GONE.

"Is rattling effective for an area's biggest bucks? I think it can be effective at the right time and in the right place. As far as timing, I think probably the best time to rattle up the best bucks is during the pre-rut."

I also asked several top hunters if they thought bucks get educated about rattling, and if they think experienced bucks quit responding. The consensus was that some bucks might eventually quit responding if there is too much rattling in a small area. However, they are likely responding. Unfortunately, they're approaching slowly and cautiously.

Conclusion

During my many years of hunting, I've often rattled up the same buck several times, season after season. But as the bucks got older, they were slower to respond. On the same ranches, I also knew of bucks that never responded to rattling. All of this simply proves that white-tailed bucks are individuals. The biggest of the herd are no less individuals.

After considering all this, only one thing seems certain: If you never try, you'll never know if you'll get lucky rattling up a huge buck!

"Rattling: Do Huge Bucks Fall for It?" was originally published in the November 1994 issue of Deer & Deer Hunting *magazine.*

OLD STANDS REVEAL SEVERAL SUBTLE SECRETS IF YOU STUDY THE REASONS FOR THEIR ORIGINAL PLACEMENT. BUT REMEMBER THIS FOR SAFETY'S SAKE: OLD TREE STANDS ARE MEANT TO BE STUDIED, NOT USED.

CHAPTER 5

OLD STANDS CAN TALK TO YOU

It would be nice if we could ask each hunter his reasons for picking the site of old stands, and why he abandoned them. But because that isn't possible, we must scout more thoroughly to find such explanations.

■ BY KENT HORNER

Old tree stands can speak volumes to deer hunters scouting new woods. Particularly, that dilapidated, rotting stand tells you another deer hunter sometime ago thought this was a good place to shoot a whitetail. Usually, old stands reveal several subtle secrets if you study the reasons for their original placement.

Recently, I acquired hunting privileges on some woodlands atop the Cumberland Plateau in northern Alabama. This also gave me access to lands at the base of the Cumberlands along the Paint Rock River. These lowlands consist of farm fields and dense woods.

Because this area was new to me, I scouted as much as possible for the coming season. During one trip I came upon a well-used deer trail. After following the trail a bit, I found a rub made the previous autumn. The tree's cambium showed a little new growth, but was still white where a buck's antlers

NATURAL FEATURES THAT CAUSE DEER TO MAKE SO-CALLED PERMANENT TRAILS CAN SOMETIMES BE OVERLOOKED. TERRAIN, GENERALLY SPEAKING, IS UNCHANGING, AND DEER REACT TO IT MUCH THE SAME WAY HUNTERS DO. THEY TAKE THE EASIEST ROUTES TO CONSERVE ENERGY.

Charles J. Alsheimer

and had obviously required time, energy and some expense to build. Such considerations indicate the builder had good reasons to justify all these efforts.

It would be nice if I could ask each hunter his reasons for picking these sites, and why he eventually abandoned them. But because that isn't possible, I must scout more thoroughly to find the explanations. Nearby cover, active trails, mast-producing oaks and beech trees, and a water source indicate, or at least imply, deer usage.

I consider many points when studying old stands. Some points are subtle, others obvious. In a few cases, you won't know the reasons behind the stand's placement until climbing to that height and viewing the terrain and cover.

Put Safety First

At this point — in the name of common courtesy, ethics and safety — I offer an explanation: By the term, "old tree stands," I mean platforms that no other hunter is using or intends to use because of ill-repair brought on by age and weathering. I no longer climb aboard old stands. Never! First, as a matter of respect, the stand belongs to another hunter. Second, I don't entrust my life to someone I've never met, let alone to a stand he's built. Stepping into a stand of unknown and untested construction could bring severe injuries or death should I break through. While I think it's OK to climb up and stand beside the stand, I never put my life in their care.

Also, keep in mind that on public wildlife management areas, it's usually illegal to build such stands — or to occupy them. On private property, however, hunters build stands that might remain in trees many years, even after the original hunter has long abandoned them. On public lands, such stands are usually destroyed eventually, if not by government foresters enforcing the law, then by other hunters who don't appreciate someone illegally trying to "lock up" a site.

Factors to Consider

What follows are some points to consider while scouting and deciding whether to follow the "advice"

rasped the bark.

Then I found several older rubs nearby. The saplings showed various stages of healing. My excitement began rising. I thought perhaps I would place one of my ladder stands nearby, and began looking at the trees for a suitable site. Just overhead, about 30 feet high, I saw an old, rotting stand.

Obviously, two deer hunters — unknown to each other and many years apart in their visits — had looked at the evidence and reached the same conclusion: This was an active deer zone and a good stand site.

Why Here?

I continued scouting the vast wooded bottomlands and found three more old tree stands. I tried to figure out why each hunter had placed his stand at the sites. Each of these "permanent" stands was made of wood, of preceding hunters on stand placement.

✓ Was the original stand built for bow-hunting or gun-hunting? Look at the stand's height, nearby cover, direction of sight, and the stand's sitting or standing accommodations. These factors give evidence of its usefulness as a bow or gun stand. If you believe the stand was placed for gun-hunting, you might find a better ambush site nearby for bow-hunting.

✓ Determine if any natural features have changed since the stand was built. For example, in Alabama where I do most of my hunting, pulpwood growers clearcut large blocks of forest. After clearcutting, planted pine seedlings soon grow into excellent cover and bedding sites for whitetails. These sites often support prolific vegetation that attracts deer until the pines develop a thick canopy. Depending on the age and composition of the regrowth, that old stand site might be improving with each passing season, or be obsolete.

✓ Was the stand overlooking a natural water or food source? Are these sources seasonal or permanent? A permanent spring, creek or pond can attract more deer than a temporary water source, which soon dries after a rain. How do you know which is which? Permanent water sources usually appear on topographical maps.

With food sources, ask yourself if the old stand was built to hunt deer in acorn flats, fruit orchards, wild honeysuckle patches or planted crops. All of these draw deer at different times and seasons, and hence vary in the number of days they'll be useful.

✓ Will you use your bow, gun or both when hunting from the stand you're proposing to build near the old structure? Your answer will usually influence your building site. Even though it's unlikely you and the original builder both misjudged a good site, be willing to fine-tune your stand placement. Sometimes five yards makes a huge difference when bow-hunting.

Other Factors

Besides interpreting the placement of old stands, consider other factors the builder might have over-

Patrick Durkin

I CAME UPON A WELL-USED DEER TRAIL. AFTER FOLLOWING THE TRAIL A BIT, I FOUND A RUB MADE EARLIER IN AUTUMN. THE TREE'S CAMBIUM SHOWED OBVIOUS GOUGE MARKS, AND IT WAS STILL WHITE WHERE A BUCK'S ANTLERS RASPED THE BARK.

looked. For example:

✓ Small, permanent water holes near cover in wilderness areas.

✓ Trail crossings that show evidence of whitetails passing through from different directions.

✓ Corridors of narrow woodlands that provide cover to connect larger tracts of deer habitat.

✓ Woodland funnels, often at the base of steep hillsides and mountainous inclines.

✓ Saddles on ridgetops where deer can easily cross from one side of the hill to the other.

✓ Game trails about 75 yards within the woods that run parallel to its edge.

✓ Small pockets of dense cover in cedars or other conifers within hardwood forests.

Richard P. Smith

✓ Any known sites where bucks historically scrape.

✓ Concentrated food sources of soft or hard mast, such as apples or acorns.

✓ And, obviously, bait piles (where legal), planted food plots or annually planted fields of corn, soybeans, alfalfa or other crops.

More on Terrain

Natural features that cause deer to make so-called permanent trails can be overlooked. Terrain, generally speaking, is unchanging, and deer react to it much the same way hunters do. They take the easiest routes to conserve energy. Following trails also requires less "psychic" energy of individual deer than if they're constantly breaking new trails. Thus, deer often walk in single file over known trails. Hunters who find an old stand overlooking such trails can bet deer will eventually come by if they build a new stand in its place.

Unless man moves through with large earthmoving machines to sculpt the land, the terrain only changes slowly over time. Excluding earthquakes and major floods, most natural terrain changes will be so modest that none of us will recognize them in our lifetime. Deer react to the terrain, choosing trails that provide cover and the most direct route between two places. Sometimes that takes them through fairly open cover, with the topography itself keeping them obscured from a predator's sight.

The best time to locate old tree stands, of course, is after the leaves fall and before spring green-up. This will also provide your best unobstructed view of terrain features. Making these observations should be part of your post-season scouting, which gives you a running start on next season.

Why So High?

While observing old tree stands for several years, I sometimes judge them to be unnecessarily high. If nothing else, excessive heights can cause increased safety hazards. Many old stands I've seen were built just when deer hunting was gaining popularity after the whitetail's post-World War II restoration in many of our nation's forests and woodlots.

I remember reading an article several years ago about a tree stand that was built about 75 feet up a huge tree. Maybe the writer exaggerated the height, but more interesting was his claim that after finishing the climb, a hunter had to swing onto the stand with a rope. Predictably, the author called the stand, "The Widow Maker."

I don't doubt a hunter gets a great view from such heights. I also doubt a whitetail would ever notice him. Unless, of course, he fell screaming from the tree and plopped onto the forest floor as the deer was walking or feeding nearby!

In either case, it's safe to assume the original tree stand was used for gun-hunting. Such heights are impractical for bow-hunting. However, several years ago I read an article in which a bow-hunter described a stand 50 feet above ground.

All I can say about both situations is that those who go that high have just about quit deer hunting. Instead, they seem more interested in rappelling to impress hunting buddies. I think it's safe to say most deer hunters are more safety-conscious than some of their predecessors who nailed and cobbled tree stands together.

Inspect Old Stands

A few years ago I was invited to hunt deer at a camp 250 miles from home. I had never been there before, so I had obviously never seen the stands. In the

pre-dawn darkness I received directions to my stand. After walking a few minutes, I directed my flashlight beam up a tree and spotted a platform about 30 feet above in the forked limbs of a huge oak. I carefully ascended, pulled up my rifle with a rope, and sat down.

After some time on stand I stood up to stretch my cramped leg muscles. The wooden stand dropped a few inches but luckily caught and held. To put it mildly, I felt fortunate.

In preparing this article, I interviewed several deer hunters and asked about their experiences with old tree stands. One of them, Russell Patton, a first-class outdoorsman, said: "I once climbed into an unfamiliar tree stand. After awhile, I stood to stretch. Immediately the bottom gave way. Luckily, the stand was above wet, muddy ground. I plummeted several feet and plunged 2 feet deep to my knees into mud, which probably saved me from serious injury."

You might recall that a 1993 hunters' survey by *Deer & Deer Hunting* found one-third of deer hunters have fallen from trees or tree stands at one time. Some accidents were caused by faulty stand repair, and in many cases involved old permanent stands the hunter had never used before.

Conclusion

To re-emphasize the cautions mentioned earlier, remember that old tree stands are to be studied, not used. Examine where and why they're placed at a site.

Most stands tell the scouting hunter that, after all, white-tailed deer are creatures of habit. That being the case, I'll possibly arrange my own stand nearby.

"Old Stands Can Talk to You" was originally published in the October 1994 issue of Deer & Deer Hunting *magazine.*

> I READ ABOUT A TREE STAND 75 FEET HIGH. MAYBE THE WRITER EXAGGERATED. EVEN SO, I DOUBT A DEER WOULD NOTICE A HUNTER AT SUCH HEIGHTS. UNLESS THE PERSON FELL SCREAMING FROM THE TREE AND PLOPPED ONTO THE FOREST FLOOR AS THE DEER WAS WALKING BY!

CHAPTER 6

THE SECOND RUT: FALSE EXPECTATIONS?

"I'm not a believer in the 'second rut' ... north or south. It is basically a writer's and hunter's phenomenon."
— *R. Larry Marchinton, professor emeritus, University of Georgia*

■ BY CHARLES J. ALSHEIMER

I'm pawing through old hunting magazines in my home, looking at articles that detail the best hunting techniques for the second rut.

Title after title suggests the so-called "second rut" is often as good as the first for bagging a decent buck. Some of the articles even convey the idea that hunters should consider passing up November's peak rutting time in favor of December's "rage in the woods." Are these writings fact, hype or a figment of some writer's imagination?

Over the years, I've been fascinated by the possibilities of hunting the second rut. After all, I grew up reading how exciting it was to hunt a rutting period after most other hunters left the woods in early December. Now, after more than 25 years of serious hunting, I wonder just how big the so-called second rut really is.

This doubt about the second rut didn't develop overnight. For years my field observations didn't match what I was reading. And with each passing year, I

AFTER THE RUT REACHES ITS PEAK EACH FALL, BUCKS SELDOM DISPLAY THE SAME INTENSITY FOR BREEDING, EVEN WHEN THEY'RE NEAR DOES THAT WEREN'T BRED THE FIRST TIME THEY WERE IN ESTRUS. BUCKS ALSO DON'T DO AS MUCH RUBBING AFTER THE RUT'S PEAK. TRYING TO HUNT NOVEMBER'S RUB LINES IN DECEMBER WILL OFTEN PROVE FUTILE.

wondered even more why I wasn't seeing the frenzied second rut so many writers praised. What was I missing?

Suppressed Action

That is not to say I have never seen rutting activity from mid-December to early January in my home state of New York. I have photographed a fair amount of rutting activity during what hunters call the second rut. This includes photos of rubbing, chasing and breeding deer. However, deer behavior I've witnessed the past 10 years of intense hunting and photography doesn't come close to rivaling the rutting activity I've seen in early to mid-November each year.

Why? Several factors determine the amount of rutting activity that occurs after mid-November's peak. Fortunately, biologists are beginning to shed more light on the rut.

In writing this article, I contacted some of the most respected white-tailed deer biologists in America. No two seemed to agree on everything, but a common thought they shared was doubt about the so-called second rut, at least as it's often described in the outdoor press.

Michigan's John Ozoga, *Deer & Deer Hunting's* research biologist, said: "I don't like the term, 'second rut.' I suppose there could be a second rut in some situations, but I'm not sure it exists the way most hunters envision it. In reality, if plotted, the rut would be a curve with a couple of blips in it."

Ozoga said many factors determine whether the rut is condensed or protracted. He says northern Michigan's rut is condensed because of the region's cold climate. However, in southern Michigan, the rut is longer because conditions allow yearling does and fawns to come into estrus and be bred in December and January.

Ozoga refers to a "window of breeding activity" to explain the rut's length. "In nature, fawns need to be born on schedule in order to survive," he said. "In Northern climates, like Michigan, that means late May and early June. As a result, the farther north one goes, the narrower the window of breeding activity.

"In the warmer Southern climates, the window of breeding activity doesn't need to be as small. Therefore,

> "I SUPPOSE THERE COULD BE A SECOND RUT IN SOME SITUATIONS, BUT I'M NOT SURE IT EXISTS THE WAY MOST HUNTERS ENVISION IT. IN REALITY, IF PLOTTED, THE RUT WOULD BE A CURVE WITH A COUPLE OF BLIPS IN IT."
> — *John J. Ozoga, research biologist*

the breeding is often drawn out, and in some portions of the whitetail's range, estrus occurs year-round."

Herd Structure

Biologist Grant Woods of South Carolina, a Ph.D. who runs a wildlife-management consulting firm, has thoughts similar to Ozoga's.

"I don't believe in a first, second or third rut because the age class and sex ratio in most deer herds is so poor," Woods said. "My findings show that when sex ratios get out of balance and a herd has few mature bucks, the rut is strung out and can last more than 100 days. When that happens, problems occur and the herd's quality drops significantly.

"However, when a herd is fine-tuned — meaning it has good nutrition and a balanced sex ratio and age structure — the rut is condensed and often lasts less than 50 days. You also find more rutting sign in a fine-tuned herd. On one property I manage, there is a 1-1 buck-to-doe ratio, and we've found 3,000 rubs per square mile. Conception in this area is tight, and the rut lasts roughly 44 days. Interestingly, the property next door has a 7-1 doe-to-buck ratio, and the rut peaks a month later and lasts more than 100 days."

The New York State Department of Environmental Conservation is studying reproduction and conception dates in two deer management units. So far, this study fits Woods' comments concerning the length of the rut when doe-to-buck ratios are unbalanced. With an adult doe-to-adult buck ratio of about 9-1, the breeding dates of sample carcasses in New York show the does were bred between Nov. 12 and Jan. 25, definitely a protracted rut.

In theory, an adult buck should be able to breed four to seven adult females (Jackson 1973). So, when doe-to-buck ratios are high, adult bucks simply cannot breed all of the does when they enter estrus. As a result, many does cycle out and come into estrus 28 days later.

With sex ratios out of balance, three things occur, especially in states where hunting pressure is intense. First, many bucks are killed during the main rut, leaving few to service the does that come into estrus 28 days later.

Secondly, with a protracted rut, bucks that survive autumn's peak rutting activity and high hunting pressure are often greatly stressed by the abundance of estrous does. When that happens, many bucks don't survive winter, especially when record cold and blizzards strike.

Lastly, when doe-to-buck ratios get out of sync, rutting activity and its associated sign diminish greatly. That and a buck's decreased desire to breed are two of several key reasons why hunting the second rut is so difficult.

Less Desire?

No doubt, many hunters will question that a buck's sexual desires decrease in December. Granted, in many cases, it depends on individual

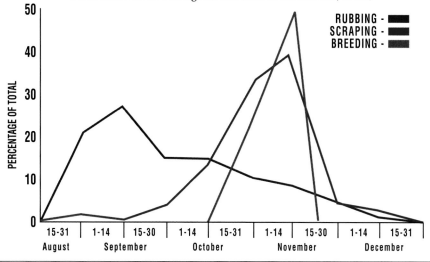

Frequency of Rubbing, Scraping, and Breeding Activity

White-tailed Bucks During the Rut. (Kile & Marchinton, 1977.)

bucks. But research (Lambiase 1972) shows that sperm production extends from mid-August through March for most bucks. The number of sperm per ejaculation typically increases through October, peaks in mid-November, drops almost in half by mid-December, and declines at a slower rate thereafter. Those facts help demonstrate why bucks go into a rutting frenzy as mid-November and the rut's peak approaches. It also illustrates why the chase phase (see "Hunting the Chase Phase," *Deer & Deer Hunting*, October 1993) and its associated rutting activity is such a good time to hunt rut-crazed bucks.

Lambiase's research also shows why less rutting activity occurs in December, even though many does are in estrus. Mother Nature plays another card during this later period. During November's peak rutting time, the bucks' physical condition slides progressively from sleek, well-muscled specimens to worn down mirrors of what they were. They deplete their fat reserves and, in many cases, lose as much as 30 percent of their weight.

Survival Mode

As a result, a buck's survival mode kicks in as their rutting ardor wanes. Rather than constantly chase does, they calm down and start eating in attempts to regain the weight they lost in November. Unfortunately, not all bucks restore those lost reserves. The subsequent winter, and what remains of the bucks' sex drive, take their toll. Death claims many bucks, especially the most active breeders.

Because survival is the main objective, a buck becomes

a different creature in December and early January. He will still breed, but generally he won't pursue does with the same intensity he showed in November. Rather, he feeds, rests and takes what comes his way.

I've seen this scenario many times during photo and hunting sessions. When December arrives, the deer's family groups begin gravitating toward known food sources. In some cases, this is cornfields. In others, it's a cedar swamp that will soon serve as a yarding area. Regardless, the objective of bucks and does is shelter, and food, food and more food. As a result, trying to hunt November's scrapes and rub lines is often futile.

I observed what often happens during this time while photographing in New York's Adirondack Mountains during a recent December. I visited a known wintering area with the intent of photographing some bucks before January's severe cold set in. Early December snows had arrived, and so had the deer. About 30 does and five or six bucks were in the area trying to bulk up on as much food as possible. On my second day, it was obvious a doe was in estrus. The biggest buck followed her around, but not overly aggressively. The other bucks, though at times interested, did not join in. They were more content to bed, rest and feed.

Though the buck finally bred the doe, he spent most of his time eating and resting. He occasionally gave a low, guttural grunt if another buck came too close, but he never showed aggressive behavior or attempted scraping activity. And only once did he rub a tree. It was almost as if the bucks knew the doe needed to be bred, but none cared which buck did it. Had it been mid-November, I can assure you the scene would have been far different.

Case in Point

Another example of mid-December, or second rut, deer activity typifies experiences I've had at that time of year. The day was Dec. 9, and about 5 inches of snow covered the ground. In the morning I sat overlooking a stream that runs through our property. About 10 a.m., I heard what sounded like deer chasing each other.

> AFTER THE RUT SUBSIDES, I HUNT FOOD SOURCES CLOSE TO THICK COVER. THAT PUTS ME CLOSE TO DOE GROUPS AND THE BUCKS THAT SURVIVED THE FIREARMS SEASON.

Unfortunately, they were out of range and were not coming closer. After an hour of silence, I headed home.

At about 3 p.m., with two hours of light remaining, I headed back to the area with my son, Aaron. Fifteen minutes into our sit I heard two bucks sparring about 100 yards away. Within minutes, with the sparring still going on, four does moved down through the woods and out of sight. A 6-point buck followed. Though the sparring grew louder and the bucks came closer, it wasn't aggressive.

With 20 minutes of light remaining, we spotted the four does coming back, with the yearling buck still in tow. All this time we could hear the bucks sparring. Hoping the combatants were larger, I let the 6-pointer walk. Soon after, the two sparring partners came into view and continued sparring in a small creek about 30 yards away.

Through my scope I could see one was a yearling and the other a heavy 6-pointer, probably a 2½-year-old buck. I decided that neither was big enough, so we sat and watched their every move. In the fading light, I brought my grunt tube to my mouth and blew on it twice. At first the bucks ignored the sound but two more grunts got their attention, and the bigger buck started in our direction. At one point, he stood 15 paces in front of our blind, trying to figure out what had called. As darkness crept in, he turned and walked off to join his sparring buddy.

Though these bucks exhibited a small amount of rutting activity, they had no interest in the four does that fed past as they sparred. It was obvious they were more interested in roughhousing than sex. Again, had it been November, I'm sure they would have behaved differently. These and many other experiences have made me doubt the hype I read about the second rut.

The Opportunist

I am an opportunist when hunting after November's rut. Though does will be bred during this time, I know deer behavior will be much different. As a result, I intensely hunt food sources close to thick cover. In so doing, I'm able to get close to doe groups and the bucks that have survived the firearms season. Remember, does, and particularly bucks, need to gain and maintain body weight to survive the winter. Therefore, everything else takes a back seat to food, even sex.

I find rattling during this time to be marginally productive because there is little competition among bucks, mainly because few survive gun season in my region. When I rattle late in the season, I make noises associated with sparring, not full-blown fighting. Seldom will two bucks really go at it after the flurry of the rut is past, so I believe less noise is better. However, I find grunting to be successful after November, and use the tube the same way I do in November (see "Rattle and Grunt Your Way To a Buck," *Deer & Deer Hunting,* November 1993).

Conclusion

So, do hunters expect too much from the second rut? I think so. There's no question this period is one of my favorite times to be in the woods, but the true rutting activity of November is long gone.

I'm not alone on that thought. R. Larry Marchinton, professor emeritus from the University of Georgia, is one of the nation's top hunters and deer biologists. He summed up his feelings on the second rut this way:

"I'm not a believer in the 'second rut' ... north or south. It is basically a writer's and hunter's phenomenon."

"The Second Rut: False Expectations?" was originally published in the January 1994 issue of Deer & Deer Hunting *magazine.*

CHAPTER 7

BIG WOODS TRACKING:

ART OR ARTIFACT?

Tracking a whitetail in fresh snow is arguably a better way to hunt than stand-hunting or still-hunting. Tracking eliminates the boredom of the former and the randomness of the latter.

■ BY JIM SHOCKEY

Dave Buckley

"TURN ON YOUR SENSES WHEN YOU ARE ON THE TRACK. TUNE INTO THE WOODS AND THE MOUNTAINS. ... IF YOU DON'T TURN YOURSELF INTO A HUNTING ANIMAL, YOU WON'T GET THAT BUCK."

— LARRY BENOIT, VERMONT DEER TRACKER
HOW TO BAG THE BIGGEST BUCK OF YOUR LIFE

N ine or so thousand years ago, a young native hunter stepped quietly through the bush. A skiff of new snow covered the ground, and the hunter crouched every now and again to inspect the trail.

Eventually his pace slowed to one almost unnoticeable step every few minutes. Then he quietly stiffened and his arm drew back. Like a snake striking, his spear darted toward something in the bush. The buck never knew what hit him.

Eight thousand years passed, a blink of time's eye. Again a native youth crept quietly through the forest. He followed the same lightly snow-powdered trail taken by his ancestor. The most obvious change was the hunter's clothing and equipment, which were more ably designed. His pace slowed and the effort of prolonged concentration began to show in tiny lines on his forehead. The youth gently nocked an arrow. Minutes later he stopped dead still and drew his bow. The buck never knew what hit him.

To the day, 900 years later, a young man of

European descent eased a branch out of the way. Though he was, to the attentive observer, less stealthy than history's moccasin-equipped native hunters, he was armed with the equalizing longer-range capability of a .45-90 rifle. Bullets were not cheap, however, and so it was with great care that he placed each foot onto the snow-covered path. Again, as did the men long before him, the young man slowed to a near stop. He searched the forest ahead for some clue, some indication of life.

And then he moved. His rifle came to bear and the forest silence was shattered by the blast of exploding black powder. The buck never knew what hit him.

Ten years ago, or was it last fall? The land lay dead calm after the night's fresh snow. Gone now was the endless expanse of forest, replaced instead with tilled open fields and pockets of bush along the deeper ravines. Still, as in ages past, no sound penetrates the gray/white stillness. Moments later, however, the barely audible steps of a white-tailed buck can be heard as he crosses a field. Suddenly the buck detects a distant hint of danger. The sound was a faraway warning at first, and the buck's sensitive ears detected the intrusion long before any other woodland creature.

He stops and waits. The sound grows to a noise that spoils the stillness. The intruder is forcing itself, rattling and clanking, upon the morning stillness. Then the sound changes in pitch, all the buck needs to hear. In a breath he is in full flight toward the cover at the field's far side.

A driver stops the noisy truck and turns out the headlights. Then he and his partner open their doors and step out, reach back inside for their rifles, and shut the truck's doors. The day is brightening in the east. They talk in low tones as they walk across the field to marked trails leading to their tree stands. Suddenly, they stop to look at the tracks in the fresh snow.

"Looks fresh," one hunter says. "I guess." The other agrees and they continue on their way.

The hunters' forefathers roll in their graves.

Why Track?

Things have changed in the hunting world the past 10,000 years, and not all the changes have been for the better. Sadly, many hunting methods early hunters took for granted have been relegated by modern hunters to the tattered bottom of their bag of tricks. I believe the age-old art of tracking must be revived before it becomes an artifact. Tracking should be more than a curiosity, and its purpose should never be forgotten.

Why? Because tracking a whitetail in fresh snow is arguably a better way to hunt than stand-hunting or still-hunting. Tracking eliminates the boredom of the former and the randomness of the latter. Take note, I said fresh snow. That is the operative phrase if you want to be a successful tracker. Those bygone hunters described at the top of this article might have been able to track deer on bare ground, but few hunters in North America today could do it. Further, tracking deer in old snow is possible, but it isn't for neophytes.

When mastered, tracking can often provide the hunter a close shot at what is normally a difficult-to-get deer. The mythical one-shot kills our forefathers took for granted can come more easily when you track down a whitetail.

Next season, stand-hunt to your heart's content if you must. But if you ever get a fresh snowfall overnight that stops around dawn, study your options. Consider tracking your next buck. You might have it made.

Tracking Bucks

First, let's agree that deer go where deer go, and if you intend to follow a deer track through the forest it might go in a straight line for miles. Therefore, you must be prepared. Johnny Cash won't be serenading you at lunch, and your buddies won't be there to discuss the football game. If you intend to track down a buck, you must realize you're going to be alone and cold, possibly all day.

And don't expect to find road signs in the bush telling you which direction to go once the day is over. Your best friend can be the sun. As long as it's visible, you won't get lost. But if it disappears, you must be on good speaking terms with your compass and, possibly, your GPS unit. Touch wood, I have never had to use my compass to find my way out of the bush after tracking a deer all day, but more than once I've had to backtrack myself out.

> IF THE BUCK YOU'RE FOLLOWING JOINS A GROUP, FOLLOW THE HERD UNTIL YOU SEE TRACKS VEERING OFF TO THE SIDE YOUR DEER WAS HEADED. IF THE TRACKS DON'T LOOP BACK TO JOIN THE HERD, THERE IS A GOOD CHANCE YOU'RE ON THE BUCK'S TRAIL.

Charles J. Alsheimer

Remember this bit of advice and follow it: At the end of every human track is a human, while at the beginning of every human track is a warm truck. If it starts to snow while you are on a buck's track and you are even remotely unsure of your position, turn around and follow your clodhopper marks home. Score Round 1 for the deer.

In the unlikely event you find yourself obligated to spending the night in the forest, you'll realize quickly the importance of a daypack filled with survival gear. I won't follow a deer for two minutes in the big woods without my survival gear. Carry a space blanket, a takedown camp saw, waterproof matches, a few cubes of fire-starter, a lighter, a candle, a few more waterproof matches, and some candy bars. Any one of these items could save your life.

Scare-mongering aside, much of the deer tracking you do will be in country you know well. And the better you know the land, the more successful you'll be on the track.

Sizing Deer

So you have your daypack and fresh snow. Now it's time to find the right deer track. You must decide what sort of deer you want to track. If any deer will suffice, obviously any track will suffice. But if you want a big buck, you must know how to identify the tracks these deer make. That's not as difficult as it seems. At least it's not always difficult to tell a buck track from a doe track.

IF YOU INTEND TO TRACK DOWN A DEER, REALIZE YOU'RE GOING TO BE ALONE AND COLD, POSSIBLY ALL DAY. YOU MUST BE ON GOOD SPEAKING TERMS WITH YOUR COMPASS AND, POSSIBLY, YOUR GPS UNIT.

If you find a single, isolated track cutting across a road or field and it's moving in a determined direction, chances are you'll find a buck at its end. If the track meanders along, as though the deer is lost or feeding here and there, chances are you'll find a doe at its end. Either that or a hungry buck. If you find a group of deer tracks together, chances are the tracks were made by does and fawns. And if there is a buck in this bunch, you might have to forget him. Trying to untangle a single track from a herd can be a tracker's nightmare.

It's tricky, however, to determine the size of the buck by his track. This is often just an educated guess. To help determine the buck's size, I try to find a track that's imprinted cleanly in the snow. Deep snow makes this all but impossible. If the snow isn't deep, you can usually determine a big deer from a small deer by the hoof size. Of course, there are exceptions. Not all big deer have matching big hoofs, and vice versa. Those familiar with Milo Hanson's world-record buck from Saskatchewan often note this buck had small to average-size hoofs. When Hanson's group was following that buck, they often had difficulty singling out its track because it was so average.

A more accurate measurement of a buck's size might be found in the length of his stride. When a buck is walking, hoof prints with a good distance between them often mean the deer is above average in size. However, I won't try to tell you how many inches will make for a big stride and a corresponding big deer. Such measurements vary greatly by region and the relative size of local deer.

It's best to determine average strides by yourself. Check out as many tracks as you can where you hunt. Pay particular attention when you actually see the deer that made the track.

Hoofs and Antlers

As to the relationship of track size to antler size, I'm skeptical it can be done reliably. I believe you'll have more chance of dating supermodel Elle McPherson than judging the size of a buck's antlers by his hoof size.

You're better off looking for other clues. Larry Benoit, Vermont's legendary deer tracker, wrote a book on tracking, *How to Bag the Biggest Buck of Your Life*. Benoit advises trackers to check the snow carefully when the buck they're tracking intersects the tracks of another deer.

"A buck will often stick his nose into another deer track to get a good scent, and if there is snow on the ground, you will see the dimple where the nose was imprinted," Benoit wrote. "If there is a good 6 inches of snow, you might even see the imprint of his tines and read how many points this particular buck has."

Benoit also examines deer beds for clues to the buck's rack. How? He says big bucks stretch out rather than curl up in their beds, and sometimes their antlers touch the snow briefly when they relax.

"If there's snow on the ground, take (a) close look. I mean really close. Look sharp, because you ought to be able to see the imprint of his antlers in the snow and maybe the spread of the antlers. (One year in Maine) I knew I was onto what I thought was a 14-pointer by seeing seven tine marks in the snow. He ended up being a 13-pointer."

The Three P's

Once you're on the track, remember the three P's. All of them are vitally important: Patience, perseverance and practice.

> AN ACCURATE MEASUREMENT OF A BUCK'S SIZE MIGHT BE FOUND IN THE LENGTH OF HIS STRIDE. WHEN THE BUCK IS WALKING, HOOF PRINTS WITH A GOOD DISTANCE BETWEEN THEM OFTEN MEAN THE DEER IS ABOVE AVERAGE IN SIZE.

Patience: Don't rush. Take your time. That deer is at the end of the track somewhere ahead. It might be close and, then again, it might be far. But it's always better to not spook the animal than to alert it to your presence. All you do by scaring the deer and glimpsing its tail is to confirm what you already knew. After all, it certainly wasn't a squirrel leaving those hoof prints!

Carefully place each foot in front of the other. If you feel a branch under your boot sole, ease back and step somewhere else. By being patient you can move through the forest much more quietly than you can imagine. It helps enormously to wear soft clothing that doesn't make scraping noises when frozen branches slide across.

Perseverance: Don't give up. I can repeat that advice 1,000 times, but nothing will reinforce that lesson as much as the first time you succeed. Every deer track will occasionally be tough to follow. It's possible the deer you're tracking will become mixed up with other deer.

Don't quit. Most likely, if your deer crossed the other tracks, it was traveling in a different direction. Most often the buck will follow the other tracks a short distance and then continue his original course. Of course, that's provided there are no hot does among the larger group.

When I encounter such situations, I follow the main herd until I see a track veering off to the side my deer was headed. In most cases, the track will loop back to join the herd, but when it doesn't, there is a good chance I am back on my deer's trail. By that time, if I have been observant, I will know the approximate length of my deer's stride. Shortly after I will know if this deer has a similar gait.

Don't give up. One time while following what I thought was a buck's track, I hit a veritable maze of tracks. It seemed more than 12 deer had spent hours in the area wandering around making tracks that led nowhere. I worked on the puzzle until the warming day nearly melted away all the tracks. When forced to make a choice, I started in the direction my buck had originally been traveling. For most of the morning, the buck had been on a beeline for a river's shoreline.

Bill Winke

Though it was a long shot, I reasoned the river's edge was my best chance. Less than 15 minutes later I spotted the buck bedded near the river. Though I can't be sure, it's likely he was the same buck I had followed earlier.

Which brings us to the last and certainly most important virtue of a tracker.

Practice: The more you practice tracking the more proficient you become. Educated guesses about where the deer is heading and where it might bed become more precise. You start to learn when you're far behind the deer and when you're getting close. You spend more time scanning ahead and less time looking at the tracks because you develop a sense about where the deer is going.

When you know this, you begin to understand where deer travel and why. Where before you might have believed deer wander aimlessly through the forest, tracking deer on a regular basis teaches you that they travel specific corridors.

When you practice tracking, you begin to see that a single deer track can lead you to forest hotspots you never knew existed. These can be sites only deer know about and where they tend to congregate.

Practice teaches you that deeper knowledge is the net benefit of tracking: Devoting one day to a deer's track can teach you more about deer than you likely learned in a career of stand-hunting.

DEVOTING ONE DAY TO A DEER'S TRACK CAN TEACH YOU MORE ABOUT DEER THAN YOU LIKELY LEARNED IN A CAREER OF STAND-HUNTING. YOU BEGIN TO SEE THAT A SINGLE DEER TRACK CAN LEAD TO FOREST HOTSPOTS YOU NEVER KNEW EXISTED. THESE CAN BE SITES ONLY DEER KNOW ABOUT AND WHERE THEY TEND TO CONGREGATE.

Conclusion

Of course, if you don't think deer hunting would be deer hunting without listening to Johnny Cash at lunch time, and if you don't care if you eat venison or beef next winter, then tracking is an artifact for you, a mere curiosity from the past.

But if you're willing to learn something new, you will quickly realize that tracking is far from an archaic pastime. For you, tracking will become a true art form. Maybe most of the masters of this art are long gone, but even an apprentice tracker outfitted with a modern rifle will find more consistent success than most stand-hunters or still-hunters.

"Big Woods Tracking: Art or Artifact?" was originally published in the March 1995 issue of Deer & Deer Hunting *magazine.*

CHAPTER 8

A CASE FOR WAITING

Assuming his shot hit the buck's chest, Bruce quickly reloaded his muzzleloader and followed the fleeing tracks. But instead of finding a dead deer within a short distance, as expected, he found a vacated bed.

■ BY RICHARD P. SMITH

GOOD HUNTERS STRIVE TO KILL AND RECOVER DEER AS CLEANLY AND QUICKLY AS POSSIBLE. SOMETIMES WAITING BACK IN CAMP BEFORE TRAILING A WOUNDED DEER IS THE QUICKEST PATH TO THAT HUMANE END.

My brother should have waited before following the wounded buck. But as many hunters do, he pursued the whitetail too quickly, not taking time to accurately determine where it was hit. Despite his mistake, we managed to recover the deer the next day, but only through persistence and with the aid of snow.

The buck had caught Bruce by surprise, coming from behind without making a sound. The deer was only 10 to 20 feet away when Bruce saw it, and the buck saw Bruce move when he shouldered his .50-caliber muzzleloader. The whitetail bounded off, then stopped to look back when 50 yards away. That's when Bruce shot. He aimed for the right shoulder, a difficult target with the buck angling sharply away.

We found hair where the buck had stood, confirming a hit. If Bruce had taken the time to examine the hair, he would have learned the round-ball hadn't hit where he aimed. Perhaps then he would have waited before trailing the buck. Instead, in his excitement to tag the buck, he rushed ahead. Assuming his shot took the whitetail through the chest, Bruce quickly reloaded and started following the tracks. But instead of finding the deer within a short distance, he found a bed the buck had vacated when it detected his approach.

The whitetail had run 200 yards after being hit, then stopped. Not detecting any pursuers, it walked a few feet and laid down where it could watch its backtrack. We found blood only where the buck had stood a few minutes before lying down.

Second Chance

Without snow, it would have been difficult for Bruce to follow the buck to its bed. At that point, he had a second chance to wait. Because the buck wasn't bleeding much externally, it was obvious the shot missed the heart and lungs. Had those organs been damaged, the animal would have been dead or too weak to continue. Still, the fact the deer laid down after going only 200 yards indicated it was seriously hurt, and that the wound would eventually be fatal.

Bruce fired at 9:45 a.m. under a clear sky and cold temperatures. I think the best thing he could have done would have been to back off and resume trailing the buck in the afternoon. But he failed to carefully consider his options. Still intent on claiming the buck quickly, he hurried along on the deer's tracks.

He had followed the buck almost a mile past the bed by the time I caught up with him. The blood sign hadn't improved. Occasionally we found a spot of red with the tracks. Fortunately, the injured deer's big prints and distinctive trail allowed us to recognize its tracks among all the others we crossed. The buck was dragging its hoofs and splaying its toes more than normal.

I persuaded Bruce to leave the trail and return later. From experience with wounded deer, I knew waiting would improve our chances of recovering the animal. Time takes its toll on internal injuries, whether a deer is on its hoofs or lying down. Mature bucks normally have the most stamina, and it takes them longer to weaken.

I think it's generally better to let a deer weaken while it's lying down, especially when the wound does not bleed externally.

As an injured deer travels greater distances on bare ground without leaving a blood trail, the chance of recovering it diminishes greatly, unless a specially trained tracking dog is available.

Even with snow, pushing a deer with an injury that isn't quickly fatal can complicate matters. At the least, pushing a deer might cause a longer drag. Worse, it might make it impossible for you to recover it, or provide a chance for an unknown hunter nearby to shoot and tag it. A pushed deer might also enter private property where you don't have access.

Waiting Philosophy

I apply this waiting philosophy to hits that rupture the paunch and/or intestines and liver. Such gut wounds often produce poor blood trails because fat and intestines plug the entry and exit holes. The farther a gut-shot deer travels, the greater the chances of little, if any, external bleeding.

When Bruce and I resumed trailing the buck in late afternoon, we discovered we had jumped it from a second bed close to where we had stopped earlier. Had we backed off sooner, I believe we would have found it there dead or too weak to continue.

Because the buck had been injured only about an hour before being jumped, however, it still had plenty of energy. We followed its tracks at least another mile without finding a third bed or seeing it. We left the track as light faded.

We returned the next morning. The deer, a 2½- or 3½-year-old 5-pointer, was dead about a quarter-mile from where we had stopped the previous night. In typical buck fashion, it died on its feet. Because its body cavity was cold, I'm sure the buck was dead when we left its trail the evening before. I concluded it took about six hours for the deer to die from its wound. Death probably would not have come sooner, but the deer wouldn't have traveled as far had Bruce waited six hours before trailing the buck initially, or

> FORTUNATELY, THE INJURED DEER'S BIG PRINTS AND DISTINCTIVE TRAIL ALLOWED US TO RECOGNIZE ITS TRACKS AMONG ALL THE OTHERS WE CROSSED. THE BUCK WAS DRAGGING ITS HOOFS AND SPLAYING ITS TOES MORE THAN NORMAL.

after jumping it from the first bed.

Because it was followed soon after the shot and subsequently pushed, the buck traveled, conservatively, more than two miles. The actual distance might have been double that. Had there been no snow, we would have been hard-pressed to find that buck's first bed, much less recover the animal.

Careful Analysis

That's why it's extremely important for hunters to make a studious effort to determine what type of hit they've inflicted before rushing after a wounded whitetail, especially without snow on the ground.

In the case above, Bruce had gut-shot the buck. The lead ball went through the buck's right ham and into its body cavity. Hairs from a whitetail's hindquarters, which we found where Bruce hit the buck, are different from those on a deer's shoulders or other regions. .

By knowing these differences in hair from various parts of a whitetail, hunters can better determine where their bullets, slugs and broadheads connect. Deer hair reference guides — either commercially published photos or actual deer hair on index cards — provide excellent tracking tools.

If you quickly recognize a gut-shot deer, you have a good chance of recovering it. After confirming the wound's location through hair identification at the site, wait up to six hours before trailing the deer. Then, in the absence of blood sign, scour the terrain in the direction the deer ran, starting at the point where it went out of sight.

In situations where you make a questionable hit on a whitetail late in the day, and when no rain or snow is expected overnight, it's usually best to wait until the next morning before starting after a whitetail. I've had excellent success recovering gut-shot deer by waiting overnight before trailing them. In most cases, they died before we resumed tracking them in the morning.

One adult doe was still alive and managed to run a short distance when jumped. She was too weak to go far, however, and I quickly finished her.

Decisive Factors

At a deer show one year, a bow-hunter told me about a gut-shot buck he recovered by waiting overnight. The buck bedded within sight after being hit, and the archer sneaked out of his stand to avoid disturbing the injured deer. Returning the next morning, he found the buck in the same place, and finished the job. Several factors influenced this hunter's deci-

BUCK ATTACKS TRACKER

Wrestling a deer was the furthest thing from Mel Thorne's mind Dec. 6, 1993, when the Michigan hunter went to track a deer a friend had shot with a muzzleloader the night before.

The buck, however, left him no choice. Thorne had to fight the deer to protect himself, and he killed it with a knife.

Thorne's friend, Mike Marble, had shot just before dark on Dec. 5. The men looked for the buck that night but didn't find any sign that Marble's shot had connected. A lack of snow also made it difficult to determine where the deer had gone.

Marble had to work the next day, so Thorne returned in the morning to look for the animal. Thorne, 47, wasn't carrying a rifle, but he strapped a sheathed knife onto his coveralls.

"I figured the deer would be dead if I found it," Thorne said. "I only brought the knife to field dress the deer."

As it turned out, Thorne never found the buck. It found him. It ambushed him, striking him from behind. He had been wandering around looking for the deer, and ended up about 150 yards from the field where Marble had shot. He was just about ready to give up, and must have walked right by the deer.

"He came out of thick evergreens 12 to 15 feet away," Thorne said. "He hit me so hard he knocked my hat and gloves into the brush. The same thing probably would have happened to a rifle if I had been carrying one."

The blow knocked Thorne to the ground. He isn't sure if the buck hit him with its head or body. Thorne stood up and waved his arms, believing the deer would leave.

"That just made it worse," he said. "I've heard deer make a blatting sound, but this one ... roared like a bull. Then he dropped his head and came right at me. I stepped aside and tried to grab him wherever I could. I ended up grabbing him behind the front shoulders, and we went down. I couldn't hold for long. The hair was slippery and not long enough to grip.

"I was still on the ground when he got up. He reared up on his hind legs like a horse. He was going to hit me with his front hoofs, but I rolled out of the way."

When the buck charged the third time, Thorne grabbed the antlers, wrestled the buck down, got on top of its neck, pulled out his knife, and cut its throat.

Thorne is an experienced hand with livestock, and credits that knowledge with subduing the buck. The attack left him badly bruised and physically drained. He also said his heavy, insulated coveralls spared him serious injury.

The buck had 4-point antlers and a dressed weight of 145 pounds. Its live weight was estimated at 175 pounds.

"I was fortunate the buck didn't have any more of a rack than he did," said Thorne, who weighs 185 pounds. "I could have been hurt worse."

The buck, which had an injured front leg, proved to be the one Marble had shot, but the wound was not life threatening. Still, the injury probably spurred the buck's actions. Most whitetails would have remained hidden and let him walk by.

"If the buck would have laid where it was, I would never have seen it," Thorne said.
— Richard P. Smith

This article was originally published in the June 1994 issue of Deer & Deer Hunting *magazine.*

Richard P. Smith

BASED ON HIS EXPERIENCE WITH WOUNDED DEER, THE AUTHOR BELIEVES WAITING WILL OFTEN IMPROVE YOUR CHANCES OF RECOVERING DEER THAT AREN'T HIT IN THE CHEST. TIME TAKES ITS TOLL ON INTERNAL INJURIES, WHETHER A DEER IS ON ITS HOOFS OR LYING DOWN. IF AN INJURED DEER IS PUSHED TOO SOON FROM ITS BED, AND TRAVELS FAR ON BARE GROUND WITHOUT LEAVING A BLOOD TRAIL, THE CHANCES OF RECOVERING IT DIMINISH GREATLY, UNLESS A TRAINED TRACKING DOG IS AVAILABLE.

sion to wait:
    ✓ Lack of snow cover.
    ✓ Uncertainty of the wound's location.
    ✓ The wounded buck appeared alert in its bed.
Had the archer approached to try another shot, the buck probably would have fled. Once on its hoofs with adrenaline pumping, there's no telling how far that

whitetail would have gone. It certainly could have traveled far, leaving little or no blood to follow.

Best to Wait

In most cases, if possible, it's best to wait four to six hours before trailing adult whitetails that have been gut-shot. Sometimes even longer is better. With fawns and yearlings, two hours might be long enough. But, I think it's better to wait longer than necessary than not long enough.

Heavy rain and snow complicate the waiting scenario, washing away or covering up blood sign. As a rule, when rain or snow threatens, wait as long as possible before trying to follow up on the animal.

String-tracking devices can help under such circumstances, but even they can't cover all contingencies. One autumn I gut-shot a spike buck on a rainy day. I was using a string tracker but, as luck had it, my first shot missed. The young buck was confused and hung around long enough for me to connect on the next shot. Unfortunately, the tracking string was connected only to the first arrow. There hadn't been time to retie it. The buck walked off slowly to the left after being hit, and then circled to the right before lying down within sight after covering 50 to 75 yards. I saw that the exit wound was plugged, and feared the buck would leave a poor blood trail.

It was 9:15 a.m. and the rain had stopped. After 10 minutes, the buck stood and walked off slowly. I waited another five minutes before leaving my tree stand to examine my arrow. I moved as quietly as possible to reduce the chances of spooking the deer if it was still nearby.

Paunch residue on the shaft confirmed a gut shot. By 10 a.m. the rain resumed with more force, so I went after the deer. I sneaked carefully to the point where it first laid down. From there, I spotted it bedded only 20 yards away! It also saw me and stood to leave.

I released an arrow, but brush deflected it. The buck moved a few feet to the left on wobbly legs before stopping. We stared at each other 10 minutes as the rain poured down. With each passing minute I sensed the deer weakening. I finally moved slightly to look for a shooting lane, and the buck staggered off.

I followed and quickly spotted him lying down nearby. Obviously weak, it would probably die where it was if I left or sat down and waited, but I decided to try to finish the job. It took me at least 30 minutes to inch within 10 yards and find an opening in the brush. My next arrow took the deer through its lungs.

Liver Hits

Whitetails often weaken and die faster from liver hits than those through the paunch or intestines, especially if the liver is seriously damaged or if the major blood vessel supplying it is severed. In the case of liver damage, it can take two to four hours for the wound to have a serious impact. I like to wait at least two hours before trailing a liver-hit whitetail.

Fortunately, liver hits often produce better blood trails than gut shots. Therefore, the risk of losing a liver-shot deer by trailing too soon is lower than with gut-shot deer. One autumn, an acquaintance liver-shot an 11-point buck with a rifle as it walked through an opening. He found plenty of dark red blood — common with liver wounds — leading from where he hit the buck.

If he had waited a couple of hours, he probably would have found the buck dead in its first bed. Instead, he followed right away. Though he soon saw it lying down, he couldn't raise his rifle fast enough to shoot before the buck jumped up and ran. His shot at the running buck missed. He continued his pursuit, jumped the buck a couple of more times, and fired two more rounds before killing it.

Because he was hunting on a large block of land owned by his uncle, he had no interference from other hunters. Under different circumstances — on crowded public ground or on private land to which he didn't have access — the hunter could have lost this buck by pushing it that far.

I also know a Wisconsin hunter who lost a buck one year by following it too soon. While hunting on his father's land near a neighbor's piece of private property, the hunter spotted a small 8-point buck. The deer moved ahead when the hunter fired, suffering a probable liver hit from the 12-gauge slug.

The hunter and his father found plenty of blood and followed it, but they jumped the deer and pushed it onto the adjoining property. Another hunter then shot and tagged it. The father-and-son team probably could have gotten that whitetail if they had waited a couple of hours before trailing it.

Conclusion

Multiple factors govern all hunting situations, especially trailing wounded deer. But you won't know which factors you're dealing with if you don't make a careful and thorough assessment at the site where the deer was hit. That's where it all starts. Before leaving that site and continuing your search, know what kind of wound you've inflicted. You're not ready to track that deer until you've obtained this information.

Good hunters strive to kill and recover deer as cleanly and quickly as possible. Sometimes waiting before trailing a wounded deer represents the quickest path to that humane end.

"A Case for Waiting" was originally published in the October 1989 issue of Deer & Deer Hunting *magazine.*

> MULTIPLE FACTORS GOVERN ALL HUNTING SITUATIONS, ESPECIALLY TRAILING WOUNDED DEER. BUT YOU WON'T KNOW WHICH FACTORS YOU'RE DEALING WITH IF YOU DON'T MAKE A CAREFUL AND THOROUGH ASSESSMENT OF YOUR SHOT AT THE SITE WHERE THE DEER WAS HIT.

THE OTHER DEER HUNTERS

*A*t times, especially when feeling I have it rough, I try to imagine what it must be like to live life as a prey species, such as a deer. Of course, no prey species can comprehend a future and past with the dread and hope humans realize. But try to imagine feeling threatened by every odd sound, sight or smell you encounter in your daily life. No wonder deer always seem to be wound tighter than a Titleist golf ball.

When can a deer truly relax? It can never know with certainty that the bow season is closed or that a coyote isn't nearby, its stomach growling. And even when no predator is present, a deer must contend with nature's indifference, whether it be extreme weather, scarce food, or another deer that suddenly turns adversary. At times it must seem everything in the whitetail's world is hunting it, not just the occasional human who stumbles through its woods or stands restlessly in the trees overhead.

In Part 3 of The Deer Hunters, we look at the other threats to a deer's existence, and revel in how deer cope with these dangers. This includes a heart-wrenching encounter between coyotes and a mule deer fawn, captured on film by Greg Pierson. We also see what becomes of deer once they've died, and are reminded that nature wastes nothing, especially in death. Some other living being will always be nearby, waiting to capitalize on the bad fate of another.

Although I hope not, some people might be offended by a few images that follow. If so, please allow that nature's beauty can be revealed in death, as evidenced by the visitors to a woodland's macabre scenes, be they jays, weasels, foxes or fishers, to name a few.

■ *PATRICK DURKIN*

CHAPTER 1

THE OPPORTUNISTS

Not until I saw the birds perched in a balsam fir 20 yards ahead did I know where the deer had died. Two gray jays were sitting there, hopping impatiently between branches, awaiting their next meal.

■ BY PATRICK DURKIN

The shot had looked true, and the blood trail in the snow told me the deer should be piled up within a few yards.

Still, it wasn't until I saw the birds perched in a balsam fir 20 yards ahead that I knew the spot where the deer had died. Two gray jays were sitting there, hopping impatiently between branches, awaiting their next meal.

Were they really marking my deer? Sure enough, after taking a few more steps I could see the deer lying still on the snow behind a small hummock. It had run about 80 yards after the slug from my .35 Whelen pierced its chest.

I circled behind the deer and watched a few seconds, making sure life's light had left its eyes. As I stood there, I was surprised to see small spikes between the deer's ears. Until now, I had assumed this whitetail was a doe.

No matter. I pulled out the old Kabar knife, validated the Michigan bonus tag, and tied it around the young buck's leg. His 2-inch spikes didn't qualify him for the regular buck license.

GRAY JAYS, OFTEN CALLED "WHISKEY JACKS" AND "CAMP ROBBERS," ARE WELL-KNOWN TO DEER HUNTERS OF THE NORTHERN FOREST. THIS GRAY JAY IS TAKING ADVANTAGE OF FAT AND SCRAPS THAT HUNTERS CUT FROM A FRESHLY KILLED WHITETAIL.

Patrick Durkin

Lucky Survivor

Stepping back, I studied the buck a moment. He was a full-chested deer, though not quite as large as a typical Upper Peninsula yearling buck. He was one of the lucky few from his class that had survived the area's previous killer winter. My hunting partner and I had found eight dead fawns (his classmates, eh?) the previous spring atop the snowpack in this little corner of the huge national forest.

Obviously, the tough winter and a lack of browse in the spring that followed had exhausted almost every ounce of this young buck's energy, slowing his growth, and leaving almost nothing for antler development. But as fate unfolded, his efforts to survive such ruthless conditions had borne venison for me and my family.

Anyway, as these thoughts flashed through my brain, the gray jays — a.k.a. "camp robbers" or "whiskey jacks" — waited in the balsam, not more than a rifle's length from my shoulder.

For those who haven't met the gray jay, she's a member of the crow family — though much prettier in looks and language — and measures 10 to 13 inches in length.

I was amazed at the birds' boldness, but also surprised how quickly they had found my deer. It had only been five minutes since I fired the lone shot, collected my gear, and followed the young buck's short, final dash.

But then I remembered hearing that gray jays perform this service on occasion for North Woods deer hunters. I chuckled to myself, mentally comparing them to Alaska's brown bears, which have been known to come running at the sound of gunfire during blacktail season. Apparently, experience has taught both creatures that an easy meal is not far away when a rifle roars.

Yearning to Eat

After studying the brazen birds some more, I figured they deserved an explanation for my leisurely pace. What the heck. I've talked with less interesting souls in my life.

"Sorry guys, but I'm in no rush," I said aloud. "I'm on vacation. You'll just have to wait."

Their black eyes just darted repeatedly from me to the deer, as if they hadn't eaten in days.

> GRAY JAYS AREN'T THE FUSSIEST OF EATERS. AFTER PICKING UP A BEAKFUL OF FOOD, THEY COVER THE MORSEL WITH A STICKY FLUID FROM THEIR MOUTHS AND SECURE IT IN A SAFE PLACE.

Suddenly feeling the peer pressure, I continued with my task. In a few minutes I had the buck's entrails out and pulled his body clear of the bloody viscera. In that time the jays' numbers had increased to about five or six, each of the new arrivals taking up a perch nearby.

When I had pulled the buck five feet from the gut pile, the first gray jay short-hopped from his branch to the dining area. Then they all descended.

They picked at the entrails, removing beaks full of food, which they stored a short flight away. Gray jays, you see, aren't the fussiest of eaters. In case you're wondering, they take the balls of food, cover them with a sticky fluid from their mouths, and secure the victuals in a safe place.

I watched the jays work a few minutes, and then remembered something. I scattered the scavengers momentarily while retrieving the buck's heart from its resting spot between the lungs. I wasn't that generous, after all. As soon as I stepped away with this rich meat, the jays were back to work.

Back to Camp

That evening, as the snows quietly resumed, I dragged the buck the mile or so back to the camper. My hunting partner, Mark Endris, came outside and helped hang the deer on the old pole between two maples. We then went inside and prepared supper. I chunked the buck's heart, and cooked it with onions, mushrooms and pineapple.

Over the next three days, the gray jays quietly worked the hide off a small portion of the buck's brisket, exposing a layer of milky-white fat. When Endris and I eventually took down the buck for the trip home, thousands of tiny beak pricks were punched into the congealed tissue.

Endris and I studied their needlepoint, shaking our heads in humored amazement.

We deer hunters are lucky the gray jay hasn't acquired a taste for venison tenderloins.

"The Opportunists" was originally published in the June 1993 issue of Deer & Deer Hunting *magazine.*

1) As the deer's attackers approached from the forest, it fled into the river. The deer stood for several minutes in the cold water, which was its only protection against the predators. The coyotes soon retreated to the forest and waited.

2) When the deer could no longer tolerate the cold water, it climbed out of the river and onto the bank. A magpie waited across the river, knowing a meal would not be long in coming.

3) ONCE THE DEER WAS OUT OF THE RIVER, THE LARGEST COYOTE BURST FROM THE FOREST, CROSSED THE RIVER, AND RESUMED THE ATTACK, GETTING A STRONG HOLD ON THE DEER'S MUZZLE.

CHAPTER 2

A VIEW TO A KILL

In early winter 1994, the author photographed a life-and-death struggle between a female mule deer fawn and a pack of coyotes. Unlike large cats that kill by suffocation or strangulation, wild canines kill their prey by tearing it apart while it's still alive.

■ TEXT AND PHOTOS BY GREG PIERSON

I frequently visit Yellowstone National Park to photograph its impressive scenery and wildlife. During a visit in early winter 1994, I traveled east from Mammoth Hot Springs to search for elk, mule deer and bighorn sheep to photograph in winter settings.

Just after I crossed the bridge that spans a gorge formed by the Gardiner River, I saw a group of female mule deer near the road. The does were highly agitated, and it was obvious something had disturbed them.

Having seen such behavior before in prey species, I suspected a predator was nearby. Investigating further, I saw many deer tracks in the snow, along with a set of coyote tracks. I walked farther to the edge of the river's gorge, and glassed the area with binoculars. I soon spotted what appeared to be a young doe, probably a fawn from the previous year, in the bottom of the gorge. It was standing at the river's edge, looking exhausted and stunned.

4) WITH ITS JAWS CLAMPED TIGHTLY ON THE DEER'S MUZZLE, THE COYOTE RELENTLESSLY PULLED AND WRESTLED WITH THE FAWN, AND FINALLY WAS ABLE TO PUSH IT TO THE GROUND (5).

Its lower lip was torn, and a great deal of its blood was visible nearby on the snow.

An Ageless Chase

Obviously, I had stumbled onto one of nature's ageless death chases between predator and prey. Soon after I spotted the young doe, a coyote ran out of the forest and headed toward her. This coyote was larger and darker than any I had ever seen before, and I at first mistook it for a wolf. At least four more coyotes soon trotted out of the forest, and began moving toward the deer.

(Curiously, one of the coyotes was wearing what appeared to be a radio-tracking collar. Apparently this individual was part of an ongoing wildlife research program in the park. If you look closely at two of the accompanying photos, you will see this device.)

Seeing the coyote approaching, the young deer fled into the river and stopped, seeming to realize the predators wouldn't resume their attack as long as it stayed there.

The coyotes, meanwhile, seemed to realize the already-weak deer could not stay in the cold river forever. They watched a few moments, and then retreated back into the forest to wait.

With this lull in the chase, I saw my opportunity to move into position to photograph the end of this rarely seen life-and-death struggle. My challenge, besides remaining undetected by predators and prey, was to quickly get down this steep and slick gorge while carrying 35 pounds of camera gear. So off I trotted, slipping and sliding down the gorge at breakneck speed to cover the half-mile distance. The instant I reached the bottom of the gorge, the young doe started to break from the river.

6 THE DEER WAS ABLE TO GET UP, AND TRIED TO RUN AWAY, BUT ITS STRENGTH WAS EBBING FAST. THE COYOTE GRABBED THE DEER BY A REAR LEG, CUTTING SHORT ITS ESCAPE.

Apparently the deer could not tolerate its cold water any longer. It climbed out of the river and onto the bank.

The Attack Resumes

The largest coyote immediately burst from the forest, crossed the river, and began attacking the deer. The coyote grabbed the young deer by the muzzle and wrestled it to the ground. The deer was able to get up, and it tried to run away, but its strength was ebbing fast. The coyote grabbed the deer by a rear leg and dragged it down again.

Soon, the deer was exhausted and could not get up anymore. The large coyote moved its grasp to the deer's throat while a second coyote moved in and began tearing open its abdomen.

After what seemed an eternity, but was probably five to 10 minutes, the deer ceased struggling and finally died. Unlike large cats that kill their prey by suffocation or strangulation, wild canines kill their prey by literally tearing it apart while it's still alive. Witnessing such a brutal — yet natural, nonetheless — death was not pleasant. The deer's pitiful distress cries had continued throughout much of the coyotes' slashing, tearing attack.

Soon after killing the deer, the coyotes took turns feeding on the carcass. Their eating order was probably predetermined by each animal's social position in the pack, with the largest coyote feeding first.

Conclusion

We'll never know how this young doe happened to be the one singled out for attack and consumption that day in Yellowstone. I suspect its smaller size might have contributed to its selection, or it might have been sick or

7 AFTER STOPPING THE DEER A FINAL TIME, THE COYOTE PULLED HARD AND DRAGGED IT DOWN FOR GOOD.

8 AS THE COYOTE CONTINUED PULLING, THE DEER STEADILY WEAKENED, AND WAS NO LONGER ABLE TO HOLD UP ITS HEAD.

injured in some manner. The snow wasn't especially deep, so, presumably, a healthy adult deer would have been able to easily flee the coyotes.

But killing is an inexact science. Researchers increasingly discuss the role of opportunity in predation, which is a departure from the once-standard belief that four-legged predators primarily hit the weak and sickly, or the young and old. For example, big bucks in winter deeryards often fall prey to timber wolves because older bucks typically live at the fringe of the yard, not its interior. Perhaps the inexperienced young mule deer, by simple fate, ended up in a vulnerable position that day, and the coyotes took advantage of the opportunity. Because I did not see the beginning of the hunt, I'll never know for certain.

Regardless, it was a wildlife spectacle that's rarely seen or photographed.

And it was a day I'll certainly never forget.

"A View to a Kill" was originally published in the special 1995 Western Deer Hunting *issue of* Deer & Deer Hunting *magazine.*

9 — AT LEFT, THE LARGEST COYOTE MOVED ITS GRASP TO THE DEER'S THROAT WHILE A SECOND COYOTE MOVED IN AND BEGAN TEARING OPEN THE DEER'S ABDOMEN. BELOW AND OPPOSITE PAGE, AFTER THE DEER WAS DEAD, THE COYOTES TOOK TURNS FEEDING. THEIR FEEDING ORDER WAS PROBABLY BASED ON DOMINANCE IN THE PACK, WITH THE LARGEST COYOTE FEEDING FIRST.

10 AS THE FEEDING CONTINUED, SOME COYOTES WALKED OFF WITH MEAT SCRAPS WHILE OTHER OPPORTUNISTS, SUCH AS THE MAGPIE IN THE FOREGROUND, WAITED FOR THEIR TURN AT NATURE'S TABLE.

Richard P. Smith

TIMBER WOLVES ARE CONSIDERED "PRIMARY" PREDATORS OF WHITE-TAILED DEER, AND DEPEND HIGHLY ON DEER FOR MEAT. THEY CANNOT LIVE IN AN AREA UNLESS DEER OR OTHER HOOFED MAMMALS ARE PRESENT IN MODERATE TO HIGH NUMBERS.

DEATH IN THE DEER WOODS

The occurrence of whitetails in the diet of predators does not necessarily imply negative effects on deer populations. Predation sometimes replaces other forms of mortality such as disease, starvation or winter kill.

■ BY ADRIAN WYDEVEN

Although man is now the No. 1 predator of the whitetail across most of its range, many other predators continue to prey on them. In North America, these four-legged hunters can be grouped as primary, secondary or incidental predators of whitetails.

Primary deer predators, such as wolves and cougars, are carnivores highly dependent on deer, animals that cannot live in an area unless deer or other ungulates (hoofed mammals) are available in moderate to high numbers.

Secondary deer predators, such as bobcats, coyotes and black bear, feed on many animals and/or plants. However, at certain times of the year or under certain conditions, they can become important deer predators.

Incidental deer predators, such as the fisher and fox, rarely prey on deer, and then only under unusual circumstances. Other incidental predators, such as the lynx and wolverine, exist mainly outside the whitetail's range.

Along with these predators, a variety of wildlife —

Richard P. Smith

bald eagles, vultures, ravens, crows, jays, chickadees — feed on deer carcasses, or carrion.

Because primary and secondary predators have the most impact on deer populations, and, because they're of greatest interest to deer hunters, they'll be discussed here.

Black Bear

The black bear ranges across much of the forested areas of North America from northern Mexico to the southern portions of the tundra in northern Canada and Alaska. Originally, black bears were found in much of the eastern United States. However, unrestricted hunting and the conversion of forest into farms eventually left bears only in the North's forests and the South's mountains and swamplands.

Until recently, black bears were not considered important predators of deer or other ungulates. Most studies found that plant materials usually make up 80 percent or more of the bears' diet, and that animal material — mostly insects, small mammals and carrion — makes up a tiny part of their diet.

SECONDARY DEER PREDATORS SUCH AS COYOTES, BOBCATS AND BLACK BEARS FEED ON A VARIETY OF ANIMALS AND PLANTS. HOWEVER, AT CERTAIN TIMES OF THE YEAR OR UNDER CERTAIN CONDITIONS, THEY CAN BECOME IMPORTANT DEER PREDATORS.

Thus, bears were thought to be unimportant predators on live deer, feeding mainly on carrion. But in 1982, John Ozoga and Louis Verme reported nine of 37 fawns born in a 1-square-mile enclosure in Michigan were apparently killed by a black bear. The bear apparently entered the enclosure in mid-May 1980 and was removed June 18. Most of the fawns were killed before they were 2 weeks old, although another bear killed a 27-day-old fawn in that enclosure in 1981.

Other studies in Wisconsin, Minnesota and Alaska have also shown that bears might, at times, be important predators of fawns and the young of other ungulates. In 1990, Lynn Rogers and others reported that five human-conditioned bears killed one to six fawns each, and that bears killed about 10 percent of the fawns in an 8-square-mile

Richard P. Smith

ALTHOUGH WOLVES FEED EXTENSIVELY ON DEER ALL YEAR, WOLF PREDATION BY ITSELF SELDOM SEEMS TO LIMIT DEER NUMBERS, EXCEPT THAT IT CAN SUPPRESS A HERD DECIMATED BY HARSH WINTERS.

area. Other studies under the direction of Raymond Anderson in northern Wisconsin suggest bears are responsible for even higher death rates for fawns.

Apparently, bears are important predators during the first two to four weeks of a fawn's life. The effect of bear predation might be more intense if fawning sites are concentrated.

Coyotes

The coyote — or brush wolf, as it's often called in the upper Midwest and Northeast — originally was found mainly in western North America from Panama north to northern Canada, and from the Pacific Ocean to the western Great Lakes. During the 1900s, the coyote greatly expanded its range eastward and northward. Strong populations were established in the mid-Atlantic states, New England and Canada's Maritime Provinces. Coyote populations also took hold in the Southeast in Alabama, Georgia and Florida.

Because the coyote is extremely versatile and opportunistic, the importance of deer to its diet varies by area. The impact of coyotes on deer populations in southern Texas is well documented. William Andelt and others conducted four food habit studies between 1961 and 1979 in the Welder Wildlife Refuge. During all periods, deer were the most important item in the coyote's diet, but the extent varied between years. In 1961-62, coyotes made high use of

fawns in June and July, while in other years fawn use was high only in June — immediately after fawning — and dropped off considerably in July. The study's early years were apparently affected by a drought that reduced the amount of wild fruit available, a food on which coyotes feed extensively in late summer and early fall. The coyote's use of deer during fall and winter varied greatly each year, but was high during times of abundant deer populations.

Deer are generally important in the winter diet of coyotes in the Northeast and Great Lakes states. Although most of the deer eaten are carrion, coyotes will kill adult deer, especially when hunting in groups. In 1988, Eric Gese and others reported that the size of coyote groups correlated with the size of prey eaten. The largest groups formed in winter, when deep snow enabled them to kill adult mule deer. Craig Huegel and Orrin Rongstad reported in 1985 that a radio-collared male coyote in Wisconsin switched its prey from mainly snowshoe hares to whitetails after the coyote began roaming with others.

Coyotes can be major deer predators in certain locales and at certain times of year, especially on newborn fawns. The increased use of deer by coyotes in fall is probably associated with unfound kills by human hunters. The increased use of deer in winter is probably caused by winter-killed deer, and groups of coyotes preying on deer made vulnerable by deep snows.

Bobcats

The bobcat's original distribution in North America ranged from central Mexico to southern Canada. During the past 100 years, bobcats disappeared from intensely agricul-

Richard P. Smith

tural lands in the East and areas with dense human populations. Bobcats have moved farther north into Canada with the cutting of virgin conifer forests and subsequent growth of brushy habitat.

As with most cats, bobcats are strict carnivores and eat little, if any, plant material. Generally the most important food items for bobcats are rabbits or hares, and the bobcat population often fluctuates with rabbit or hare populations. Bobcats can occasionally be important deer predators. In 1986 David Maehr and James Brady summarized 20 bobcat food-habit studies, and determined deer were most important in the diet of Northeastern bobcats. Deer made up an average of 26 percent of the volume of the cats' scat and stomach contents. Elsewhere, deer in bobcat diets were 3 percent along the Coastal Plain, 7 percent in the West, and 11 percent in the southern Appalachians. High use in the Northeast, including the Great Lakes region, was attributed to greater vulnerability of deer to bobcats in deep snow, and the more limited availability of small mammals in winter in Northern climates.

The age, sex and weight of a bobcat appeared important in the animal's ability to kill and feed on deer in New Hampshire (Litvaitis et al., 1984.) Adult males fed more on deer than did juvenile males or adult females. Deer made up 64 percent of stomach contents in male bobcats weighing more than 26 pounds but 36 percent or less for male bobcats weighing less than 25 pounds. Large male bobcats

IN THE FAR NORTH, ABOUT 15 TO 20 ADULT-SIZED DEER ARE KILLED EACH YEAR PER WOLF.

could kill deer and were better able to prevent other bobcats from feeding on their kills. Sometimes, though, an adult male tolerated feeding by a female bobcat and her kittens.

The hunting of deer fawns in summer seems much less frequent for bobcats than for coyotes. Bobcats hunt some fawns in late summer or fall, in contrast to coyotes and bears, which hunt fawns more intensely in early summer. That might be because cats hunt more by sight and sound, while bears and canids hunt more by scent. During a fawn's first two weeks, it remains mostly motionless and, although it carries little scent, it would be more susceptible to predators that hunt by smell.

Cougar

The cougar was originally the most widely distributed mammal in the Western Hemisphere, ranging from southern Canada to the southern tip of South America. While cougars originally were found across the United States south of Canada, they're currently restricted to the Rocky Mountains and westward. Small breeding populations of cougars occur in southern Florida and southern Manitoba, and scattered cougars have been seen across the East and Midwest in recent years.

The cougar goes by many names: mountain lion, puma,

panther, painter, catamount, American lion and American panther. Although cougar sightings in the East are often called "black panthers," no specimens of totally black cougars have been verified.

Throughout their range, cougars are heavily dependent on deer or other ungulates. Porcupines and hares might be locally important in some areas. In the western United States and Canada, mule deer and sometimes elk are the most important food items. Farther south into Mexico and Central America, peccaries — pig-like animals — also become important foods. Guanacos and several deer species are major food items in southern portions of South America, while white-tailed deer was the most important food item in the cougar's original range in eastern North America. The relic cougar population in Florida feeds extensively on deer and feral hogs. Cougar distribution in Manitoba seems to be correlated with the distribution of white-tailed deer.

Selectivity studies of cougar predation on deer have been done mainly on mule deer in Western states and provinces. Maurice Hornocker indicated in 1970 that 14 to 20 deer per year were needed to sustain an adult cougar. Cougars seem to favor young deer and adult males. Mature bucks appeared more susceptible because they used more of the rugged habitat where cougars hunted, and because adult males often enter winter in poor nutritional condition after the rut.

Gray and Red Wolves

Gray wolves once ranged across most of North America from central Mexico northward. The southeastern United States, where the gray wolf was absent, was occupied by the red wolf. Today the gray wolf still inhabits the whitetail's range in Minnesota, Wisconsin and Michigan, and deer range in southern Canada.

Although the red wolf was eliminated from the wild by the mid-1970s, populations are being re-established in coastal North Carolina and the Great Smoky Mountains National Park.

Many studies have noted the importance of deer in the wolf's diet. In 1984, David Mech concluded that wolves are the primary natural mortality factor on deer where the two species live together. About 15 to 20 adult-sized deer are killed each year per wolf. Wolves tend to focus their attention on fawns in summer, and fawns and older adults in winter. Although wolves feed extensively on deer all year, wolf predation by itself seldom seems to limit deer numbers, except that it can suppress a herd decimated by harsh winters.

The red wolf, since being reintroduced in the

Michael H. Francis

ALTHOUGH MOST DEER EATEN BY COYOTES ARE CARRION, COYOTES WILL KILL ADULT DEER, ESPECIALLY WHEN HUNTING IN GROUPS. THE LARGEST COYOTE GROUPS FORM IN WINTER, WHEN DEEP SNOW ENABLES THEM TO KILL ADULT DEER MORE EASILY.

Connolly also illustrated seven studies where predators (two wolves, two coyotes, two dogs and one mixed carnivore) didn't control deer numbers.

Mech later pointed out that coyotes might sometimes be a more limiting factor on fawns than wolves because coyotes can exist at densities 5 times higher than is possible for wolves. Also, because fawns are relatively small prey for wolves, wolf predation would probably also include more larger prey such as beavers and adult deer.

Although predator control might increase fawn survival in some situations, its overall benefit to deer might be limited. In 1987, William Andelt cited a study where deer in a predator-free enclosure had nutritional problems, suffered higher mortality for fawns more than 3 months old, experienced late copulations, carried increased parasite loads, carried antlers in velvet longer, and dropped antlers earlier. The impact of coyote predation generally was greatest when prey populations were above carrying capacity, under poor nutrition, and during severe winters.

Clearly, the occurrence of deer in the diet of predators does not necessarily imply negative effects on deer populations. Predation sometimes replaces other forms of mortality such as disease, starvation or winter kill. Also, because most predators readily use carrion, much of the deer use at times might be deer already dead from other causes.

Predator Interactions

Along with the potential impact on deer herds, predators can also affect each other. A recent study of cougars, bobcats and coyotes in Idaho showed that cougars were a major mortality factor on bobcats and coyotes, especially near kills. All three predators killed deer, but cougars killed more elk, and coyotes more readily scavenged on deer.

Studies of coyotes and wolves generally find some level of intolerance between the species. Wolves have apparently eliminated coyotes from Isle Royale and might suppress their numbers in saturated wolf range in northeastern Minnesota. Coyotes and wolves coexist in Manitoba's Riding Mountain National Park, but wolves are usually a major mortality factor for coyotes. In 1991, Paul Paquet reported that of 23 coyotes killed by wolves, 11 were killed near ungulate kills. Apparently, wolves and coyotes are better able to coexist when multiple ungulate populations are available. Where these canids depend mainly on the same ungulate

Richard P. Smith photos

COYOTES AND BEARS HUNT FAWNS MORE INTENSELY IN EARLY SUMMER, SHORTLY AFTER THE FAWNS ARE BORN. BOBCATS, HOWEVER, HUNT FAWNS IN LATE SUMMER OR FALL. THE DIFFERENCE IN HUNTING PERIODS COULD BE BECAUSE CATS HUNT MORE BY SIGHT AND SOUND, WHILE CANIDS AND BEARS HUNT MORE BY SCENT.

Southeast, seems to feed less extensively on deer than gray wolves. Whitetails, raccoons and rabbits seem to be their most important foods. As red wolves become better established and form larger packs, their deer predation might increase.

The Predators' Impact

In 1978, when he evaluated several studies on the impact of predators on white-tailed deer, Guy Connolly listed six studies where predators controlled deer populations, including two by wolves, one by wolves and cougars, two by coyotes, and one by coyotes and wolves.

species, wolves tend to beat out coyotes. In areas where healthy populations of several ungulate species exist, wolves seem more tolerant of coyotes. This was probably what occurred on the Great Plains before settlement.

Although coyotes and bobcats seem able to coexist by using different habitats, coyotes seem to exclude red fox in the same way wolves exclude coyotes. In Maine, for example, bobcats and coyotes existed in the same area while foxes usually had home ranges outside of coyote territories.

Predator Management

In the early years of wildlife management, predator control was often perceived as an important tool for improving game populations. Studies conducted over the past 50 years have often pointed out the value of predators to ecosystems and their benefits to prey populations.

Some disruptions of natural predator populations by humans might even have worsened predation on deer populations by decreasing large predators such as wolves and cougars, while increasing populations of effective fawn predators such as coyotes.

Predator controls should only be considered after evaluating predator and prey populations. In his 1978 study, Connolly examined some factors to consider when planning predator control. These include whether ungulate populations are below carrying capacity, whether predation is compensating for other mortality factors, whether habitat can support higher ungulate populations, the cost-effectiveness of predator control, and the ability to control predator populations. Mech in 1984 suggested that philosophical considerations are also important. As more of the public becomes aware of the complex role predators play in ecosystems, and others view predator control as an animal-rights issue, support for such programs is likely to decline.

Conclusion

Broadly speaking, no complete, fully functional ecosystem exists in North America except, perhaps, the high Arctic. Therefore, all wild lands are somewhat under the control of humans. All human-controlled environments might need occasional adjustments of large animal populations to fulfill human needs, as well as maintain the ecosystem's health. Scientifically controlled and managed hunting and trapping seasons are probably the best way to manage deer populations and the various predators that prey on them.

SELECTED REFERENCES

Andelt, William, John G. Kie, Frederick Knowlton and Kean Cardwell. 1986. Variation in coyote diets associated with season and successional changes in vegetation. *Journal of Wildlife Management* 50:273-277.

Andelt, William F. 1987. Coyote Predation. Pages 128-140 in M. Novak, J.A. Baker, M.E. Obbard and B. Malloch (eds.) *Wild Furbearer Management and Conservation in North America*. Ontario Ministry of Natural Resources.

Connolly, Guy E. 1978. "Predators and Predator Control." Pages 369-394 in J.L. Schmidt and D.L. Gilbert (eds.) *Big Game of North America*. Stackpole Books, Harrisburg, Pa.

Gese, Eric M., Orrin J. Rongstad and William R. Mytton. 1988. "Relationship Between Coyote Group Size and Diet in Southeastern Colorado." *Journal of Wildlife Management* 52:647-653.

Hornocker, Maurice G. 1970. "An Analysis of Mountain Lion Predation Upon Mule Deer and Elk in the Idaho Primitive Area." *Wildlife Monograph 21*. The Wildlife Society. 39 pp.

Huegel, Craig N. and Orrin J. Rongstad. 1985. "Winter Foraging Patterns and Consumption Rates of Northern Wisconsin Coyotes." *American Midland Naturalist* 113:203-207.

Kodhler, Gary M. and Maurice G. Hornocker. 1991. "Seasonal Resource Use Among Mountain Lions, Bobcats and Coyotes." *Journal of Mammalogy* 72:391-396.

Litvaitis, John A. Clark L. Stevens and William W. Mautz. 1984. "Age, Sex and Weight of Bobcats in Relation to Diet." *Journal of Wildlife Management* 48:632-635.

Maehr, David S. and James R. Brady. 1986. "Food Habits of Bobcats in Florida." *Journal of Mammalogy* 67:133-138.

Mech, L. David. 1984 "Predators and Predation." Pages 189-200 in L.K. Halls (ed.) *The White-Tailed Deer Ecology and Management*. Wildlife Management Institute.

Major, John T. and James A. Sherburne. 1987. "Interspecific Relationships of Coyotes, Bobcats and Red Foxes in Western Maine." *Journal of Wildlife Management* 51:606-616.

Ozoga, John J. and Louis J. Verme. 1982. "Predation by Black Bears on Newborn White-tailed Deer. *Journal of Mammalogy* 63: 696-697.

Paquet, Paul C. 1991. "Winter Spatial Relationships of Wolves and Coyotes in Riding Mountain National Park, Manitoba." *Journal of Mammalogy* 72:397-401.

Rogers, Lynn L., Patrick S. Beringer, Robert E. Kennedy and Gregory A. Wilker. 1990. "Fawn Predation by Black Bears." Page 214 in 52nd Midwest Fish and Wildlife Conference, Minneapolis, Minn.

Wydeven, Adrian P. 1991. "Deer and Wolves." *Deer & Deer Hunting* magazine 15:94-102.

"Death in the Deer Woods" was originally published in the March 1993 issue of Deer & Deer Hunting *magazine.*

PROBABLY THE MOST FREQUENT
ANIMALS TO SCAVENGE DEAD DEER
ARE ALSO THE WHITETAIL'S MAJOR
PREDATORS, SUCH AS WOLVES,
BOBCATS, BEARS AND COYOTES.
COYOTES — SUCH AS THE ONE
HOWLING OVER THE FORKHORN —
READILY FEED ON DEAD DEER YEAR-
ROUND, INCLUDING ROAD-KILLS AND
WINTER-KILLED DEER. THE GRAY
WOLF, INSET BELOW, RIPS A PIECE
OF HIDE FROM A DEAD BUCK.

Tim Christie

CHAPTER 4

SCAVENGERS OF THE DEER WOODS

Today, most humans are not responsible for killing the meat they consume. Therefore, the difference between being a scavenger or predator is a fine line, and depends mainly on who does the killing.

■ BY ADRIAN WYDEVEN

The dictionary defines scavengers as organisms that feed habitually on refuse and carrion. Carrion is defined as dead and putrefied flesh.

Scavengers, in contrast to predators, search for animals already dead instead of killing on their own. As a group, scavengers are often viewed with disdain and disgust, but they play vital roles in the health of wildlife communities.

Although some animals specialize in searching for dead animals, most animals that scavenge also are predators at other times. In fact, most anthropologists believe early humans were major scavengers, stealing prey from lions, cheetahs and hyenas before these humanoids became hunters. Even today, most humans are not responsible for killing the meat they consume. Therefore, the difference between being a scavenger or predator is a fine line, and mainly depends on who does the killing.

Most carnivorous birds and mammals in the white-tailed deer's range feed on dead deer at some time.

Tim Christie

Richard P. Smith

Richard P. Smith

BEARS OCCASIONALLY KILL DEER FOR FOOD, BUT IT'S MORE COMMON FOR THEM TO SCAVENGE ALREADY-DEAD DEER. THIS BLACK BEAR, LEFT, DRAGS AWAY A ROAD-KILL. ABOVE IS A FAWN'S HEAD, ALL THAT'S LEFT OF A BLACK BEAR'S MEAL. AT TOP, A YOUNG GRIZZLY IN THE ROCKIES CHEWS ON A BUCK'S HEAD.

Probably the most frequent animals to scavenge dead deer are also the whitetail's major predators, such as wolves, cougars, bobcats, bears and coyotes. Coyotes readily feed on dead deer year-round, including road-kills, winter-killed deer and unretrieved hunter-kills. Winter-killed deer provide food for bears emerging from hibernation in spring. Wolves, cougars and bobcats most frequently kill deer, but they also eat deer that died from other causes.

Mammals that scavenge white-tailed deer carcasses include opossums, red squirrels, skunks, weasels, badgers, fishers, martens, foxes and raccoons, to name a few. Bird scavengers include eagles, vultures, gulls, woodpeckers,

Leonard Lee Rue III

chickadees, nuthatches, ravens, crows, magpies and jays. Deer dying near waterways, especially in the Southeast, might occasionally be eaten by snapping turtles or alligators. Generally, though, reptiles rarely scavenge deer. Numerous insects such as carrion beetles, dermestid beetles and botflies also scavenge on any decaying carcass.

Role of Scavengers

Scavengers play important roles in the transfer of energy and nutrient cycling through an ecosystem. Scavengers finish the work started by predators, or other causes of death. Along with the overall benefits to ecosystems, scavengers also provide immediate services. They eliminate carcasses that otherwise spread disease or contaminate waterways. Humans often interpret deer deaths from winter-kill or vehicle collisions as waste, but in the workings of natural ecosystems, nothing is wasted.

Let's discuss some of the whitetail's major scavengers.

Weasel

The weasel, properly called an ermine, is also known as a stoat or short-tailed weasel. It lives in the forested and tundra zones of North America, and is most commonly seen and photographed when it's in its winter coat — pure white with a black-tipped tail.

Weasels hunt largely above ground or under snow. They are active day and night, appearing to nervously dart about looking for food or prey. They eat large numbers of voles, mice, rats, rabbits or other rodents that expose themselves from cover. But they will not pass up a chance to scavenge from a deer carcass or other carrion, including that of birds.

BOBCATS, LIKE OTHER PREDATOR/SCAVENGER SPECIES, WILL MAKE USE OF DEAD WHITETAILS THEY HAPPEN UPON.

Their teeth are highly adapted to killing and cutting up prey.

Skunk

Skunks, a member of the weasel family, coexist with foxes, raccoons and coyotes. They will often use the same burrows as these species, but at different times of the year.

The striped skunk lives in southern Canada, the United States and northern Mexico. Skunks are mainly nocturnal, foraging at dusk, night and dawn. They are opportunistic feeders, and are largely carnivorous. They will scavenge upon dead deer, but their main food is insects, small mammals, grubs, birds' eggs and fruit seasonally. They use their long front claws to root out food.

Opossum

The opossum is the only marsupial (pouched mammal) that lives in the United States and Canada. It lives across most of the eastern United States. Its range has gradually expanded northward and westward over the past 100 years.

The opossum's diet is one of the most diverse of any mammal in North America. Although regarded as an omnivore, the opossum's diet varies greatly by location. Human development, including roads and buildings, are probably major factors in the animal's range expansion. Deer carcasses and other kills along roads provide major food sources. Opossums will readily take advantage of any carcass, and deer represent a superabundant food source.

Leonard Lee Rue III

Richard P. Smith

Unfortunately for opossums, vehicle collisions are often the most common cause of death for them, also. Therefore, in their scavenging efforts, opossums often become food sources for other scavengers, including other opossums.

Red Squirrel

The red squirrel inhabits the coniferous forests of much of Canada, and the Rocky Mountain region and northern portions of the United States. The antics of this Northern Forest squirrel are frequently observed by deer hunters.

Although the red squirrel is better known for eating conifer cones, tree seeds and nuts, it occasionally eats meat. In fact, recent studies in the Yukon showed red squirrels at times might be major predators on young snowshoe hares. The degree to which they feed on deer

BALD EAGLES, INSET PHOTO, GENERALLY USE DEER CARCASSES MOST FREQUENTLY IN WINTER AND EARLY SPRING WHEN FISHING OPPORTUNITIES ARE LIMITED. BUT BALD EAGLES ALSO EAT FROM DEER CARCASSES AT OTHER TIMES OF THE YEAR. GOLDEN EAGLES ARE SPECIALIZED HUNTERS OF MEDIUM-SIZED MAMMALS, ESPECIALLY RABBITS, HARES, GROUND SQUIRRELS, MARMOTS AND PRAIRIE DOGS. BUT THEY WILL SCAVENGE FROM DEER CARCASSES.

carcasses isn't well known. Probably the greatest use of deer carcasses occurs in late winter and early spring after the squirrel's caches of conifer cones are exhausted, and before new seeds develop. More research is needed to understand the role of deer carcasses in the ecology of red squirrels.

Richard P. Smith

Foxes

The gray fox and red fox live across much of the white-tail's range in Canada and the United States. Gray fox live across most of eastern and southwestern United States, and a small portion of southeastern Canada. The red fox lives in most of Canada except northern Arctic Islands, and across most of the United States, except the arid Southwest and Intermountain Region.

Foxes are best adapted to feeding on small mammals, especially voles, mice and rabbits, but they also eat many other animals and plant materials, such as fruits. Both foxes readily feed on carrion, including white-tailed deer. Red fox, especially, seem to eat deer carrion during winter. The availability of deer carcasses might affect distribution, abundance and survival of foxes in certain areas. Recent increases in red fox in the northern Great Lakes region might be partially caused by greater food availability with high deer numbers.

Feeding on deer carcasses poses some risks to foxes in areas inhabited by larger predators. Wolves sometimes kill foxes living near carcasses of prey animals. Coyotes also might displace foxes from deer carcasses, and fox numbers are often reduced in areas where coyotes are abundant.

Fisher

The fisher is a large member of the weasel family, weighing 5 to 16 pounds. It lives in the Northern forests of the United States, and across southern and central Canada.

RAVENS AND CROWS HAVE HIGHLY VARIED DIETS. RAVENS ARE MORE DEPENDENT ON CARRION AND CROWS FEED MORE READILY ON GRAINS. STILL, BOTH SPECIES EAGERLY FEED ON CARCASSES OF DEAD DEER.

Many fisher populations were extirpated or reduced to low numbers by the early 1900s. Through restoration programs, restrictive trapping regulations, and reforestation of the Northern Forest, the fisher has returned to many of its old haunts. Fishers might be the most abundant medium-sized predator in most of the Great Lakes forest region.

Fishers are versatile predators. Although they most frequently hunt on the ground, they are also at home in trees. Major foods of the fisher include snowshoe hare, porcupines, squirrels and mice. In summer the diet is supplemented with fruits and mushrooms. The fisher also feeds on a variety of birds, including bald eagle chicks and young red-shouldered hawks.

In recent years some hunters have become concerned about the potential impact of fishers on deer populations. Although parts of deer are frequently found in fisher scats, most are considered to be carrion. Fisher especially seem to seek deer carcasses in winter. A fisher was reported to have attacked a fawn, and fisher might occasionally kill deer within a few days of birth. But the period during which fawns are vulnerable to fishers is so limited that noticeable impacts on deer populations are not likely. Additional research might be necessary to better understand the impact

Richard P. Smith

THE GRAY JAY, OR CANADA JAY, ABOVE, SCAVENGES MORE OFTEN THAN OTHER JAYS, PROBABLY AN ADAPTATION TO THE NORTHERN FOREST, WHERE FOOD IS SCARCE IN WINTER. MANY NORTH WOODS HUNTERS HAVE SEEN GRAY JAYS PERCH IN NEARBY TREES WHILE WAITING TO FEED ON THE GUT PILE OF A FRESHLY KILLED DEER. WOODPECKERS, SUCH AS THE HAIRY WOODPECKER, BELOW, ARE NORMALLY INSECT EATERS, BUT IN WINTER THEY ALSO FEED ON ANIMAL CARCASSES, ESPECIALLY FATTY PORTIONS.

Richard P. Smith

of high fisher populations on deer and other prey species.

Fishers frequently use temporary dens such as tree cavities, brush piles and snow dens, especially during inclement weather. These temporary dens are often found near food sources such as carcasses. In fact, the deer carcass itself sometimes becomes the temporary shelter.

Pine Marten

The pine marten is the fisher's smaller relative, and weighs 1 to 3 pounds. It lives across the coniferous forest region of Canada, Alaska, northern United States and Rocky Mountains. Martens were extirpated along the southern portions of their range in the late 1800s because of unregulated harvest and habitat loss. Marten populations have been restocked in many areas of former range and, along with regrowth of older forest habitat, have re-established. Unlike the fisher, marten populations have not expanded far, and many have remained somewhat local. Martens in several states are listed as "endangered" or "threatened."

Martens differ from fishers in being more adapted to older coniferous forests. They spend more time in trees (arboreal habitats), hunt under snow more frequently, and feed more heavily on mice and birds.

Major foods of martens are mice, voles, red squirrels, chipmunks, flying squirrels, snowshoe hares, birds and their eggs, fruits, nuts and berries. Martens also readily feed on carrion, including road-killed deer and moose. Although a large carcass can represent a bonanza for martens, such meals also represent a risk because larger predators that prey on martens are readily attracted to these sites.

Eagles

Two species of eagles live in North America, but the bald eagle is found across more of the whitetail's range. The golden eagle is a bird of wide open spaces, living mainly in the West and northern Canada. Golden eagles occasionally visit the eastern United States and southeastern Canada, especially in late fall or winter. Populations of golden eagles are relatively stable, although many were killed in the past as potential sheep predators.

Bald eagles live in forested areas and near waterways. Bald eagles nest in northern portions of the United States, across Canada, and along the Atlantic and Gulf coasts. Bald eagles winter in the central and

Richard P. Smith

southern United States, and along the Pacific Coast. Bald eagle populations were drastically reduced during the mid-1900s by excessive use of pesticides. After DDT was prohibited in the 1970s, bald eagles recovered extensively across the Great Lakes region and other areas.

Golden eagles are specialized hunters of medium-sized mammals, especially rabbits, hares, ground squirrels, marmots and prairie dogs. The young of hoofed mammals such as pronghorn antelope, bighorn sheep and mountain goats are sometimes killed by golden eagles, and occasionally even adult ungulates are killed.

Bald eagles tend to feed most frequently on fish, but they also hunt water birds and small mammals such as rabbits, squirrels and young otters. Because bald eagles live more regularly in areas occupied by whitetails, they probably feed more often on deer carcasses than golden eagles. Bald eagles generally use deer carcasses most frequently in winter and early spring when fishing opportunities are limited. But bald eagles also eat from deer carcasses at other times of the year. In May 1993, for example, I spooked an adult bald eagle from a carcass that was being used to attract wolves in a research project in northern Wisconsin.

Vultures

Two species of vultures live within the range of white-tailed deer in the United States. The turkey vulture is found

WEASELS WON'T PASS UP A CHANCE TO SCAVENGE FROM A DEER CARCASS OR OTHER CARRION. THE WEASEL'S TEETH ARE ADAPTED TO KILLING AND CUTTING UP PREY.

across most of the United States and southern Canada in summer, and in the South during winter. The black vulture lives in the Southeast. Both vulture populations are expanding and moving northward.

Of all the bird scavengers of white-tailed deer, vultures are perhaps most specialized for locating and using dead animals. Turkey vultures are unusual among birds in that they have a strong sense of smell, which helps them locate carcasses. Both vultures have naked heads, which allows them to more easily stick their heads inside the carcasses of large animals. Neither vulture is well suited for killing prey on its own, although black vultures occasionally make some kills on young birds or small mammals.

Ravens and Crows

The raven is the largest member of the crow family, and is also the largest songbird in the world, although its voice does not sound much like a song.

Ravens live in most of Canada and the Northern Forest and mountainous West of the United States. In the eastern United States and Canada the raven lives mainly in forests.

The crow is the raven's smaller cousin, and lives across

Charles J. Alsheimer

much of the United States and Canada. It is especially abundant in areas highly modified by humans. Before European settlement of places such as Wisconsin, crows were rare, and ravens were the more abundant species. The range of ravens retreated northward after forests were converted to farmland in the Midwest and Northeast.

Although ravens and crows have highly varied diets, crows feed more readily on grains, and ravens are more dependent on carrion. Both species readily feed on carcasses of road-killed deer.

The raven plays an ecological role in the Northern Forest that is similar to vultures of the east African savannas. During winter when food supplies are limited, ravens become dependent on carrion. Ravens become closely associated with wolves where the two species coexist. This is similar to African vultures that follow prides of lions or packs of African wild dogs.

Ravens follow wolf packs to their kills, and either fly about or perch in nearby trees, waiting for wolves to finish feeding. Individual ravens will sometimes sneak in close to steal meat scraps while wolves feed. Ravens remain behind to finish scavenging kills after wolf packs abandon them. To find the wolves, ravens follow the pack's tracks.

Ravens also have an elaborate communication system

SCAVENGERS ENSURE ALMOST NOTHING GOES TO WASTE IN THE DEER WOODS. IN EFFECT, SCAVENGERS SUCH AS THIS PORCUPINE, WHICH IS CHEWING A DEER ANTLER FOR ITS CALCIUM, ARE NATURE'S GREAT RECYCLERS.

that allows them to gather at kill sites. Generally, ravens can eat more safely and effectively in a large group. The raven/wolf association is probably most distinct in areas where wolves hunt large prey such as moose or bison. Wolves generally will more completely consume deer carcasses and spend less time at these than at larger carcasses. Therefore, feeding opportunities for ravens are generally better on larger carcasses.

Deer carcasses can cause short-term concentrations of ravens in winter. In February 1991, I followed wolf tracks to a recently killed deer in northern Wisconsin. I could hear ravens more than a half-mile away before reaching the kill site. When I approached within 50 yards of the carcass, the air swooshed with the sound of 40 to 50 ravens taking off.

Jays and Magpies

Seven species of jays and two magpies live in North America north of Mexico. The gray and blue jay are the main species within the whitetail's range. Blue jays live across most of the deer's range, and gray jays occupy Northern deer range. Magpies live mainly in the West and occupy some deer range from the Dakotas westward.

Jays and Magpies are members of the crow family. This family is well known for destroying bird eggs and killing young birds. They also readily use carcasses, but magpies are perhaps more intense scavengers. The gray jay or Canada jay appears to scavenge more frequently than other jays, probably an adaptation to the Northern Forest, where food is restricted in winter.

Many North Woods deer hunters have seen impatient gray jays perched in nearby trees, waiting to feed on portions of a freshly killed deer. Gray jays will feed on the whole carcass or just the gut pile left behind.

Other Birds

Along with the large birds already mentioned, numerous small birds also feed on carrion. Woodpeckers normally eat insects, but in winter they feed on animal carcasses, especially the fatty portions. Nuthatches and chickadees feed on insects, insect larva, and nuts and seeds, but occasionally feed on carcasses. I have located deer gut piles on several occasions by listening for nuthatches and chickadees.

Most people who feed birds in winter know suet (hard fat) will attract woodpeckers and other birds. I have found at my home in northern Wisconsin that deer fat and venison trimmings attract the hairy woodpecker, downy woodpecker, red-breasted nuthatch, white-breasted nuthatch, black-capped chickadee, common crow and starlings.

Carcass Values

The aforementioned scavengers make up a partial list of animals that feed on deer carcasses. The variety of insects and microbes that feed on animal carcasses would be a much longer list.

It is apparent the availability of deer carcasses provide food for a variety of animals. Throughout much of its range, the white-tailed deer is now the largest animal in the wild. Therefore deer carcasses are especially important for scavengers.

The abundance and occurrence of deer carcasses might affect the numbers of many scavengers. As deer have become more abundant in the Midwest's agricultural areas the past 40 years, opossums and turkey vultures have increased and moved farther north.

The increase in deer numbers in the northern Great Lakes region has paralleled increases in fisher and foxes. Raven abundance is probably affected by the regular distribution of deer or other large mammal carcasses in winter.

Richard P. Smith

SKUNKS ARE MAINLY NOCTURNAL, FORAGING AT DUSK, NIGHT AND DAWN. THEY ARE OPPORTUNISTIC FEEDERS, AND LARGELY CARNIVOROUS. THEY WILL SCAVENGE UPON DEAD DEER, BUT THEIR MAIN FOOD IS INSECTS, SMALL MAMMALS, GRUBS, BIRDS' EGGS AND FRUIT SEASONALLY.

The Feasts of Dead Deer

Normally we humans don't get excited over carcasses of dead deer along the roadway or in the woods after severe winters. But to many wildlife species, rotting carcasses represent major feasts. Deer carcasses provide opportunities to view a variety of wildlife species. Most deer hunters are intrigued and fascinated by the many wildlife species that inhabit the woods. It might be interesting to keep a list of animals that visit deer carcasses.

Tracks of many local predators and scavengers can readily be observed near deer carcasses in winter. And road-killed deer can provide opportunities for seeing the majestic bald eagle or the sly, secretive fox.

In addition, fat and unusable portions of harvested deer might be useful when placed near bird feeders in the winter to feed several bird species.

Scavengers of white-tailed deer include a variety of interesting wildlife species. Observation, study and examination of signs made by these animals can further enhance the deer hunting experience.

"Scavengers of the Deer Woods" was originally published in the September 1994 issue of Deer & Deer Hunting *magazine.*

CHAPTER 5

AGGRESSIVE BEHAVIOR OF DEER

Deer exhibit many types of aggressive behavior, and much of it plays a role in a herd's social organization and helps perpetuate the species' survival.

■ BY AL HOFACKER

In February 1976, a white-tailed doe demonstrated to me a behavior that dramatically differed from the notion that deer are docile. That afternoon I climbed into a tree stand overlooking a pulpwood cutting that provided excellent winter browse.

At 4:15 p.m. a doe and fawn walked up to the crown of a felled white birch and began feeding. At first, the fawn fed about 10 yards away from the doe. It then moved alongside the doe and reached for a mouthful of birch browse. The doe raised a front hoof and gently nudged the fawn, which backed off a few steps. About 30 seconds later, the fawn returned to the doe's side. The doe lashed out with her hoof, striking the fawn's shoulder. The fawn was startled and jumped back, and then stood behind the doe and watched for nearly one minute.

Again the fawn moved close to the doe. The doe swiftly lowered her head, swung it sideways and upward, and struck the fawn slightly behind its left front leg with her forehead. The blow lifted the fawn about one foot off the ground. It then trotted to a different treetop to feed and made no further attempt to approach. An hour later, the doe and fawn departed.

TYPICALLY, AS THE FEROCITY OF THE WHITETAIL'S AGGRESSION INCREASES, THE FREQUENCY OF ITS OCCURRENCE DECREASES. BEFORE COMBAT BEGINS, A DOMINANT DEER WILL USUALLY EMPLOY A SERIES OF ESCALATING WARNINGS TO GIVE THE SUBORDINATE A CHANCE TO BACK OFF. THEREFORE, MOST ENCOUNTERS END BEFORE A FULL-FLEDGED FIGHT ERUPTS. MOST FIGHTS END WITH THE WEAKER DEER BREAKING AND RUNNING AWAY.

GLOSSARY OF AGGRESSIVE BEHAVIOR

Aggressive Behavior: Bucks and Does

Walk Toward: Aggressor walks toward another deer. Lowest intensity aggressive pattern exhibited by deer.

Ear Drop: Deer presses ears back along neck with the orifices directed away from the neck. Low intensity, frequently used aggressive pattern.

Head-High Threat: Deer stands erect, holds head high, tilts nose upward, and lays back ears. A seldom-used threat.

Head-Low Threat: The aggressor lowers the head and extends the neck toward the foe with ears laid back along the neck. Sometimes termed "Hard Look."

Lunge: The deer abruptly jerks its head forward toward the recipient and back without contact.

Head Raise: The head, oriented toward the recipient, is quickly snapped up and backward, then brought back to a resting posture while the ears are held out horizontally.

Front Leg Kick: Dominant deer strikes out at subordinate with a forehoof one or more times. Forehoof does not necessarily make contact with subordinate. Also termed "Strike."

Charge: Deer runs rapidly at another from a distance of three to 15 feet, but stops before making contact. Deer usually performs another threat at the end of charge.

Chase: Subordinates that do not respond to lower level aggressive displays are sometimes chased by the dominant. Head low threat posture frequently used during the chase.

Rake: Used by dominant deer to displace a subordinate from bed. Deer lifts a foreleg about 18 inches above the ground and scrapes hoof across back of the bedded deer.

Poke: One deer contacts another with its nose. Commonly used to direct group movements or supplant another deer.

Head Shake: The deer lowers its head and separates stiff forelegs to lower the anterior portion of the body while shaking the head side to side with ears relaxed. A high-intensity threat performed at a distance from the recipient.

Body Push: The aggressor approaches from the rear and pushes its front shoulder against the flank of the recipient while laying its throat on the back.

Sidle: Sidling deer stand with broadside toward each other in head-high threat posture and move slowly together. A buck usually turns head and body about 30 degrees from his adversary. If neither deer retreats, sidling is usually followed by flailing or a rush.

Rear Up: A deer rears up on its hind legs into a vertical position. Usually preceded by a head-high threat.

Flail: Adversaries stand on their hind legs and strike out at each other with both front hoofs. Flailing continues until one deer submits. Most intense form of aggressive behavior exhibited by does and bucks without polished antlers.

FLAILING IS THE MOST INTENSE AGGRESSION SHOWN BY DOES, AND ALSO BUCKS WITHOUT HARDENED ANTLERS.

Aggressive Behavior: Bucks Only

Nose Licking: The buck constantly licks his nose. He protrudes the tongue alternately from each side of the mouth and flicks it quickly upward.

Crouch: The buck lowers his head and tilts antlers toward opponent. Involves a hunched posture; hind legs partially flexed, shoulder and elbow joints also partially flexed with the combined effect of lowering the height of the buck. Erectorpili effect, or raised hair, frequently used. The walk is slow, stiff and stilted. The crouch is a dominance display performed only during the breeding season by high-ranking bucks.

Circling: The aggressive male slowly circles his opponent while assuming the crouched position.

Rut-Snort: Rut-snort not as loud as that of mule deer and performed rarely.

Antler Threat: A buck lowers his head so the antlers point directly toward the rival. If the adversary duplicates the antler threat, the "rush" normally follows.

Antler Thrust: The buck rapidly lowers his head so the antlers point toward the rump or side of the opponent, and then abruptly raises the head. Directed toward males and females. Does not always result in contact.

Sparring: Two bucks engage antlers and push and/or twist their heads back and forth. Relatively nonviolent contests. Bucks of all antler sizes participate. Bucks frequently remain nearby afterward.

Rush: This rare aggressive behavior involves hostile combat between two, usually large, males. Both bucks lunge at each other in a violent antler clash from a distance of about six feet. A buck might try to pull opponent backward or swing him sideways. Erectorpili effect frequently present. Usually of short duration, the rush ends when one turns and bolts.

Many Aggressions

That episode prompted me to examine aggressive deer behavior more intently. Deer exhibit many types of aggressive behavior, and much of it plays a role in the herd's social organization.

Professor Valerius Geist of Calgary, a noted wildlife biologist, defines aggression this way: "Behavior by which individuals create and maintain access to scarce resources against the actions of conspecific competitors. It is active competition in which one individual, in some fashion, displaces another."

Scarce resources might include food, living space or

sexual partners. Competition for resources occurs mainly at three times. Competition for food becomes most intense in times of shortage, typically winter in the North and severe summer drought in the South. At fawning time, does might compete for living space. Dominant does secure habitat that provides the best cover for fawns and food supplies for the doe. Aggressive encounters between bucks peak during the breeding season when they compete for mates.

All deer, regardless of age or sex, exhibit aggressive behavior to some degree. Aggressive behavior ranges from low-intensity, non-contact confrontations to high-intensity, violent combat. Its many forms can be listed as dominance displays, direct threats or combat.

Dominance displays, and subtle and indirect threats substitute for combat, which can be costly to loser and winner. Both antagonists expend great energy and risk serious, even fatal, injury. A dominant buck usually performs a dominance display and uses this indirect threat to intimidate his opponent — usually another buck — with his superior size, height and weapons. Geist, in *Mule And Black-tailed Deer of North America*, describes a typical dominance display:

"At the appearance of an unfamiliar, medium-sized buck, a large one fixes him with his eyes while at a distance. Only at this time will the dominant look at the smaller male. At about 100 paces, the large buck begins his advance. His head will be held low, with neck in line with the body, ears back and folded out, hair erect, tail held horizontally and whipping up and

ALTHOUGH IT'S RARE, BUCKS WILL SOMETIMES BECOME ENTANGLED BY THEIR ANTLERS WHILE FIGHTING. A LONG, ANGUISHING DEATH IS THEN INEVITABLE. THIS PHOTOGRAPH, TAKEN BY BOB ZAIGLIN OF TEXAS, WAS ON THE COVER OF THE OCTOBER 1989 ISSUE OF *DEER & DEER HUNTING*. ZAIGLIN MANAGED TO RELEASE THIS BUCK AFTER FITTING IT WITH A RADIO TRANSMITTER, BUT IT DIED SOON AFTER. THE MAGAZINE ON WHICH THIS PHOTO APPEARED WAS THE NO. 1 SELLING ISSUE IN *DEER & DEER HUNTING*'S FIRST 20 YEARS.

down with each step, and back slightly arched. His movements will be stiff and somewhat slow. At a distance, owing to the erectorpili effect, the displaying dominant looks very dark. Periodically the tongue will lick over the lips and nose. At first, his approach will be directly at the smaller buck, but within 30 paces the dominant will swing outward and approach at a tangent, averting his head slightly. The tarsal and preorbital glands are not likely to be flared.

"During the approach phase, the smaller male, in all likelihood, will watch the larger buck while standing alert, slightly splay-footed, tail pinched in and back caved downward. His hair will be appressed, and therefore he will look lighter in color than the approaching dominant. As the dominant approaches tangentially, the subordinate is likely to evade by circling to the former's rear. The subordinate might attempt to get downwind of the dominant while looking directly at him. This is an unmistakable behavior of the subordinate. As the dominant buck continues his advance, the smaller buck avoids him by moving away, head erect, back depressed, and so forth, showing the submissive behavior of the species. The dominant keeps his head averted, and the subordinate continues to look at the dominant — with either raised or lowered head — as he sneaks past. Glancing up from a lowered head is infrequent in mule deer but common in the white-tailed deer. In whitetail encounters, the subordinate might crawl on its belly around the dominant, with neck extended and, from a crouched position, look upward at the larger deer."

Dominance displays also function as attention-gathering behavior, almost comparable to showing off in humans. Besides the dominance displays, a dominant buck might thrash bushes, saplings or overhanging tree branches. Whitetails also frequently paw or scrape the ground. High-ranking mule and black-tailed deer sometimes rut-snort at a subordinate, invariably causing the lower-ranking deer to retreat. Whitetails rut-snort less often.

Dominance displays don't always convince subordinates that they're of lower rank. As a result, direct threats might be mixed with or follow the dominance display.

Direct Threats

Direct threats are warnings, and include several signals that allow threatened deer to predict the outcome of doing combat with the deer making the threats. Males and females of all ages make direct threats, but if a subordinate threatens a dominant animal, the dominant threatens more

> AN ENCOUNTER BETWEEN BUCKS USUALLY BEGINS WITH A LOW-INTENSITY EAR DROP. IF THERE IS NO RESPONSE, THE AGGRESSOR MAKES THE HEAD-LOW THREAT.

strongly, and the lower-ranking deer usually retreats.

Of the many aggressive behaviors, direct threats comprise most interactions between deer. Some threats are so mild, however, that they aren't noticed by a casual observer. For example, Debra L. Koutnik, after studying aggressive behavior in mule deer, reported that the lowest intensity aggressive pattern — walk toward — was often enough to make a subordinate back down.

A deer often uses a series of aggressive postures of increasing intensity before a threatened foe retreats or assumes a submissive posture.

One research group (Jack W. Thomas, et al.) noted a distinct pattern of aggressive actions involving two white-tailed bucks. An encounter usually began with the low-intensity ear-drop. If this threat produced no response, the aggressor made the head-low threat. He lowered his head, extended his neck toward the threatened buck, and pressed his ears along his neck . He stared intently at his foe while performing this threat.

The adversary often duplicated this posture which, in turn, prompted a third action: sidling. If the adversary still failed to retreat, the aggressive buck lowered his head and pointed his antlers at the opponent, which is the antler threat. Retreat nearly always followed this threat, but if the other buck duplicated the action, the two bucks engaged in combat, or the rush.

Low-intensity threats, whether performed by bucks or

Aggressive Interactions of White-tailed Deer at Winter Cuttings

Interaction	Total Number	Ear Drop/ Hard Look	Strike	Rush	Sidle	Snort	Flail
		TERMINATING AGGRESSIVE ACTION (PERCENT FREQUENCY)					
Buck over Buck	39	28	18	36	5	3	10
Buck over Doe	84	32	33	22	1	7	5
Buck over Fawn	59	41	41	12	0	6	0
Doe over Buck	20	15	35	40	0	10	0
Doe over Doe	98	21	40	26	1	7	5
Doe over Fawn	85	21	47	24	0	8	0
Fawn over Fawn	28	15	46	32	0	0	7
Fawn over Doe	4	0	75	0	0	0	25
Total	417						

From Journal of Wildlife Management (1972)

does, usually make an adversary retreat. Thus, aggressive deer behaviors we see are low-intensity threats — ear drop and head-low threat — and infrequent severe threats — sidling and antler threat.

Combat

However, threatened deer don't always bolt or retreat, even after being severely challenged, and combat ensues.

Deer use two types of weapons when fighting. Sharp front hoofs are used by deer of all sex, age and species. While moose commonly strike at opponents with their hind and front legs, deer only use their front legs. Bucks also use their hard, polished antlers in autumn. Several species of Old World deer bite each other when fighting, but that seldom occurs in North American deer.

Front hoofs are used in two forms of hostile behavior: flailing and the front leg kick. The front leg kick varies from a nudge to a vicious blow or series of blows. Flailing is considered the most ferocious form of aggression used by does, and bucks without polished antlers. After studying aggressive behavior in white-tailed bucks, Edwin D. Michael said hoof fights seem more vicious than antler fights. He wrote: "At times of the year when bucks were antlerless or when antlers were covered with velvet, bucks fought in a different manner. A challenge similar to that used in antler aggression was made by one of the bucks, and if the other accepted, each reared on his hind legs and struck with his forelegs at the opponent's head (flailing). Most blows were met by the opponent's hoofs, but the head and antlers appeared to be struck frequently. Hoof fights seemed more vicious and more dangerous than antler fights. In antler aggression, the skin was seldom, if ever, touched by the opponent, but this was not the case with hoof fights."

Antler combat occurs as sparring or a rush. Sometimes referred to as pushing contests, sparring appears to be a relatively non-violent trial of strength. One buck, not necessarily the dominant, initiates sparring by lowering his head and presenting his antlers to the other. The second buck responds in similar fashion, and both bucks walk slowly toward each other until their antlers meet. Then they push against each other, sometimes forcefully, for as little as a few seconds to more than 15 minutes.

Bucks of all antler sizes spar, but a rush, or antler fight, usually involves two large bucks and occurs mainly during the peak of the rut. Sidling typically precedes the rush, and then both bucks assume the antler threat posture while up to 10 feet away from each other. As if on cue, the bucks lunge at each other and clash their antlers together violently. With antlers meshed, the bucks push and pull

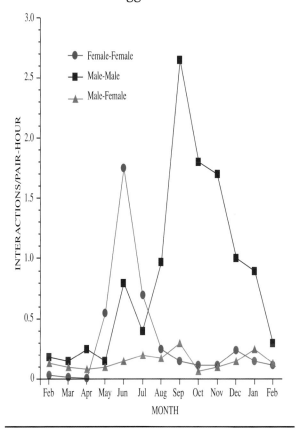

Rates of Aggressive Interactions

THIS CHART SHOWS THE SEASONAL CHANGES IN THE RATES OF AGGRESSIVE INTERACTIONS BETWEEN FEMALES, BETWEEN MALES, AND BETWEEN MALES AND FEMALES OF MULE DEER IN THE CHATSWORTH RESERVOIR IN CALIFORNIA, FROM FEBRUARY 1977 TO FEBRUARY 1978 (FROM THE *JOURNAL OF MAMMALOGY*).

against each other and try to throw the opponent sideways. Antler combat can be dramatic. Both bucks breathe heavily and strongly exhibit the erectorpili effect — hair standing erect — as they fight, throwing clods of dirt into the air and trampling vegetation. The combat ends when one buck suddenly turns and retreats. The victor might thrust his antlers at the departing foe, sometimes inflicting serious injuries. Antler combat can be dangerous for bucks, but relatively few suffer fatal injuries, but it's not for lack of trying. Bucks are incredibly quick in their reflexes, and seldom present an easy target for their foe.

Why do bucks fight with such ferocity? Geist writes: "Close observation of fighting ungulates indicates their actions appear to have two aims: making the opponent withdraw by putting leverage on his body, distorting it, or piercing it, which are pain-evoking actions and quite likely aim at triggering the withdrawal reflexes; making the opponent lose control over his own body, which is not so much a painful as traumatic experience and would lead to flight from the source of the trauma."

Aggression Factors

In general, as the ferocity of the aggression increases, its frequency decreases. Further, aggression fluctuates in relation to several factors. Does become more aggressive shortly before and after the birth of fawns. During the breeding season, encounters between bucks reach an annual peak. At times of limited food supplies, bucks and does also become more aggressive.

ADULT DOES DIRECT MUCH OF THEIR AGGRESSION TOWARD THEIR YEARLINGS. CONFLICTS BETWEEN ADULT DOES AND YEARLINGS DECREASE ALL SUMMER AND ARE NEARLY NON-EXISTENT BY AUTUMN.

Does associate freely with other deer most of the year, but desire solitude at fawning time. This leads to a dramatic increase in adult-doe aggression. Koutnik's study of mule deer aggression revealed "aggressive behavior by females during the fawning season increased up to 17.6 times that of the annual interaction rate."

Adult does direct much of this aggression toward their own yearlings. As fawning time approaches, adult does drive away the yearlings. In many cases, they use threat behaviors such as sidling, the ear drop, a head-low threat or chase in driving away their yearlings. If a yearling balks and remains nearby, the doe increases her hostility by striking or flailing with her front hoofs. Conflicts between adult does and yearlings decrease through summer and become almost non-existent by mid-autumn.

Few confrontations occur between adult does because they seem to adopt a policy of mutual avoidance, but there are exceptions. As reported in *The Oak Creek Mule Deer Herd* (Robinette, et al.), "We observed two obviously pregnant adults on June 12 traveling together, and yet one was hostile toward the other. As they moved along they came within 20 feet of another doe with young fawns. The third doe moved menacingly forward, causing the intruders to hurry away. Within a short time the original does resumed their bickering. We suspect one of the does was a 2-year-old daughter of the other and, because she was fawning for the first time, had not yet established an independent home range. The foregoing indicates that antagonism may contribute to spatial distribution among adult does during fawning, but we have observed many non-hostile contacts between transients and does with young fawns."

Studies indicate aggression between adult does and adult bucks is rare. Encounters between adult does and small bucks occur more often. Michael reported: "On a few occasions bucks were seen pushing with does. The bucks were usually small and the does seemed reluctant. When a buck continued to place his antlers in the doe's face, she usually cooperated and half-heartedly pushed against him for a brief period of time."

Buck Aggression

Bucks are only mildly aggressive most of the year. This changes during the breeding season when aggression between males increases significantly. An instigating factor is the new generation of males entering the buck population: yearlings sporting their first antlers. These bucks create conflict in establishing the pecking order among bucks.

Despite relatively high aggression between adult and yearling bucks, its intensity is usually low. In his study of whitetails, researcher David H. Hirth found more than 70 percent of aggressive interactions between adult and yearling bucks were chases and head-low threats. Likewise, the low intensity head-low threat accounted for nearly half of the aggressive interactions between adult bucks.

While biologists report significant aggressive behavior during the breeding season, most of it still consists of non-hostile displays or threats. Sparring matches occur primarily between the time bucks shed their velvet and the peak of the breeding season. These bouts far outnumber hostile antler combat, which occurs primarily during the peak of the rut. For example, Hirth observed 167 sparring contests on Texas' Welder Refuge, but only five rushes. And Geist writes: "These serious fights (rushes) are so rare that, in the time I collected data on social behavior, I recorded 718 interactions among bucks but not a single dominance fight. Those seen were observed incidental to gathering data on aspects other than social behavior or while filming."

Aggressive behavior among males during the breeding season establishes a dominance order, with high-ranking males servicing the females. Still, bucks seldom need hostilities to establish their rank. Michael presented a logical explanation for the rarity of hostile combat:

"Although relatively few deer are seriously injured in hostile fights, these fights are can inflict lethal injuries. Some get their antlers inextricably locked and both individuals die. Thus, it seems a behavioral pattern of eliminating hostile fights has evolved in the form of preseason sparring matches, which prevent the need for many such injurious incidents. ... Nonessential aggressive behaviors tend to be eliminated so that, in the end, the dominant animal makes only a threat and the subordinate moves away."

Food Fights

While increased aggression occurs at fawning time and breeding season, food shortages also trigger higher levels of aggression. Food shortages are caused by prolonged drought, severe snow depths, or excessive deer populations. Food shortages inevitably lead to competition.

When competing for food, deer exhibit many of the same aggressive behaviors as at other times of the year. Wisconsin deer biologists describe aggressive behaviors in a Northern deeryard during severe winters:

"The deer competed aggressively for food. One animal would approach another, neck erect and ears laid back, and, should the other fail to retreat, would rap it sharply with one front hoof, or even rear up on both hind legs, bringing both front hoofs down on the other deer. Sometimes, the attacked deer would fight and both animals would rear up on their hind legs, and slap each other with their forefeet.

"Occasionally, a smaller deer would attack a larger deer from behind, but at once retreat when the larger individual turned upon it. Rarely when one deer was about to attack another, a low harsh bleat or threat sound from the latter caused the former to 'change its mind' and suddenly veer off. The deer also showed a tendency to pass along punishment received. Occasionally one deer, after being driven from a pile of food, would at once attack some subordinate animal in its vicinity."

John J. Ozoga conducted research to study aggressive white-tailed deer behavior while competing for food at winter timber cuttings.

These deer displayed seven basic aggressive actions: ear drop, hard look, sidle, charge, snort, strike and flail. Bucks and does frequently interacted aggressively at these cuttings.

Besides tabulating 417 deer interactions, Ozoga quantified how often each aggressive behavior ended interaction between two deer. Although fawns rarely win aggressive encounters, they're not necessarily excluded from feeding. Ozoga said dominant deer usually tolerated subordinates as long as they did not exhibit aggressive postures.

Conclusion

Aggression, of course, isn't done for mere recreation. It serves important purposes. Generally, aggression establishes dominance. Aggressive males and females benefit in different ways from their behavior.

Aggressive, or high-ranking, does get the best resources at fawning time, thus enhancing their offspring's survival. A doe that aggressively repels other deer from her fawning sites also reduces the risk of losing her fawns to predators.

Aggressive males, meanwhile, gain access to breeding females. Because deer are polygamous, high-ranking males breed most of the females. The species, as well as the high-ranking males, benefits because the superior males reproduce with the females.

In doing so, the survival of the species is perpetuated.

References

Cowan, I. McT. and V. Geist. 1961. Aggressive behavior in deer of the genus Odocoileus. *Journal of Mammalogy* 42(4): 522-526.

Dasmann, R.F. and R.D. Taber. 1956. Behavior of Columbian black- tailed deer with reference to population ecology. *Journal of Mammalogy* 37(2): 143-164.

Geist, V. 1971. *Mountain Sheep: A Study in Behavior and Evolution.* University of Chicago Press: Chicago. pp. 2 pp.1 28-238.

_____. 1981. Adaptive strategies in mule deer. In: Walmo, O.C. (Ed.), *Mule and Black-tailed Deer of North America.* University of Nebraska Press: Lincoln. pp.177-195.

Hirth, D.H. 1977. Social behavior of white-tailed deer in relation to habitat. *Wildlife Monograph* No. 53.-55.

Kabat, C., N.E. Collias, and R.C. Guettinger. 1953. Some winter habits of white-tailed deer and the development of census methods in the Flag Yard of northern Wisconsin. Technical Wildlife Bulletin No. 7, Wisconsin Conservation Department. pp. 15-18.

Koutnik, D.L. 1981. Sex-related differences in the seasonality of agonistic behavior in mule deer. *Journal of Mammalogy* 62 (1): 1-11.

Linsdale, J.M. and P.Q. Tomich. 1953. A herd of mule deer. University of California Press: Berkeley. pp. 193-202.

Michael, E.D. 1968. Aggressive behavior of white-tailed deer. *The Southwestern Naturalist* 13(4): 411-420.

Ozoga, J.J. 1972. Aggressive behavior of white-tailed deer at winter cuttings. *Journal of Wildlife Management* 36(3): 861-868.

Peterson, R.L. 1955. *North American Moose.* University of Toronto press: Toronto. pp. 103-105.

Robinette, W.L., N.V. Hancock, and D.A. Jones. 1977. The Oak Creek mule deer herd in Utah. Utah division of Wildlife Resources: Salt Lake City. p. 72.

Skinner, M.P. 1929. White-tailed deer formerly in Yellowstone Park. *Journal of Mammalogy* 10(2): 101-115.

Thomas, J.W., R.M. Robinson, and R.G. Marburger. 1965. Social behavior in a white-tailed deer herd containing hypogonadal males. *Journal of Mammalogy* 46(2): 314-327.

"Aggressive Behavior of Deer" was originally published in the April 1982 issue of Deer & Deer Hunting *magazine.*

CHAPTER 6

WALKER YARD

The wildlife manager was concerned about deer wintering in the yard. It held many of them, but contained only limited amounts of coniferous cover and that, including the red pine, showed a heavy browse line.

■ BY GEORGE HARTMAN

That late February day and the crusted snow were meant for snowshoeing. The day was bright and windless, and the temperature about 10 degrees when we got out of the car and into our snowshoes.

The walk into the Walker Deeryard started in an open sedge marsh with only scattered shrubs. The 14 to 16 inches of crusted snow covered the rip-gut, and only the seed stocks of the bullgrass showed. The few scattered shrubs, hardhack, bog birch and willow presented no problems. Our snowshoe frames bit into the snow just enough to give excellent traction. The webs left their imprint only near the toe of the shoe harnesses.

High Browse Line

Ben, the local wildlife manager, was concerned about deer wintering in the yard. It held a large number of them. The yard contained only a limited amount of coniferous cover and that, including the red pine, showed a heavy browse line after the previous winter. High browse wasn't much, mostly aspen, scrub oak and birch. The area contained few good browse plants such as red maple, chokeberry and Michigan holly. Here, wintering deer depended mostly on ground cover and other low-growing plants. These, chiefly swamp dewberry, wintergreen, bearberry and blueberry were covered by crusted snow.

We hiked a quarter-mile or so across the marsh to its meeting with the highland. Here there was a narrow band of pole-size tamarack with a few scrubby black spruce. No fresh deer sign here. Ben mentioned there were few lichens, or old man's beard, on the dead lower branches because deer had eaten it the previous winter.

Leaving the tamarack, we shoed through a stand of defective off-site aspen. Being pole-size, these trees were too big for deer browse and too scrubby and small for pulpwood. No deer tracks here.

> WE LIKED WHAT WE SAW AND WE TALKED ABOUT OAKS AND ACORNS. WE LAMENTED THE FACT THERE ISN'T A BUMPER CROP OF ACORNS EVERY YEAR AND THAT HERE OAKS OFTEN HAVE TOTAL CROP FAILURES.

The ground elevation raised a few feet as we came onto a vegetation-fixed sand dune of the old glacial lake bed. This sandy, higher land was covered with large limby oaks — "scrub oak" — which botanists key down to the name of Hill's oak. Here we saw deer, a dozen or so. The many tracks and packed trails told us they had been here a long time. These deer were wintering almost entirely on acorns.

A Bumper Crop

The forest had produced a bumper crop of acorns the previous fall, the best crop in 10 or more years. The deer started feeding on acorns in early fall, built up fat and kept feeding on acorns even after the snows came. Increases in snow depths were gradual and the deer, by smelling and pawing, progressively extended their feeding area. The winter's initial feeding was done at the base of the highlands' south-facing slopes and extended as winter progressed. The churned and refrozen snow of earlier feedings indicated that while the deer were feeding mostly on acorns, they were getting a bit of other feed too: wintergreen, bearberry and blueberry.

Using a snowshoe, Ben dug into the deeper snow ahead of deer pawings. Here he found several of the characteristically small Hill's oak acorns in about a square foot area.

We liked what we saw and we talked about oaks and acorns. We lamented the fact that there isn't a bumper crop of acorns every year and that here, up near the northern end of oak range, we often have total acorn crop failures. We discussed possible reasons. Are spring frosts the major cause? If so, is it just the freezing of the oak flowers or do

the pips, the tiny first-year acorns, sometimes start growth and then freeze? I recalled a discussion at a wildlife seminar years before on favorable and unfavorable carbon-nitrogen rations in trees. We talked too of our different oaks, the white and burr oak, which produce acorns after a single year's growth, while black oak species need two years for their acorns to mature.

Here on the poor, sandy soils of the glacial lake dunes, all oaks are scrubby. Only the size and shape of the acorns of the black oak group identify their species. White Hill's oak is the most common. Under these oaks we, and the deer, too, like to find the bigger acorns of the red and black oaks. Sometimes the acorns are of intermediate size, indicating natural hybridization.

We snowshoed through the oaks and through a growth of poor aspen. As the ground raised, we came to more oaks and much more deer sign. A sandstone ridge told us we were on an outcropping rather than a fixed dune. This stand of oak was more extensive and not quite as scrubby. There were scattered white oaks mixed with the others and, at the base of the ridge, there was about an acre of white oaks. The absence of deer sign under these trees told us they had produced no acorns the past fall.

The deer were concentrated on the southern exposed slope, and here, too, the extensiveness of the worked-over snow attested to them being here most of the winter.

Return Trip

We circled the ridge and worked our way back toward the car. We rested when we came to the marsh. I remember Ben saying, "Now all we gotta worry about is a seal-in ice storm or a 2-foot snowfall."

Ben, like all good wildlife managers still do, worried about wintering deer.

"Walker Yard" was originally published in the March 1988 issue of Deer & Deer Hunting *magazine.*

ONE FAWN, JUDGING BY WHAT LITTLE WAS LEFT BY THE SCAVENGING RAVENS AND MAMMALS, WAS LIKELY A VICTIM TO LATE JANUARY'S BITTER COLD.

Patrick Durkin

CHAPTER 7

IN WINTER'S WAKE

All the signs told us these adult whitetails had just recently died, probably late into that cruel, endless April. After all, while snowshoeing here in late March, we had found countless deer beds but only two dead fawns.

■ BY PATRICK DURKIN

The calm after a pounding storm sometimes seems so peaceful I struggle to believe the snow ever fell and the wind ever roared. The cracked, twisted damage strewn in its wake is the only link to reality.

That feeling struck me in mid-May one year while walking with my three daughters in a forest in Michigan's Upper Peninsula. Overhead, the lime-green of emerging aspen leaves and the fuzzy red of budding maples signaled spring. But at our feet were patches of snow, shaded by white cedars and balsam fir, which reminded us of a North Woods winter that had stretched deep into April.

A more grim reminder of the brutal winter lay ragged, withered and brown where a small ridge tapered into a swale choked with tag alders. It was a dead deer, the second we had found in the past 30 minutes. After walking about 50 yards farther, I

Richard P. Smith

looked up the hill and spotted another brown form stretched in death.

All the signs told us these whitetails had just recently died, probably late into that cruel April. After all, while snowshoeing that same swale edge in late March, we had found countless deer beds but only two dead fawns. One fawn, judging by what little was left by the scavenging ravens and assorted mammals, was likely a victim to late January's bitter cold.

> DEATH'S PECKING ORDER IS LOGICAL AND PRACTICAL. THE HERD'S SURVIVAL DEPENDS ON THE DOE, AND NATURE PROVIDES HER THE SIZE, STAMINA AND FAT RESERVES TO SURVIVE HARSH WINTERS.

Adult Victims

The first three dead deer we found during our mid-May visit, however, were adult does. None had yet been found by the forest's scavengers. Obviously, the forest was thick with carrion. A scavenger didn't have to search far for food. Only the first flies of spring were working these victims of winter and degraded habitat.

I crouched over the third doe we found, slid my pocket knife into the corner of its mouth, and cut a line back toward its jaw socket. After prying slightly on the stained teeth, I studied the wear on the lower molars to estimate the deer's age. I'm not an expert on that technique, but I tell myself I'm not bad, either.

"I think she's about 4 years old," I told the girls, who watched with morbid curiosity. "This isn't good."

We had expected to find dead deer, maybe even lots of dead deer. What we hadn't expected was this many dead adult females. Typically, an adult doe is the most capable deer of surviving a rough winter. Fawns are the first to go, followed by mature bucks. In previous springs, it wasn't unusual to find dead fawns scattered in this forest. But never before had we found adult does.

Death's Pecking Order

But death's pecking order is logical and practical. The herd's survival depends on the doe, and nature provides her the size, stamina and fat reserves to survive harsh winters.

Fawns? Forget it. When times are tough, their own mothers kick them aside when finding food. And because they're smaller, fawns can't reach as high to nip cedar fronds, arboreal lichens and white pine needles. In addition, fawns enter winter at about 7 months of age, so they haven't accumulated much fat. Most of their intake had gone toward bone growth.

The mature buck? Not to stereotype, but he was a typical male the previous fall. His need to breed dominated his life in late October and through November. He hardly ate while pursuing available females, and he literally ran off all of his fat reserves. He entered winter in lean shape, never fully replenishing his energy.

Therefore, when does are widespread victims of winter's hazards, it's clear the herd had been far beyond the forest's carrying capacity. Winter merely proved a punishing point.

We found further mortal evidence of harsh times when cresting a small ridge nearby. There lay the top half of a mature maple, which had broken off during winter, possibly from high winds and wet, heavy snows. Every branch deer could reach was stripped bare. Deep tooth marks and ragged strips of bark distinguished this as deer, not hare, feeding.

Conclusion

Biologists and serious hunters have long warned of what's left of deer herds in the wake of winter's brutal rule. Too bad so few people witness the scenes firsthand for themselves. The sights might shock them back to the realities of responsible deer management.

One can hope.

"In Winter's Wake" was originally published in several Wisconsin newspapers in June 1996.

THE DEER HUNTER'S BONDS

I'm not as pessimistic as some of hunting's top supporters, nor as optimistic as some of its most mouthy foes, that deer hunters are a dying breed. That deer hunters will be different is guaranteed, but that hardly qualifies as insight. Heck. I'll be different, too, 20 days, 20 months or 20 years from now.

Why do I have faith in its future? Well, call it blind faith, if you want. I can't support it with trend indicators, projections, cross-tabs and computerized charts. Besides, all it takes is one societal hiccup, and all those color-coded arrows on a sociologist's graphs shoot off course faster than if they carried poor broadheads.

But I feel the hunt beating too strongly in my heart and churning too intensely in my guts to believe society can so easily kill it through shallow scorn and intellectual neglect. I reinforce those feelings when I look around at other hunters, and feel the buckskin bonds they've tied, not only to each other, but also to the land, the deer and autumn's frosty air and flaming leaves. Those are things that can't be measured, projected or predicted. They can only be felt. But what is deer hunting if not feelings and emotions?

Don't worry. This section won't turn mushy on you as we examine the deer hunter's varied bonds. It was every author's intention to stay somewhere north of maudlin. After all, while deer hunting is a study in complexities, deer hunters typically aren't ones to sit around trying to "bond" and "get in touch with their feelings." They realize their love of the woods, deer and their families has never been forced.

Nor has it been false or easily forsaken.

■ *PATRICK DURKIN*

CHARLES J. ALSHEIMER IS THE NORTHERN FIELD EDITOR FOR DEER & DEER HUNTING MAGAZINE. HE IS SEEN HERE WITH HIS SON, AARON, WHO WAS THEN 14.

ALSHEIMER SHARES A SUCCESSFUL DEER HUNT WITH HIS SON DURING AARON'S NINTH AUTUMN. BESIDES IMPARTING HUNTING KNOWLEDGE AT SUCH TIMES, ALSHEIMER USED THESE OPPORTUNITIES TO TEACH DEER ANATOMY AND BIOLOGY.

CHAPTER 1

THE JOURNEY

"We make a living by what we get, but we make a life by what we give."

— Winston Churchill

■ TEXT, PHOTOS BY CHARLES J. ALSHEIMER

As Aaron ran toward me, he excitedly said: "Dad! Dad! I got one! I got a deer! Boy, Dad, it was something. Two does walked by my stand, and I shot one when it stopped about 10 yards from me. I made a perfect shot through both lungs."

Listening to his story caused me to have a rush of emotion. I was getting as excited as he was. Before he could go on with the story I said, "Well, where is she?"

Aaron replied, "She ran about 75 yards before dying just above the creek."

I put my arm around his shoulder and said: "This is something you'll remember the rest of your life. You know, I was 30 when I killed my first deer with a bow and arrow, and you did it at 15. Let's go get her."

Upon reaching the downed doe we exchanged high-5s and began field dressing her. Though Aaron had watched me gut many deer, this one was special. Slowly, I took him through the process. We paused at one point to open the stomach to see what the doe had been eating, and then cut through the diaphragm to remove the heart and lungs. As we studied the way the broadhead sliced the lungs, I explained why the hit was so lethal.

We then loaded the doe onto our tractor and headed for the house. Aaron was on Cloud 9, and I wasn't far below. As we rode down the hill toward home, my mind raced. I thought back to the first deer I killed when I was 17, and I thought about everything that had led to this day. This was a high point in life's journey, a journey pieced together with hopes, plans, pains and dreams.

Early Memories

I was raised on a potato farm in the heart of New York's Finger Lakes region. My dad enjoyed deer hunting, though he wasn't serious about it. This was partly because of the fact he took me along, beginning at age 7. I was

hyperactive, and I often drove him nuts in the woods. He could sit for long periods of time, but not me. I was always fidgeting and making noise, and more than once I spooked a deer before dad could shoot. If he tried still-hunting, I was right behind him, stepping on the back of his boots and noisily scuffing the legs of my frozen jeans.

In spite of this, he continued to take me along. We were buddies, and regardless of what I did, he still wanted me with him. In 1955, when I was 8, he killed his only white-tailed buck, and I was beside him on that cold, slate-gray November day. I don't know who was more excited, he or I. The buck carried only five points, but as far as I was concerned, it was the trophy of a lifetime.

As I got older I often roamed the farm's woodlots and fields with my .22 single-shot. Woodchucks were the quarry, and I killed enough to help out the potato and bean crops. Our farm and its surrounding it were my sanctuary. I knew the hummocks, gullies and ravines as if they were

ABOVE, IN 1979, CHARLIE ALSHEIMER GIVES AARON, SEEN HERE AT AGE 2, AN EARLY LESSON IN NATURE. "ONCE AARON WAS OLD ENOUGH TO SIT UP AND CRAWL I TOOK HIM EVERYWHERE I WENT."

RIGHT, IN 1988, AARON, AT AGE 11, HELPS HIS FATHER DRAG OUT A BUCK.

BELOW, IN 1985, CHARLIE AND AARON, AT AGE 8, EXAMINE A BUCK RUB ON THEIR FARM IN WESTERN NEW YORK.

extensions of my bedroom.

But life's journey made a drastic turn when I was 13. My parents split, and my dad went into the construction business 70 miles away. Our hunting time dwindled and I didn't see much of him at a critical point in my life. For nearly four years I stopped hunting and immersed myself in athletics. Then, at the urging of a friend, I became interested in hunting again when I was 17. That four-year absence proved positive. It made me realize how much I missed hunting and he woods.

Early Adulthood

This appreciation was magnified in 1969 and 1970 when I spent 14 months in Vietnam with the U.S. Air Force. Many negative things have been written about Vietnam. But war's horrors gave me a reference point, providing a positive influence on my life. War made me appreciate America and all it stands for.

"Life, liberty and the pursuit of happiness" took on new meaning after I came home in 1970. My dad and I became closer than we had been in years, and we hunted deer together for the first time in nearly a decade. The smells and sights of the woods helped rekindle the bond we knew when I was a youngster.

I also came home with a new companion, the 35mm camera. I was introduced to these cameras in Vietnam, and now I desired to hunt whitetails with them. The more I photographed whitetails, the more I wanted to be in the woods. The true journey had just begun.

In 1973 my wife, Carla, and I bought a farm a couple of miles from where I grew up. We turned it into a wildlife sanctuary. Then, after five years of marriage, God blessed Carla and me with our only child, a son. Once Aaron was old enough to sit up and crawl I took him everywhere. If I went scouting on a warm summer evening, he went along. If I went someplace to photograph deer, he went along. At

THE MOST CRUCIAL ASPECT OF HUNTING IS NOT WHETHER A WORLD-RECORD WHITETAIL IS KILLED. IT'S PLANTING THE SEED SO FUTURE GENERATIONS CAN ENJOY THE WORLD'S GREATEST OUTDOOR EXPERIENCE: HUNTING WHITETAILS ON CRISP AUTUMN MORNINGS.

times he was noisy in the woods but I didn't care. We were learning together. Those times together often caused me to reflect. My childhood flashed in front of me. I saw my dad and myself back on the farm.

When Aaron was nearly 2, Carla returned to teaching, and I resigned my position in corporate sales and marketing to pursue a full-time career in the outdoors. Rather than hire a baby-sitter, we decided Aaron would spend the days with me.

Needless to say, we had some interesting times.

A New Direction

As a traveling lecturer, photographer and writer, I saw America changing rapidly in its views toward hunting. I was concerned and wanted to do something about it. The pen can be powerful, but I learned early there is only so

much you can do to influence people about hunting. For me, hunting is more than words. It's amber sunrises and the smell of leaves in an October forest. It's fluffy snowflakes landing on a cold gun barrel, and the smell of wet wool at the end of a day's hunt. It's the rapid heartbeat as a white-tailed buck gracefully moves through the woods, and the "fummmp" sound of an arrow's release. It's the skinning, butchering and cooking process of getting the deer from the woods to the table.

In short, hunting is being there. It's experiencing all that nature offers.

It was these things and more that I wanted Aaron to see and experience. Hunting and nature had given me so much, and I wanted him to understand and experience all of it. I'm sure we must have looked like a peculiar pair, a guy with a big camera and his little kid moving through the woods. After stopping to photograph a scenic setting, I often found Aaron picking flowers for his mom. On other occasions we would just sit in the woods, and he would ask me all kinds of questions about leaves, birds and trees. In a way, Aaron wasn't introduced to nature; he was born into it.

The finality of hunting came for him at age 4. I came home and fetched him before I gutted and dragged a buck out of the woods. I'll never forget his words upon seeing the downed deer: "Daddy, is the deer sleeping? Why doesn't he get up?"

Aaron had seen deer hanging in the barn, but that scene was far different from seeing one lying in the woods. I slowly and patiently explained that I had killed it for us to eat.

He said, "You mean this is what they look like before we eat supper?"

I chuckled and explained to him what went into getting a deer from the woods to the supper table. As I took my knife from its sheath, he said, "Can I watch you take its insides out?"

"Of course," I said, and we squatted beside the buck. Even though Aaron was only 4, this first biology class was fascinating for him, and for me. He wanted to know about the various organs, and I carefully dissected the heart to show him how it worked. Once done, he helped me drag the deer out of the woods.

In those days we butchered our own deer, and Aaron wanted to be in on the process. One of his tasks was to carry the meat from the cutting table to the grinder. Carla then let him cut some of the tape to seal the packages for freezing. It was a family affair, from the woods to the freezer. After that, Aaron wanted to help with all the deer I killed.

Hunter/Trapper

Besides deer hunting, I also trapped fox on the farm. Before Aaron started kindergarten, he and I had a ritual during trapping season. Each morning after breakfast we headed for the back 40 to check my trap line. It was during the trapping sessions that he learned much about nature's balance. We would often discuss why animal populations must be kept in check. That would occasionally be reinforced when I found a mangy fox in a trap. It allowed him to see firsthand that nature's way of killing is often cruel and prolonged. I would use these times to illustrate the importance of trapping and hunting.

When Aaron was 4½, we went to the Rocky Mountains on a working vacation. After speaking for a week at a camp in Jackson Hole, Wyo., we headed for Yellowstone National Park. One afternoon, Aaron and I climbed to the summit of Mount Washburn. Along the way we photographed a big bull moose that was bedded near the hiking trail. Once at the top, we sat and gazed for 100 miles in every direction. When a band of bighorn sheep grazed past us 30 yards away, I started taking pictures. As the camera's motor drive hummed, Aaron whispered, "Dad, didn't God make us a beautiful world?" It was enough to melt my heart. It made me realize that adults need to slow down to see nature through the eyes of a child, and appreciate what God has given us. That trip didn't involve hunting, but it laid the groundwork for Aaron's appreciation of nature, and set the stage for his understanding of stewardship. Though I was trying to teach him, I began realizing he was also teaching me. Since then, our trips throughout North America have solidified our deep love for nature.

When Aaron turned 6, I started taking him hunting. I

AT AGE 14 IN 1992, AARON FINALLY GOT THE CHANCE TO CARRY A BOW INTO THE WOODS WHILE HUNTING WITH HIS FATHER. "HUNTING IS BEING THERE. IT'S EXPERIENCING ALL THAT NATURE OFFERS."

began slowly at first. I knew all too well that staying quiet and motionless is difficult for a youngster. I picked situations where we would not be sitting long. He would get off the school bus, and we would often head to a favorite ground blind to sit the last hour of the day. In the mid-1980s he was with me when I grunted in my first white-tailed buck using a new invention called a grunt tube. Then, when he was 7, he was with me when I killed a white-tailed doe. We watched the deer more than 30 minutes before I clicked off the shotgun's safety and fired.

I viewed taking him with me on photo trips, lectures and backyard hunting sits as "seed" time. My goal was to make each trip a positive experience. I made it a point not to push guns and bows on Aaron. I was a baseball coach for 20 years, and saw too many parents push their favorite sports on their children. I knew how much he loved nature, and how he always wanted to go with me. But I didn't know if he would like to hunt and actually kill an animal. If he didn't want to, I was prepared to live with his choice.

When he was 9, Aaron asked if we could shoot the .22 rifle. Then when he was 10 he wanted to start shooting a bow. That Christmas he got his first bow and we began shooting in our basement. Since then he's been involved in much of what I do, from modeling for hunting photos to helping with the farm's wildlife habitat work. In many ways our life has been a script written in heaven.

AARON, AT AGE 15 IN OCTOBER 1993, IS CONGRATULATED BY HIS FATHER AFTER SHOOTING HIS FIRST DEER WITH A BOW AND ARROW. "I MADE IT A POINT NOT TO PUSH GUNS AND BOWS ON AARON. ... I DIDN'T KNOW IF HE WOULD LIKE TO HUNT AND ACTUALLY KILL AN ANIMAL. IF HE DIDN'T WANT TO, I WAS PREPARED TO LIVE WITH HIS CHOICE."

Heavy Stuff

In 1992, Aaron was a finalist in his school's public speaking contest. When he began preparing for it I asked what his speech was on. He said, "The Animal Rights Myth."

"Why'd you pick that topic?" I asked.

"Because I want to share the positive side of the issue. All anyone ever hears is the negative side of hunting, and I want to share my perspective."

I looked at him and thought, "Wow, that's pretty heady stuff for a high school freshman."

I went to the contest not knowing what his chances would be. He was going up against experienced seniors, so I knew winning would be difficult. Well, Aaron didn't win, a senior did, but as I sat there and watched him address the entire school I thought to myself: "Man, he's articulating things better than most could dream of doing. Today, hunting is a big winner."

As I reflect on hunting in America, I think of our country's youths. Unfortunately, too many parents don't have the time or desire to share the outdoors with their kids. There is a familiar quote that says, "We have filled our lives with meaningless trophies." Sadly, that too well sums up America.

For many, the quest for more gadgets, gizmos, money and positions has caused family and traditions to be cast aside. Unfortunately, parents baby-sit their kids with a TV, Nintendo and computerized junk instead of showing them what the outdoors is all about. In other cases, kids with loving, but single parents can only dream of what might have been. I know this one all too well.

Gifts of Time

On my office wall is a sign with the following quote: "In the eyes of a child, love is spelled TIME." My father gave me the time when I was his "little shaver," and I learned from his gift. As a result, I made the time when Aaron came along. When I think of the memories my son and I have shared, my eyes well with tears. It's the greatest investment I ever made, and the dividends have been worth more than silver or gold.

The other day I took the long way to town, over the hill and past the farm where my life began. I pulled off the road at the top of the hill, got out of my van, and crunched through the snow to get a better vantage point.

"FOR ME, HUNTING IS MORE THAN WORDS. IT'S AMBER SUNRISES AND THE SMELL OF LEAVES IN AN OCTOBER FOREST." ALSHEIMER TOOK THIS PHOTO OF AARON AT FULL DRAW DURING THE 1994 SEASON AT AGE 16.

The view from the hilltop was just as I remembered it. Stretched before me was a sea of snow-covered fields gouged here and there with tree-choked ravines. In the distance my boyhood farmhouse stood out like an island. Through the bright sunlight I focused on the long hedgerow behind the house. It still looked as I remembered it. There are loads of memories in that slice of brush.

Even though more than 30 seasons have come and gone, it seemed like only yesterday that I was testing my hunting skill on the woodchucks that called it home. It was there that my love for hunting was born when a potato farmer and his son found time to be together with a single-shot .22 rifle.

THREE GENERATIONS OF THE ALSHEIMER FAMILY GET TOGETHER TO HUNT DEER EACH AUTUMN. PICTURED HERE ARE AARON, CHARLES H. AND CHARLES J. ALSHEIMER. "IN THE EYES OF A CHILD, LOVE IS SPELLED TIME."

Conclusion

The longer I live, the more I realize the brevity of life's journey. Winston Churchill was so right: We truly do make a life by what we give and not by what we get.

The most important thing for hunting is not whether record whitetails fall. It's ensuring future generations can experience the world's greatest outdoor experience: hunting whitetails on crisp autumn mornings. That's a journey that requires an investment of time, but it's worth the trip. I know. I've been there. And I try every day to appreciate the journey because none of us knows how long it will last.

"The Journey" was originally published in the August 1995 issue of Deer & Deer Hunting *magazine.*

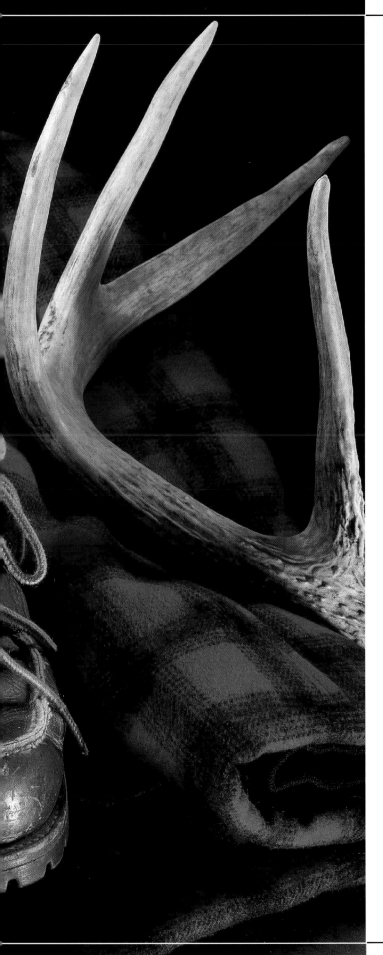

CHAPTER 2

WALK A MILE IN THE OLD MAN'S BOOTS

The old boots were in good shape, though the leather laces were frail, the stitches slightly frayed, and the toes subtly curled. I was proud to inherit them. They were my link to a man I had hardly known.

■ BY PATRICK EDWARD DURKIN

We buried the Old Man one spring; May 16, 1990, to be exact. He was 88 when he took it down the trail. Afterward, his four kids, then in their 60s, gathered to divide his few possessions.

One son put some money toward the small estate and claimed the .30-06. Noticing a pair of old Red Wing boots, he claimed those as well. Why the son wanted the boots isn't clear. Their size, 9EE, made them too small for him or his own boys.

Scratched on the boot heels were E.P.D, the Old Man's initials. The Old Man had poked periods after the E and P, but not the D. No great significance there. Just a curiosity that only a petty copy editor would worry about. The son oiled the Red Wings and put them aside for the summer. Eventually, he thought, he would find someone in

Patrick Durkin

the family to fill those boots.

In early autumn, I stopped by to visit that son, who happens to be my uncle. As we talked, the discussion turned to the Old Man. After a thoughtful pause, my uncle asked my foot size.

"Eight-and-half or 9 double-E," I said. "The wider the better."

Knowing nothing about the boots, I was puzzled by the question. Then my uncle turned and grabbed the Red Wings from the corner.

"How would you like these?" he asked. "They were your grandfather's."

The old boots were in good shape, though the leather laces were frail, the stitches slightly frayed, and the toes subtly curled.

"We think he bought them for a hunting trip out West back in the '60s," my uncle said as my eyes and hands inspected the boots.

A Missing Link

Why my grandfather had bought them didn't matter much, I guess. I was just proud to inherit

I HAD SEEN COLOR PICTURES OF THE OLD MAN AND SOME PEOPLE I DIDN'T RECOGNIZE OUTSIDE A DEER SHACK IN THE NORTHERN WISCONSIN FOREST. A GRAY BUCK HUNG NEAR THE DOOR. I HOPED HE WOULD SOMEDAY SHARE SUCH A SETTING WITH ME. BY THE TIME I WAS 15, I KNEW THAT WOULDN'T HAPPEN. THE OLD MAN, WHILE ALWAYS SOLITARY, SEEMED TO GROW EVEN MORE RECLUSIVE WITH AGE.

them. They were my link to a man I had hardly known.

The Old Man, you see, was never close to most of his family. When my father and uncles referred to him, they rarely called him "Dad." It was either "Grandpa Durkin" or the "Old Man."

They say the heart can only hold so much love. Maybe the Old Man rationed that quota to his work, his friends, his hootch and a few select kin. In fact, he and my grandmother hadn't shared the same house, let alone the same pillow, since the early 1930s. But they never divorced. Grandma had principles, you understand. She said she had taken God's vow to love and cherish the Old Man unto death. And she did.

When the 92-year-old matriarch learned her husband was dead that spring day in 1990, she told a son, "Well, now I can finally live with him."

We laughed at her wit when hearing the story, but her simple profoundness spoke for all of us. Memories are often easier to accommodate than the person who inspired them. Memories can be generous. They don't pick at quirks and defects. They tend to find the good that's so often hidden in real life.

That autumn, because I now wore his boots, I hunted deer with the Old Man for the first time. As we hunted, I recalled that he had provided my first taste of venison, my first feel of tanned buckskin.

> I KNEW THE OLD MAN AND I WOULD NEVER BE CLOSE. BUT BY BEING WHO HE WAS, HE HAD TAUGHT ME HOW COMPLEX PEOPLE COULD BE. HE COULD TOUCH SUCH GREAT EXTREMES, AND ALMOST AT THE SAME TIME.

Or, should I say, the Old Man provided the first venison and buckskin that I remember. My father killed four deer in seven hunting seasons, but he quit the woods and sold his .270 before I was old enough to remember his hunts' rewards.

First Venison

That first venison meal from the Old Man takes me back to about age 10. I realized with those steaks that I was a deer hunter, even though I had never worn a red wool jacket or lined up the sights of an '06. My three brothers and two sisters poked and pushed the venison around their plates. I just grabbed the salt-shaker, sprinkled the appropriate amount, and chewed.

I thought about the Old Man when I ate that supper. I had seen color pictures of him and some men I didn't recognize outside a deer shack in the Northern Forest. A gray buck hung near the door. I hoped he would someday share such a setting with me.

By the time I was 15, I knew that wouldn't happen. The Old Man, while always solitary, seemed to grow even more reclusive with age. And I now realized we would never be close. He didn't need my companionship, then or before. But the Old Man, by being who he was, had taught me how complex people could be. He could touch such great extremes, and almost at the same time.

When he was around, he loved to tell stories. Over time, some tales evolved with such flourish that listeners didn't recognize old standbys gussied up in formal wear. The Old Man's eyes radiated Irish wry all through the performance, warming his audience of grandchildren and their polite, tolerant parents. The next minute, though, the same eyes could frost some unlucky whelp and clear a suddenly frigid room. Everyone knew to seek shelter when the boar was loose.

That's how I remember the Old Man, the one who provided the deer hunting genes that skipped a generation before settling in me. He had great pride in his family and its name, yet he couldn't translate much of it into affection.

But no one except family is allowed to make such charges. He was my grandfather, you see, flaws and all. I didn't pick him and he didn't pick me. I just loved him, for better or worse. I assume something in his background, something he possibly couldn't control, made him what he was — great and otherwise.

Maybe after I've walked a mile in his boots, and shared a few deer seasons with him, I'll get a better measure of the man named Edward Patrick Durkin.

May you rest in peace, Old Man, wherever you may be.

"Walk a Mile in the Old Man's Boots" was originally published in the June 1991 issue of Deer & Deer Hunting *magazine.*

URSULA DURKIN (1898-1994), THE INSPIRATION FOR THIS ARTICLE, ENCOURAGED THE DEER HUNTING PASSION IN MANY OF HER DESCENDANTS. TWO OF HER GREAT-GRANDCHILDREN, LEAH URSULA DURKIN AND CASE DIBBLE, ARE SHOWN HERE WITH CASE'S FIRST DEER.

CHAPTER 3

URSULA'S INFLUENCE

The harsh times she endured caused her to despise waste, whether of food, time, talent or money. She strived to pass on those hatreds to descendants. When a grandson took up hunting and fishing, she ensured his meager catches were cleaned and eaten.

■ BY PATRICK DURKIN

For as long as I knew her, she was ready to die. Damn her, no one treasured work, love, laughter, family and devotion more than she. But for her last 30-plus years she knew if the bucket were sitting there, she would kick it without fear.

There was no bravado in her attitude. That's just the way she was. She knew life and death to be impartial, and that once she passed 60, she "dasn't" ask for too much more, lest she look ungrateful.

But she would occasionally let down just enough to hint she might have been keeping score. She told of life in the early 1900s, when chronic asthma kept her stooped and wheezing, and ignorant neighbors warned sons to keep their distance.

"There goes the walking dead girl," they'd say. "Probably has TB. Don't want to marry her. She'll die young on you."

She outlived those people, parents and sons alike.

Patrick Durkin

A COMMON DISCUSSION AMONG TODAY'S HUNTERS IS HOW TO ENSURE THE FUTURE OF HUNTING. **A** GROWING NUMBER OF PEOPLE REALIZE THE BEST BET LIES WITHIN OUR FAMILIES, NOT IN TRYING TO RECRUIT OUTSIDE OUR RANKS. **W**ITHOUT A FAMILY REINFORCING THE HUNTING ETHIC, "RECRUITS" SOON DEPART THE RANKS. **W**HEN TWO OR MORE GENERATIONS GET TOGETHER TO HUNT DEER, THEY ESTABLISH TIES AND TRADITIONS THAT ARE DIFFICULT TO BREAK. **S**HOWN IN THE **N**OVEMBER **1991** PHOTO ABOVE, ARE THE AUTHOR'S UNCLE, **J**OSEPH TERRANCE **D**URKIN, AND THE AUTHOR'S OLDEST DAUGHTER, **L**EAH, WHO JOINED HER FATHER THAT YEAR FOR HER FIRST DEER HUNT ON HER GREAT-UNCLE'S FARM.

her about living off tomato soup their entire childhood, she evenly replied, "You didn't starve, did you?"

Firm Roots

Still, she valued fresh meat in her home. She told grandkids how her brother often provided their only meat some weeks: fish from a nearby lake, and rabbits from nearby fencerows.

And, of course, in her day, the meat seldom came wrapped, including the chickens, which they butchered themselves. Quite simply, if families wanted meat in the early 1900s, they often had to kill the animal on whose bones it had grown.

When reflecting on those times, she would sometimes voice displeasure at today's judgmental hindsight. As those harsh times faded from society's memory, she heard people cluck their tongues when discussing the widespread killing of deer and other wildlife 100 years ago. But let's remember, not all of it went to wasteful commercial uses. For many rural people, she pointed out, wild animals provided a rare source of meat. Therefore, maybe conservation of those wildlife resources had to wait for more prosperous times. And who's to say it will remain in vogue when times get rough again?

All such things caused her to despise waste throughout her life, whether of food, time, talent or money. And she tried hard to pass on those hatreds to descendants. When a grandson took up hunting and fishing, she ensured his meager catches were cleaned and eaten.

That wasn't hard for her to monitor. After all, she lived with a son's family most of her final 30 years, and she usually knew when to slip into sermon, or skip to the next page. When she was left home to cook for the grandkids, she quietly directed the young hunter toward the freezer.

"And don't let your brothers and sisters see you," she whispered with an amused look on her face.

She then quietly prepared her chicken dish, adding

Maybe she survived because she never took anything for granted. After becoming a mother, and discovering her husband to be an irregular mate and father, she raised four kids by herself during the Depression. When her kids became adults and teased in chunks of rabbit and squirrel after plucking out the No. 6 pellets.

While washing the dishes after supper, she relived her trick with the boy, saying with a laugh, "Well, they'd never eat it if they knew what was in it."

True Values

Just as importantly, she valued independence. But unlike many, she knew toil, knowledge and responsibility made it possible. She never relied on a store for all her food. She vigorously tended huge vegetable gardens, moving in quickly after each rain to pull and hoe out weeds while the ground remained soft.

And she never missed a chance to collect rain water for her plants, or add fallen leaves and grass clippings to her compost pile, long before the musty heaps became a '90s fashion statement for yuppies.

All the while, she never shied from opinion. Late in life, when too weak to do much outdoors, she still watched "Meet the Press," "Face the Nation" and the belligerent screamers on "Crossfire." But she once confided to a daughter-in-law that life stopped being fun after 88, when the pain of age never ceased.

The Fall

Still, it took a fall from bed, which broke her hip at age 96, to finally weaken and kill her on March 28, 1994.

So now she's gone, buried at the gravesite she had chosen long before most of us were born. Ursula Fischenich Durkin was one hell of a woman, and at least one grandson will never forget her lessons.

Not to mention her plates of "chicken."

"Ursula's Influence" was originally published in several Wisconsin newspapers in April 1994.

Patrick Durkin

The Meeting Place

The tremor in his voice made me realize his adrenaline rush was as strong as mine. He appeared to be hooked on deer hunting. On the way home we relived the day's hunts, and the excitement of being surrounded by deer.

■ BY JOEL M. SPRING

The faint sound came from above. Clip-clop. Clip-clop. Like horses on a dusty trail. I couldn't believe it. A deer was crossing the road above. I heard twigs gently snapping as the deer entered the woods, yet could still hear hoof-falls on the blacktop. More than one! It had been five years since I hunted this spot, and six since I had seen a deer here, yet there they were, coming toward me five minutes before sunset.

I hoped Dad was in place. Please let him see this.

We had spent the first day of our first deer hunt together trudging through the swamps and dense conifer stands of the Adirondack Mountains in northern New York. We would stop and set up in a good-looking area, and I would rattle the big 6-point antlers and blow my grunt tube. This was Dad's first deer hunt since he was a teen-ager, and I wanted him to think I knew what I was doing. But from the sideways glances I sometimes got, I'm sure that's not what he was thinking. Inside his camo face mask he was probably laughing. We covered lots of territory that first day but saw nothing besides red squirrels and moss-covered trees.

I slept fitfully that first night in the iced-over cap of my truck. I plotted as Dad snored. The Adirondacks are rough to hunt, and not so loaded with whitetails that seeing even one a weekend is guaranteed. But I wanted to get my father close to deer and excited enough so I could talk him into taking a vacation in two weeks for a bow-hunt in the Catskills. I figured once he had seen deer up close, he would get hooked on hunting as quickly as I had.

When dawn broke Sunday morning, both of us were sore, and I wasn't well-rested. After a miserable breakfast hastily prepared over a propane burner, we headed into the woods. The icy morning turned quickly into a sticky, uncomfortable day as we headed along another unexplored ridge. To the right the ridge angled suddenly and steeply upward. Straight ahead lay a small draw that looked like a natural funnel from the mountains to a swamp below. We hiked into the draw, letting the towering beech trees and smattering of hemlocks swallow us.

> A DEER HAD BEEN COMING DOWN THE HILL INTO OUR AMBUSH WHEN WE DECIDED TO MOVE. IF IT HAD STAYED ON COURSE IT WOULD HAVE PASSED WITHIN YARDS OF DAD. WE DIDN'T EXCHANGE WORDS. NONE WERE NEEDED.

Time to Call

"Let's set up to call here."

Dad agreed, but I swear he had a look of weary amusement dancing across his face. Even so, he climbed a little farther up in the draw and sat on a log that leaned against the base of a massive, gnarled tree. I had trouble picking him out from the lush surroundings when he donned his camo mask, but the white tips of his recurve eventually betrayed his presence.

I began to rattle. A warm breeze had picked up, and so I rattled louder to make sure the sound would carry. I banged a small hemlock with the antlers, and stomped the ground with my right foot. I tried to picture an old buck on that hillside hearing the noise and reacting to it. I stopped after rattling only about five minutes. I gave the antlers a gentle tick about 15 minutes later, and blew two short, deep "uuughs." I then tucked the grunt call back into my shirt and hung the antlers on a branch.

Ten minutes later, Dad looked in my direction and I decided it was time to move. A year had passed since a buck had come to my rattling, and my confidence on this

warm September day — with the rut still so far away — was low. I stretched and hefted my compound, thinking how much nicer it would be to carry the light, graceful recurve my father balanced so effortlessly.

"Did you hear that?" he asked in a hushed voice as we reached each other.

"No," I said, puzzled.

"Maybe it was nothing."

I suggested we sit a few more minutes. I blew gingerly on the grunt call a couple more times, and strained to see into the midday shadows of the huge woods. After 30 minutes, we began climbing the steep draw to see what was over the ridge. We went about 100 yards and then I spotted the tracks. A single dark line was visible in the draw's damp leaves, and it stopped in a small clump. I moved the leaves to reveal a huge hoof print gouged into the black earth. Obviously, a deer had been coming down the hill into our ambush when we decided to move. If he had stayed on course he would have passed within yards of Dad.

We didn't exchange words. None were needed. It had been my decision to move, and we knew I was the more impatient of the pair. Dad would have sat there all day.

We followed the buck's tracks back up the mountain, finally losing them when the damp earth gave way to rock. Suddenly I was cool. We had climbed a long way — several hundred feet — and the wind was blowing harder up here. We spent a couple of hours exploring this mountain with no name, stopping occasionally to try to call our buck back. We knew it was futile. As we neared the road, Dad finally asked, "So, are you ready to go home?"

Delayed Departure

"No, let's take a ride and sit until dark," I offered.

When we parked the truck we had less than 30 minutes of light remaining. Dad, being a good partner, didn't give me much of an argument when I had him sit against a tree, not 50 yards down the edge of the roadside. I took my bow and sat about 70 yards away. I couldn't see him through the thick wall of chest-high hemlocks.

When the deer crossed the road and stepped into the woods, I prayed they would go his way. I could see them momentarily silhouetted against the sky as they stepped off the pavement. Picking leisurely at the vegetation, they

Charles J. Alsheimer

slowly came in my direction. The lead deer, a huge doe that would surpass 200 pounds, passed broadside at 10 yards. Instinctively, I drew as she neared, but let her pass, hoping she would work toward Dad. After she passed, I looked around and saw the other deer, all smaller does, facing away from me. I silently let my bow back down. However, I had failed to see a small button buck watching me from about eight yards away.

"Whoosh!"

His loud snort signaled the end of the bow-hunt. The big doe blew a return warning, and I think I heard a hoof stomp in the wet leaves. In seconds, the woods were alive with crashing, snorting deer and their bobbing white tails.

When I eventually found Dad, sitting stock-still in the darkening woods, he said he hadn't seen the deer but had heard the whole thing.

I started to apologize for the day's second blown chance, but then noticed his smile. The tremor in his voice made me realize he was having as much of an adrenaline rush as me.

Hooked

He looked hooked. On the way home we relived the day's hunts, and the excitement of being surrounded by deer at sunset. I told him about the first time I hunted the spot we had just left, and how an 8-point buck had strolled into the middle of the road at dark to watch me put my gear away, and how that experience hooked me on deer hunting.

He then told stories about hunting these mountains with his older brother when they were boys. I had never heard these stories, and I hung on his words. I could see by the gleam in his eye and the excitement in his voice that I had found a new hunting partner.

"The Meeting Place" was originally published in the June 1995 issue of Deer & Deer Hunting *magazine.*

CHAPTER 5

CHANGES

Tall trees blocking the sun will wall me in from the outside world. I will need to change to fit in here. Creek water flowing quietly by the trail will make me slow down to the pace of the woods. It'll be a welcome change.

■ BY JOEL M. SPRING

The hot coffee is good on this cool September morning. I walk over to turn off the air conditioner that's been running needlessly all night. Looking out the front window, I notice that a tree in the creek bed across the road has turned brilliant red.

The lone maple stands out like a flame against the green background. It seems the tree changed overnight, but I realize I haven't noticed it because I've been on the midnight shift the past week and have slept away the days. Walking into the yard, I notice the crisp air. The chill is welcome after a long, hot summer. I notice the other trees aren't as green as they were a few weeks ago. The change is happening to them, too.

The next few days are as cool as the weatherman said they would be. Switching back onto the day shift isn't as easy as usual. The cold nights make me want to hit the snooze button a few extra times each morning. Flannel shirts and sweatshirts are replacing T-shirts and shorts. My old truck shudders and spits and smokes, acting like a tired old man on these cold mornings. It senses the changes coming too, I think.

Staging Time

One of these days, if money ever allows it, I'm going to have to get a new truck. But I'm going to have to buy another bright red one with a dent on one side and a bad muffler so the farmers know who I am when I'm walking around on their land during deer season.

The shorter days make it harder to get the yard mowed when I get home from work. I guess it's a combination of less daylight and less desire to labor, as my thoughts turn more toward the hunting season. At least keeping the grass cut helps me find my arrows during my practice.

In the basement, my office has become a staging area for fall's first deer hunt, which will happen less than a month from now. Stacked in one corner is bow equipment and broken arrows in need of repair. My desk is piled with maps and license applications and hunting schedules. Another pile consists of hunting clothes I need to try on to see which ones will go back into storage. I swear, next year I'll lose 15 pounds.

As I try on my camo I notice, as I do every year, how much more comfortable the faded, years-old green stuff is than the newer, crisp stuff with the fancy photo finish. I wonder if I drove over the new stuff with my truck a couple of times if it would soften up a little.

The Last Mosquitoes

I dismiss the idea because I probably couldn't get the truck started anyway. In another corner sits my new ladder stand. The ugly piece of gray carpeting that I glued to the metal platform is oozing glue onto the floor.

With the cool weather, Dad and I will make more frequent trips to the rifle range. The black flies that plagued the range during summer are a thing of the past. And the mosquitoes, what few there are left, are sluggish. Two more weeks and they'll all be gone.

I'll shoot the rifles and shotgun, which is still perfectly sighted in from six years ago, over and over at the little paper targets until I know I'll be prepared when the season comes. It won't be long now. The changes happen more quickly every day.

Soon the little orange maple tree across the road will be joined in its brilliance by its neighbors. The hills will burn with October fire.

Soon the wind will begin its slow swing from the south to the north, bringing down cold air from places I wish I could be right now.

> THE CHANGES ARE HAPPENING MORE QUICKLY EVERY DAY. SOON THE LITTLE ORANGE MAPLE TREE ACROSS THE ROAD WILL BE JOINED IN ITS BRILLIANCE BY ITS NEIGHBORS. THE HILLS WILL BURN WITH OCTOBER FIRE.

The Hunter's Moon

Soon the hunter's moon will hang in the cold night sky, guarded by Orion and hidden occasionally by the first hints of gray snow clouds.

Soon the deer will begin their changes, too. Polished antlers will rub saplings. Does will move through the thick woods, leading their fawns to feed in the fields a little earlier each evening, feeling the urgency of the season. The bucks will follow them passively at first. A few weeks later they'll pursue them with an urgency all their own. Food, for them, will be forgotten for a while. Ground will be pawed, branches will be licked. Miles of woods will be traveled. The elaborate courtship ritual will rise to a feverish pace lasting day and night until the continuity of the herd is assured.

The deer also will sense the changes will bring another visitor to the woods. Long boot prints will mark the trails only visited by raccoons and bears and deer during summer. Strange, strong smells will waft from odd places at odd times, betraying the location of a stranger, or maybe just the hint of his earlier passing.

To the deer, I'll be the stranger, even though I feel at home in the woods. Beech leaves underfoot will crunch in familiar rhythms. Tall trees blocking the sun will wall me in from the outside world. I will need to change to fit in here. Creek water flowing quietly by the trail will make me slow down to the pace of the woods.

Needed Change

It's a change I very much need. A glimpse of brown and white on the way to my stand will speed up my heartbeat. My nose will be filled with the smells of moist earth and leaves, moss and pure air. These things never change.

But now, on this cool September day, there's just the single red tree against the dark green woods. But that's all about to change.

"Changes" was originally published in the October 1995 issue of Deer & Deer Hunting *magazine.*

Patrick Durkin

CHAPTER 6

LIKE A BALD MAN'S HEAD

Solid bush is never solid bush. The land on which it grows contains valleys and knolls, swamps and rises. Thick forests always have bumps and furrows where deer are more likely to rest or move.

■ BY JIM SHOCKEY

There were times during the learning years when frustration seemed to be the day's only lesson. I would have given anything to have Old Pete there at times to guide me along this or that deer trail.

Down on my knees, I was a detective, searching for the track, unraveling the puzzle, deciphering the code. After each false lead, I felt less like Sherlock Holmes and more like Mr. Magoo. I let the thought slip a moment, and instead searched the trees for any telltale wisp of brown.

Where was He?

Where was Old Pete when I needed him? What rule would he want me to apply? He wouldn't tell me his favorite, "At the end of every deer track there is a deer." No, not that rule. I learned that one the hard way long ago. My mentor had spoken those words a hundred times, easily. And I had listened, but in the end, the lesson within the words had only come the hard way.

How many times had I given up a track, rushing ahead, thinking the buck was long gone? Even as I

Bill Marchel

reached to move aside another willow twig, I knew the answer. It was the same number of times I had seen the flag of a fleeing buck.

Without thought, even as I stepped forward, I stopped. The reaction had come instinctively at the first indication of pressure on the sole of my leading boot. A dead branch was hidden beneath the snow, waiting to spoil my hunt, waiting to serve a hard lesson should I be careless. That was another lesson learned long ago.

I gently lifted my foot and placed it beyond the branch. For a fleeting second I was off balance, forced to step beyond my reach, but just as quickly my leading foot was down firmly. Perhaps gritting my teeth helped, and perhaps not. But I was balanced again, and gave only the barest hint of sudden movement. I didn't bring my back foot forward. With legs scissored, I waited. Old Pete had told me once, "The best way to track a big whitetail is to stand still." Another rule.

I scanned the terrain ahead and then to the sides. Nothing was holding me to the spot, at least nothing obvious. The tracks were no fresher than when I picked them up early that morning. It was noon now and, by all indications, the buck was moving to nature's command. He was in full rut and looking for does.

The Wait Continues

Still I didn't move, though for the tenth time my slow scan of the snow-laden forest turned up nothing. Old Pete once told me that when I met the lady to share my life, I would have no question about it. He said there is no way to explain in words how I would know. I just would. In the same breath, he said if I hunted alone — quietly and slowly, as he taught — there would be times when I would know a buck was close. Just as surely, there would be no way to explain how this knowledge would come.

I suppose I am not the romantic Pete is, because I believe the feeling comes from a lifetime of hunting, a lifetime of experience. The clues are there but we can't see them with our eyes. Instead, our memories register the information and dictate our response.

If we listen.

It had been minutes now since I first stepped forward. My legs began to show the first signs of fatigue at being held awkwardly for so long. My eyes followed the tracks up the incline. What had Pete told me? I thought back to other hunts, to other lessons.

"No deer ever grew wings," he once said. Days later,

he added, "But sometimes they jump a long way."

Eventually, I understood. I was tracking a buck one day when his tracks suddenly disappeared. Deer don't fly, so I searched to pick up the thread of his trail in the scattered snow patches. I finally found the trail again, 200 yards from where I had lost it. Don't ask how he did it. I found no tracks between the two bits of trail. I would have quit if not for Old Pete's wisdom.

Obvious Tracks

But such was not the case on this trail. The tracks had been obvious since I picked them up. There was no way to mistake the buck's swaggering, toe-dragging step. Another lesson. I had asked Old Pete how to tell the difference between a buck and a doe track. Instead of answering directly, he asked how I knew the difference between a man and a beautiful woman walking down the street.

"Pete," I said with a wink. "They walk differently."

"Exactly."

But today, deep in the woods with my muscles cramping, the question was not whether the track was made by a buck or a doe. I wondered if I was wasting valuable shooting light standing still when I should have been moving along the trail. Again I searched my mind for the right lesson. Pete had told me about a bald man's head. How had he put it?

I remembered the day I had complained about the nondescript terrain I was hunting. "Solid bush," I said. I claimed there was no way to see, and the deer were impossible to hunt because they wandered randomly.

Pete looked sadly at me a moment and said, "A bald man's head is still a bald man's head ..." He paused to let his words sink in, and added, "whether it's covered with hair or not."

The Revelation

Poor senile Pete, I thought. I continued thinking he had spoken nonsense until I found myself in a movie theater one day. In front of me was an enormous man with a bald head. Watching the movie was all but impossible because of the big head, so I studied its features. Before long, I had a revelation. The man's bald head wasn't smooth, as I had assumed. Instead, as light from the screen danced across its surface, I noticed the head was a bumpy, ridgy affair

> THE SPOT WHERE I STOOD WAS NOT IN A THICKET, NOR DID IT BISECT A GLADE. IT WASN'T A RIDGELINE, EITHER. IT WAS THE BASE OF A GENTLY SLOPING, TREE-COVERED HILL. THE KNOB, MAYBE AN ACRE IN SIZE, WAS HARDLY NOTEWORTHY.

with the odd deep furrow. Even if hair had covered this head, it would still be ridged, furrowed and creased.

That was it! Solid bush is never solid bush. The land on which it grows contains valleys and knolls, swamps and rises. Thickets and clearings dot the greater forest. More importantly, natural runways and bedding areas occur in the bush just as they do in farm country. The thickest forests always have bumps and furrows where deer are more likely to rest or move.

The spot where I stood was not in a thicket, nor did it bisect a glade. It wasn't a ridgeline, either. It was the base of a gently sloping, tree-covered hill. The knob, perhaps an acre in area, was hardly noteworthy. Most likely, it was a mere bit of dirt left behind by the last ice age. But whatever else it was, it was a hill. A vantage point! How many times had I walked up hills in the bush, exactly like this one, only to find one or two large deer beds on top?

Forever Stilled

Yet there was no sound, no clue to confirm what I felt. If the buck were there, and if he heard me step across the dead branch, I knew that he must — at that very second — be searching his innate memory for some ancient bit of information to help recognize whatever had intruded his space below. Being the world's foremost survival machine, the buck had a thousand generations of his own mentors guiding his actions.

And I had mine. The best way to track a buck is to stand still.

Suddenly, the buck stood up, no doubt to see what had made the whisper of noise on his back trail. One second there was no buck. The next second, there he stood. As the buck rose, so, too, did the rifle to my shoulder.

The buck never felt a thing.

"Like a Bald Man's Head" was originally published in the March 1997 issue of Deer & Deer Hunting *magazine.*

CHAPTER 7

CHRISTMAS DAY

He felt like a left-out kid again. He had received many great presents, including a compass and knife. But the one thing he wanted most hadn't materialized. He wanted a deer rifle. A man needed his own deer rifle.

■ BY BRYCE M. TOWSLEY

Jeff felt guilty. He was trying to conceal his disappointment as he polished silver for his mom. He knew he had no right to feel this way, but he couldn't help it.

The room was filled with the aroma of a cooking dinner. He liked that. This dinner was the wild turkey shot a few weeks before. Dad's bird was a 17-pound gobbler that had come to raspy yelps that imitated a fellow bachelor. Jeff shot the other bird, a 12-pound tom that had poked its head over the rise in front of the 12-gauge shotgun. He was as proud of his first turkey as any 15-year-old could be.

It had been a good year, the turkey and six partridge falling to his shotgun, and a mess of squirrels to his .22 rifle. He used the .22 because it was more sporting, and good practice for deer.

To top off the autumn hunts, Jeff shot a 6-point buck on opening morning. The buck came the right way and Jeff felt good about outsmarting him. He had scouted his territory and picked the ambush site himself. He had placed his dad's portable tree stand 15 feet up a poplar tree on a trail between the buck's feeding and bedding

Patrick Durkin

areas. At 8:30 a.m., a doe came by, stopping often and looking back. Jeff had a doe permit but he waited. He had killed a doe last year, but when he went to dress it out, a buck charged off. He hadn't forgotten the lesson.

Not long after the doe passed, the buck came along with his nose on her trail. After making the shot, Jeff wanted to do the rest of the job alone. But the buck weighed more than he did and, after dressing it out, he got his uncle to help drag.

Shooting Times

The hunting seasons were now over except for rabbit hunting. Today was Christmas, and Jeff was glad it was Dad's turn to play host to the family. It was OK when Uncle Bob had it at his house — the guys still talked hunting and guns almost all day — but his uncle lived in town and, of course, you couldn't shoot there.

When Dad's turn came to be host, they went to the range out back, which had a bench, an automatic trap machine, and steel gongs all the way to 300 yards. To reach the range you merely stepped out the back door of the heated garage. With the wood stove roaring and sweet cider mulling on top, they had a grand time each Christmas. The shoots were with shotgun, rifle and handgun. They made up the rules as they went along, each taking turns inventing new games.

Grandpa still was the best rifle shot, and Uncle Bob pointed a handgun the best of any (except maybe Dad), but Jeff won more than his share of shotgun matches. Two years ago he won all but one shotgun match. Grandpa insisted he was the most natural shotgun shooter he had ever seen. Jeff thought they were letting him win because he was a kid, but Dad insisted they didn't. Jeff finally felt like one of the men that day.

Today, though, he felt like a left-out kid again. He had received many great presents, including a compass and a Buck knife from Mom and Dad. They also bought him school clothes, a pair of wool hunting pants, and several record albums, some of which he liked.

But the one thing he had wanted most never materialized. He wanted a deer rifle, but not just any rifle. Jeff had killed two deer with Dad's old .32 Special, but a man needed his own rifle. Jeff studied catalogs and gun maga-

zines, and knew exactly what he wanted. He could quote ballistics tables for all his favorite calibers, and even knew which bullets were available for reloading. The rifle he craved was a Remington Model 7 in 7mm-08 caliber. He had prayed for it this Christmas, but it wasn't under the tree.

Dad popped his head into the kitchen, saw Jeff working on the silver, and said: "Jeff, your uncle will be here any minute, and I'm not about to let him beat me again this year. I need a little warmup. Go down to the reloading bench and get me some 44s."

The Gift

Trying not to look glum, Jeff walked off to the cellar room he and Dad had fixed up into a reloading area last winter. When he turned on the light, there on the bench was a note and a new Remington Model 7. The note said:

"The owner of this gun must be responsible and must act like a man, but he should never forget how to be a kid. To own a gun is a serious responsibility and must be taken as such, but life must never be taken too seriously. Therefore, the owner should never forget how to have fun, no matter how old he gets. Use this gun safely and remember the power it represents over life and death. Never kill something just to kill, and always put back into the hunt more than you take out. Use this gun and remember to pass on the thrill of the hunt, the sadness of the kill, and the joy of nature to your own children some day. Merry Christmas, Jeff.

—Love, Dad.

P.S. Mom and I decided that next year you can come to deer camp and hunt, not just on the weekends, but the first week of the season. But you must square it with your teachers and make up all the lost work. Also, you must have a "B" or better average, or the deal is off!"

Jeff ran up the stairs and burst into the den. "Even algebra?" he cried.

Dad grinned.

"Especially algebra!"

"Christmas Day" was originally published in the January 1994 issue of Deer & Deer Hunting *magazine.*

> HE COULD QUOTE BALLISTICS FOR MANY CALIBERS, AND EVEN KNEW THE BULLETS AVAILABLE FOR RELOADING. THE RIFLE HE CRAVED WAS A REMINGTON IN 7MM-08 CALIBER. HE HAD PRAYED FOR IT THIS CHRISTMAS, BUT IT WASN'T UNDER THE TREE.

CHAPTER 8

THE BEST MARINADE

Folks up at the nearby taverns were full of stories about big bucks they had shot. Only when asked did I say that I had a good hunt, but no, I hadn't bagged a deer. That's happened before, I said. It's no big deal.

■ BY RON LEYS

For some reason, the venison chops taste sweeter this year than ever before. The flavor of venison chops, of course, comes from the mind and heart as much as the taste buds. Pork chops are only pork chops, but venison chops contain the hunt's very flavor and essence.

If, as the French say, hunger makes the best sauce, then surely memories make the best marinade.

It's kind of funny, in a way. The marinade this year holds no memories of a magnificent stag with head and rack worthy of gracing a wall of my home. There is nothing there to mark a perfect 300-yard shot that killed a Wyoming buck before it could wake from its nap. No horseback trips into the Rocky Mountain wilderness with close friends and guides flavor this year's marinade. And there are no smells and tastes of a hunt with my son from a log cabin that he and I built.

Past venison dinners have contained all those memories. However, this year's marinade reminds me of shots that missed, and long, often-boring

Patrick Durkin

hours in the woods near my farmhouse.

But it reminds me also of persistence, perseverance, of refusal to give up.

Free Advice

I sometimes give free advice, worth every penny, of course, to a neighbor's teen-age son who is somewhat obsessed with hunting and fishing. When we go out together and get skunked, I have been known to tell Andy that it's not supposed to be easy. That if it were, we wouldn't value our outdoor sports so. It's the possibilities, not the certainties, I tell him, that keep us coming back.

I've been known to forget that, but this year, for some reason, I took my own words to heart.

The hunt began on a friend's sheep farm just east of my home. Farmers had been complaining that the area was overrun with deer, so state biologists flooded the area with extra hunting permits. I obtained one permit that allowed me to shoot any deer that walked by, plus a second tag for an antlerless deer.

My plan was to shoot a doe on opening morning to satisfy my wife, who is more impressed with tender venison than big antlers. Then, the plan continued, I would be free to take my time and hunt for a big buck. That plan had worked the previous year. I had not shot a big buck, but I had the enjoyment of hunting for one.

So when a trio of does came walking along the hillside across from my tree stand at 8 o'clock on opening day, it all fit into the plan. But things began to unravel when the lead doe stopped behind a big tree and then eased herself out to investigate a sense of danger. I took careful aim through the scope of my .30-06 and fired.

When I walked the 100 or so yards to the scene, I found not a drop of blood and not a single deer hair. Although I searched for a while, I knew immediately I had missed. Well, it was a clean miss, I told myself.

Plenty of Season Left

Ah, well, it was still the beginning of the season. Since I retired from my city job, I have plenty of time to devote to deer hunting. And that's why they make the season more than one day long.

There were more deer to see on that opening weekend, bucks, does and fawns. But for some reason, mostly having to do with running deer, I didn't take another shot.

The middle of the week was spent on another friend's farm, hour after hour, day after day. Once again there were deer to watch, but none to shoot at. The final weekend was spent back at the sheep farm, with similar results.

Folks up at the nearby taverns were, of course, full of stories about the big bucks they had shot. I nursed my beer or Diet Coke mostly in silence. Only when asked did I say that I had a good hunt, but no, I hadn't bagged a deer. That's happened before, I said. It's no big deal.

But the coals had not been quenched. The desire still smoldered. So I bought an archery license for the December portion of the bow season.

I spent that cold season on my own farm, in a tree stand back in a patch of woods that joins a much bigger thicket. Not as many deer here, but it was just a short walk from the house and I could pick the hours when the weather was somewhat kind.

Again, I saw some deer. Again, I took a shot at a doe. And again I missed cleanly — at about 30 yards. Should have practiced more, I thought. And then I found the severed branch, about as thick as my thumb, that had caused the arrow to veer off.

When the thermometer plunged to 10 below, I was back in the house after feeding my beef cattle. But when it soared to 10 above, I was back in the woods.

A Late-Season Opportunity

The end of December crept up, and it was becoming clear that it was written somewhere I would not kill a deer this year.

Late in the afternoon of the second-to-last day of the season, as snow silently sifted down through the barren trees, a couple of deer came by. But they saw me from about 50 yards and ran off, tails high. But then, as though drawn by curiosity, they came back,

slowly, cautiously, one step at a time.

The buck took one step too many. For the third time in that long season, I took careful aim and fired. The deer ran off.

Normally I wait a half-hour after shooting an arrow before I begin tracking a deer. But darkness was not far off, and the new snow would quickly cover his trail.

So I came down from my stand, found a good blood trail and came to a dead buck 100 yards away. Death had come quickly, for which I am always grateful.

Dinner was late that night as I walked home to report in, fired up the tractor to fetch the deer, and then registered the deer at the *Rolling Ground* tavern.

> WE HUNG THE BUCK HIGH IN A TREE, AND THE NEXT MORNING I USED A FILLET KNIFE AND A SAW TO BUTCHER THE BUCK, UNDER MARILYN'S CAREFUL SUPERVISION. SHE WRAPPED AND LABELED THE CUTS, AND FOUND ROOM FOR THEM IN THE FREEZER.

My wife, Marilyn, and I hung the buck high in a tree in the front yard. Rusty, our cow dog, stood watch all night. Perhaps she was on guard to protect the deer. More likely, she was praying the rope would break while everybody but her was asleep.

Making Venison

That didn't happen, and the next morning I used a fillet knife and a carpenter's saw to butcher the buck, under Marilyn's careful supervision. She wrapped and labeled the cuts, and found room for them in the freezer.

It wasn't a trophy buck. It didn't win the big-buck contest at any neighborhood tavern. You'll never see its antlers on a wall or in a photo.

But I earned this venison. And it tastes ever so sweet. Even the memories are sweet. That might have been the best hunt ever.

"The Best Marinade" was originally published in the January 1997 issue of Deer & Deer Hunting *magazine.*

CHAPTER 9

DRY BONES

Usually bare bones just denote death. Deer hunters revel in the exception. Yet there is more. The doe perceives it. Hunters share in the spell. Go and hear the pop of dry bones, see the glint from polished tines, and imbibe the magic of the antler.

■ BY AL CORNELL

In 1892, Francis Parkman wrote of the millions of bison, "Nothing is left but bones." Likely they were similar to the bones of a prophet's vision, "...and lo, they were very dry."

The bison's bones symbolized the West's transition, and they symbolized death. Usually bare bones just denote death.

Deer hunters revel in the exception. They examine and speculate about the antler's every curve, twist, knurl, burr and blemish. Are these bones the sometimes painful artwork of genes, good health, freak injuries, a doe's influence, or merely time and chance in all?

Members of the deer family tote bared and drying bones, ones exterior to the body. Outside the flesh and veins. Dry, dead bones, becoming bleached. Yet sutured to the living. Unique in the world of bones.

If nothing living wore dry bones, in what manner would we imagine them?

Charles J. Alsheimer

Absolutely weird, practically unimaginable, grotesque? Certainly grotesque, and subject for a modern cartoon.

But bones do grow outside the body. They live and grow, then die and dry. Still firmly attached to the living, they dry and shrink and bleach. Antlers are unique.

If something living wore dry bones, how would we view them? Trophies, pieces of art, elegant? Certainly elegant. Worthy of the mantel.

Prudent Nature

Again, if there were no bone growth forming an exterior appendage protruding from the head, how would we imagine it grew? We might envision a similarity to horn, continuing to grow from the base so that more mature animals would tote larger appendages.

Nature is conservative and rarely expends energy in the manner associated with the annual renewal of antlers. We might well ponder their existence. Are bones as deciduous as a maple leaf? Both are firmly attached until the time is right. Then they loose the grip with the death of one layer of cells. Both shed quickly at the proper time.

As with the tooth-edged structure, so with the tined appendage. One is cast away as the petiole lets go, the other as the pedicle undoes its hold. Come May, beneath a branch of swelling buds, bulbous masses begin their regrowth.

Late spring paints abundance into the landscape. Yet, the doe's ribs show as her body pours energy into the rapid development of the newborn. Bucks use this luxury of plenty to produce an extravagant structure of new bone.

All other mammals, from the least to the greatest, lack the ability to regenerate an appendage. It happens only on the frontal bone of the cranium in members of the deer family. Velvet, that thin, fine-haired skin, can quickly grow to amazing dimensions as it supplies most of the calcium, phosphorous, protein, and other essentials to the antler.

Veins shrink, velvet dries and sloughs. The new

> NATURE IS CONSERVATIVE AND RARELY EXPENDS ENERGY IN THE MANNER ASSOCIATED WITH THE ANNUAL RENEWAL OF ANTLER. WE MIGHT WELL PONDER THEIR EXISTENCE. ARE BONES AS DECIDUOUS AS A MAPLE LEAF?

appendage retains no characteristic of continued life. A layer of living cells bonds this dead bone to the skull.

Regular visitors to the deer woods begin to perceive messages from these dead and drying bones. Antlers, attached or cast, communicate by their shape and dimensions.

First, they answer the species question, and then they go beyond to address individual matters. A yearling's antlers will often clearly telegraph the age, but not always. While this set of antlers tells little about genetics, it can reveal more about nutrition and winter severity.

Conclusion

Large antlers might broadcast a combination of traits, such as maturity, genetics, nutrition and social status. Antlers with similar shapes and oddities, found over a few-year period, might announce the continued survival of a particular individual.

Yet, beyond those normal messages from this strange appendage there is more. You have to be there to grasp it. The doe perceives it. Hunters share in the spell.

Go and hear the pop of dry bones, see the glint from polished tines, and imbibe the magic of the antler.

"Dry Bones" was originally published in the August 1995 issue of Deer & Deer Hunting *magazine.*

CHAPTER 10

TO HUNT THE SNOW

He was glad to be alone. It was his private dream, spawned by the hunting stories he had read as a boy. The great hunts, spectacular whitetails, and precious moments always took place in ancient deer camps and deep, pristine forests.

■ BY MICHAEL L. DUARTE

The man stood at the tent's door, his gaze fixed on the thin flashlight beam that probed the darkness. Specks of ice crowded the air around the light. A small smile crossed his face.

To hunt the snow. For 20 years he had dreamed of this hunt, imagining its look and feel, its smell and taste. He closed the door flap and huddled next to the gas lantern, watching tiny, half-frozen beads of condensation sparkle across the white canvas roof. He was a long way from Louisiana — 1,500 miles across the middle of America — far from the cypress and Spanish moss, and the sweet and sour odor of methane rising from swampy bogs.

Closing his eyes, he again pictured the 12-

Charles J. Alsheimer

pointer moving slowly below his stand, its swollen neck bent to the ground as it drew strong drafts of pheromone from the doe's fresh track. How had he missed? Fifteen-hundred miles to hunt the North's huge bucks, and he had cleanly missed a 20-yard shot — not a branch or leaf to share the blame.

At least he would have tomorrow; in fact, three more tomorrows, before having to pack it in. In the end, it would matter little whether he killed a good buck. He had already spent four magnificent days in the land of his boyhood dreams; four days bathing in the crimson and scarlet hue of maple, and the rich, golden glow of popple; four frosted nights around the campfire, and the pungent aroma of birch smoke clouding the Northern air like incense. And now the snow.

Private Dreams

The man was glad to be alone. It was his private dream, spawned by the hunting stories he had read as a boy. In those magazines of the '60s and '70s, the great hunts, spectacular whitetails and precious moments were always the grand moments shared in the ancient Pennsylvania deer camps or deep forests of the far North. He had promised himself that one day, while blood still pulsed strongly in his veins, he too would sit in a blind surrounded by the autumnal explosion of the North Woods. And when he wasn't doing that, he would start out a morning by silently tracking a buck — its heavy hoof and dew-points crushed into the fresh snow.

"Why the hell would you drive 2,000 miles to hunt deer?" his friends asked. "Got plenty-enough whitetails sneaking right behind Old Man Colter's store down the road."

There was no way to explain the dream, no way to explain the alluring intangibles of sights and scents. To a Southern lad weaned on North Woods deer stories, only one life-long desire burned brightly.

"Now if you was heading to Alaska to hunt grizzly, or up to Colorado for elk, hell, we could understand," friends said. "But to go that dang far for a whitetail. Hoo boy, that's twisted."

Again, the man opened the tent flap, this time reaching down to scoop a small pile of the sparkling white into his hands. The snow was letting up. A small sliver of moonlight escaped from between dark, rolling clouds, casting a soft glow on the darkened forest. Good. He had always read that deer moved willingly on the tail-end of a snowstorm. Tomorrow might be the day.

The man squinted into the night, shaking his head in child-like wonder. Just five hours earlier, this very forest was alive in spectacular colors that defied description or name — brilliant shades of autumn intensity he had only glimpsed in pictures. Now, a strange and alien landscape returned his stare. Strange and white, but quietly inviting.

Awaiting Dawn

He thought morning would never come. The anticipation of knowing he would finally hunt the snow robbed the man of deep sleep. Though he was tired, anxiety's adrenaline rush fueled his morning ritual. With stoic, practiced patience, he forced himself to eat a small breakfast, supply his day pack and give his bow a thorough, last-minute check.

Soon, he was outside in the pre-dawn darkness, moving toward the stand he had placed in a grove of hardwoods by a spring. As his feet bit into four inches of November's first snow, he was glad he had

decided on the luxury of felt-pac boots. They were expensive and would serve little purpose back home, but they were worth their weight in gold these past few frozen mornings. Today, they were priceless.

The storm was not quite over. Little flakes fell and spotted his camo. Shortly after getting into the stand, he was watching the antics of two squirrels when he spotted a doe picking her way through the grove. Though he had seen several deer over the past few days, he was still astounded by the size of Northern deer. This lone doe was easily the largest he had ever seen. He watched her nervous twitch; head turned to watch her back track, the white flag of her tail bent to the side in a hormonal-spurred invitation.

> HOW HAD HE MISSED? FIFTEEN-HUNDRED MILES TO HUNT THESE HUGE BUCKS, AND HE HAD CLEANLY MISSED A 20-YARD SHOT — NOT A BRANCH OR LEAF TO BLAME. AT LEAST HE WOULD HAVE TOMORROW. IN FACT, HE HAD THREE MORE TOMORROWS BEFORE HAVING TO PACK IT IN.

The man knew what was coming next and, within minutes, he spotted the buck. The grace of hunting luck was smiling down upon the man. It was the same huge 12-pointer. With a pounding heart and little chills of excitement crawling across his neck, he drew the bow and sighted on the 30-yard pin. A tumbling veil of white, silent flakes blinked past his eyes.

No, the boys back home would never understand; never feel the vibration of thrill the man knew; never know the rare, sweet gift of a dream fulfilled.

It was his chance to hunt the snow.

"To Hunt the Snow" was originally published in the March 1996 issue of Deer & Deer Hunting *magazine.*

INDEX

ABOUT THE EDITOR

Penny Durkin

Patrick Durkin, editor of *The Deer Hunters: The Tactics, Lore, Legacy and Allure of American Deer Hunting*, also serves as editor of *Deer & Deer Hunting,* an award-winning, nationally honored magazine.

In addition to his work on *Deer & Deer Hunting* magazine, Durkin serves as editorial director for the Krause Publications outdoors group, which includes — in addition to *Deer & Deer Hunting — Whitetail Business, Turkey & Turkey Hunting, Wisconsin Outdoor Journal* and *Trapper & Predator Caller* magazines.

Durkin makes his home in Waupaca, Wis., a rural community 11 miles south of the Krause Publications offices in Iola. He lives with his wife, Penny, and their three daughters: Karsyn, Elle and Leah (from left, above). Deer hunting has always played a large role in the Durkin family. Leah, for instance, has accompanied her father on many deer hunts since she was 6, and often sits with him on stand for hours, no matter what the weather. She was honing her shooting skills for her first gun- and bow-hunts as this book was being edited in Spring 1997.

Although Penny Durkin isn't a hunter, she helps butcher and package each deer her husband brings home, sometimes with the help of all three daughters. The family allows no cuts of beef in their home as long as there is

venison in their chest freezers. That means if you're invited to dine with the Durkins, the main course will usually be venison.

Durkin, a Wisconsinite by birth, began his journalism career in 1982 as a sports and outdoors reporter for the *Oshkosh Northwestern* daily newspaper. He earned numerous state and national awards for his reports, photographs and opinion columns on outdoor topics.

During his work in Oshkosh, Durkin became an admirer of *Deer & Deer Hunting* because of its practical, thoughtful and well-researched articles about his passion: deer hunting. He especially appreciated the magazine's frank approach, which meant seldom ducking controversy while encouraging open debate. Durkin frequently contacted the magazine's original editor, Al Hofacker, while seeking insights, opinion and information to include on the *Oshkosh Northwestern's* outdoors pages.

Durkin's newspaper work eventually caught the magazine's collective eye, and he assumed the associate editor's position at *Deer & Deer Hunting* in January 1991. A year later, he was promoted to the editor's chair. While Durkin has put his own stamp upon the magazine's pages, he strives to hold the magazine true to the course set down when it was launched in 1977 by the Stump Sitters.